Business Management and Administration

Business Management and Administration

Geoffrey Whitehead, BSc (Hons) (Econ)
Graham Whitehall, BA (Hons) (Econ)

The Institute of Commercial Management

First published in 1989 by Hutchinson Education
New edition 2000
Reprinted 2000
Reprinted with revisions 2003

Published by
The Institute of Commercial Management
PO Box 125, Christchurch, Dorset BH23 IYP, England
Tel: +44(0)1202 490555 Fax: +44(0)1202 490666
Email: info@icm.ac.uk   Web site: http://www.icm.ac.uk

British Library Cataloguing in Publication Data
A catalogue record for this book is available from the British Library

ISBN 1 903260 00 0
Printed and bound in Great Britain
by Antony Rowe Limited, Chippenham

Preface

As we move through the first decade of the new millennium, the global activities of management extend and every year sees the corps of management recruits grow ever larger. For this new edition we have separated off the text of *Business Management and Administration* from the many exercises and other activites provided for the various groups of students. These have been provided in a separate *Student Handbook*, which is more manageable.

The result is a core text book which makes easy reading for middle management staff, uninterrupted by activites and exercises designed to recapitulate the subject matter and give practice in written work. We hope readers of the core text will still dip into the student handbook, and that students themselves will make a really detailed study of both the core book and the revision tests, self-assessment questions and other assignments provided.

This book covers the syllabuses of the leading institutions in these fields and is particularly directed at new entrants to the profession who need a broad background at an introductory level rather than a detailed analysis of any specialist section. It will also be helpful to business studies students of these subjects in a variety of courses. The book is written for intermediate professional, A level, HND, AVCE Business Foundation Degree and other undergraduate students.

In preparing this book we have received considerable support from a number of individuals and firms who have given help with particular aspects and in many cases permitted the use of charts, diagrams, and so on. These are acknowledged elsewhere, but we should particularly like to thank Stephen Wellings for help and advice on the planning stages. We should also like to thank Alistair Somerville-Ford, of the Institute of Commercial Management for his encouragement of the project.

Geoffrey Whitehead
Graham Whitehall

Contents

Part Two
Functions within organisations

8 The information technology (IT) function 137

9 Personnel department 153

10 The accounting function 179

Part Three
The administrative officer's role

Acknowledgements

The assistance of many individuals and firms is gratefully acknowledged. In particular we should like to thank:

British Telecom PLC
Chancellor Formecon Ltd
Edding Lega International BV
Flexiform Ltd
Institute of Commercial Management
K & N International Ltd
The Simpler Trade Procedures Board (SITPRO)

Part One

The organisational background to business administration

1 The management framework to business administration

1.1 What is business administration?

Defining terms is not easy, particularly in the field of management and administration where ideas change from time to time and popular usage of words may vary. The consensus in recent years is that 'administration' implies some fairly detailed involvement in the activities of an organisation, and certainly business administration syllabuses seem to have developed into quite detailed lists of aspects of business organisation which students should study. We may therefore define business administration as '**that part of the management of a business organisation which seeks to implement the decisions made by top management and achieve the objectives which it has specified**'. Its true representative is the managing director, who is both the representative of the board to the ordinary workforce, and the representative of the workforce in any feedback to the board. As the representative of the board, the managing director must communicate the objectives to the staff and, no doubt, in the process arranges to break them down into a sequence of activities which can be achieved as time goes by. In the process of attempting to realise the objectives specified, some comparison between the results achieved and the plans made will become possible. This may call for reporting back to board level about various aspects: the difficulties encountered, the unrealistic nature of the original plans or possibly their inadequacy in view of the potential revealed. The managing director would present such a report, or arrange to have it presented by a suitable executive.

The managing director cannot, except in the very smallest organisations, do all the work of administration personally, and will be assisted by a team of senior executives, several of whom may have boardroom status. They will usually be known as **executive directors** to distinguish them from **part-time (non-executive) directors**. The latter have an advisory capacity, bringing certain types of expertise to the boardroom, but not having any part to play in putting the plans into execution. The executive directors are of a lower status than the managing director, and in most day-to-day situations report to him/her. They may be referred to as 'managers', for example the marketing manager or sales manager, the personnel manager, the factory manager, and so on. A typical board of directors is discussed more fully later in this chapter.

1.2   What is management?

If business administration is only part of management, what exactly is management? The term is used loosely to describe many activities. It is often said that every soldier has a field marshall's baton in his knapsack, and similarly every employee may aspire to management. It is not long before the new employee begins to feel that he/she is management material and the slightest supervisory role encourages claims to be 'middle management'. We shall see that where staff are coming in at fairly mature levels after long educational programmes, authority on particular matters (say, computerised systems) may lie with the newest recruit. It is therefore unwise to deny anyone's claim to be management material: there are many grades of management.

When we try to define management we must therefore limit the definition to what is usually thought of as 'top management'. A suitable definition today might be:

Management is the process of determining the objectives of an enterprise; deciding how these objectives are to be achieved in general terms; devising an appropriate organisation to pursue the objectives; providing funds which will enable the organisation to be adequately supplied with staff, equipment and other items necessary; making initial arrangements to commence operations and then keeping them under constant review.

It will be seen that these top-level activities are initially above the level of 'business administration' as defined in 1.1 above but merge into it once the first top-level decisions have been made. Some at least of the top management team become mere administrators when the chairman of the board declares the board meeting adjourned.

1.3   The board of directors

In business life today most important organisations are limited companies or public corporations which have a rather similar structure. We will therefore leave out of our discussion such firms as sole traders and partnerships which are run on rather personal lines in accordance with the wishes of the individuals who own them. In considering large-scale organisations we seek to see the framework of the organisation, and how it is organised to fulfil its objectives, rather than the individuals concerned. Individuals come and go, but the organisation persists. Indeed, this continuity of the enterprise is one of the most important features of the limited company and similar organisations. The death or departure of any individual makes no real difference to the organisation, which continues to offer its products for sale and to employ the rest of its workforce even though the head of the firm is no longer present.

The board of directors is the most important part of any limited company, and the **chairman of the board** is the true head of the firm. Although frequently he/she is only a part-time member, who is not in attendance at head office all the time, the chairman is a person of the very widest experience and absolutely familiar with the activities of the company and its objectives as stated in the 'objects' clause of its Memorandum of Association.

There may be a deputy chairman, whose function is obviously to replace the chairman should he/she be absent or called away from a meeting temporarily. If there is no such person appointed, there will usually be in standing orders a formula for the appointment of a deputy chairman in a temporary capacity as and when required. This might mean that any other director could be appointed, according to the nature of the main subject matter of the meeting – a person who was not hotly contesting the main subject being desirable so that a proper debate could take place, without bias.

The other members of the board are called directors. The most powerful director after the chairman is the **managing director**, who is charged by the board with the task of running the firm, and putting the decisions taken at board meetings into effect. Other directors may be the heads of important departments, so that like the managing director they are full-time employees, with important functions to perform. All such directors are called **executive directors**. Frequently the factory manager, the marketing manager, the chief accountant and the general administration officer are executive directors. Other directors may be only part-time directors, who have experience which will be of service to the company. Financial expertise, legal knowledge, technical expertise in various fields, and so on, are thus made available to the company relatively inexpensively since many directors serve for a thousand or so pounds per year only. The contribution such directors make may be invaluable, and although a particular director only attends perhaps once a month he/she is usually available for consultation at any time should a situation calling for his/her type of expertise arise. A typical board is illustrated in Fig. 1.1.

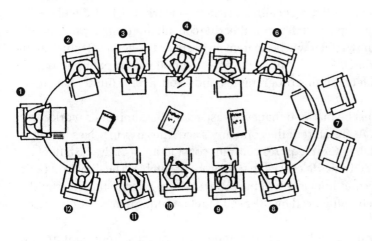

❶ Chairman
❷ Financial advisor
❸ Legal advisor
❹ Former general manager
❺ Environmental advisor
❻ Company secretary, *responsible for the minutes – possibly taken by a minuting secretary*
❼ *chairs for non-members called in for consultation on a particular item of agenda*
❽ Chief accountant
❾ Personnel and general administration officer
❿ Factory Manager
⓫ Marketing manager
⓬ Managing director

Fig. 1.1 A board of directors

Functions of the board of directors

Everything that happens in a company takes place through the authority of the board of directors. The minutes of a **board meeting** embody resolutions passed by the directors which authorise the managing director and the other executive directors to perform such acts as are necessary to implement board policies. The functions of the board may therefore be listed as follows:

1   The determination of policy, the clarification of the company's objectives and the formulation of plans to achieve them.
2   The establishment of a proper organisation, with a suitable executive structure, including the appointment of appropriately qualified executives to fill the posts thus created.
3   The board must ensure compliance with the detailed legal requirements of the country concerned. In the United Kingdom the rules are contained in the Companies Acts 1985–9. There are hundreds of points in the Acts which carry penalties if they are not performed. A typical phrase from the Acts reads:

   If a company fails to comply with any provision of sections (1) to (7) above, every officer of the company shall be liable on summary conviction to imprisonment for a term not exceeding six months, or to a fine not exceeding £1000 or both.

   Such phrases are to be found on almost every page of the Acts.
4   Compliance with a wide range of other Acts of Parliament, such as the Factory Acts, the Health and Safety at Work Acts, the Finance Acts, and so on, are major functions which the board must allow for in its organisation. Thus the Health and Safety at Work Act requires every employer who has more than five employees to draw up a written statement on the firm's general policy on health and safety at work. The board will need to appoint someone to draw up this statement, after due consultation with representatives of the employees, and no doubt it will be an item on the board's agenda at which all the implications are considered – for example, the need to publicise the policy among the staff and to carry out safety training programmes, and so on. Every country has similar regulatory legislation.
5   Financial provision must be made so that every aspect of the company's work can be carried out effectively. At the start of the company's activities this involves the provision of the initial capital. Later it requires constant consideration of the cash flow and appraisal of the firm's activities to ensure that they are profitable. The dividend policy of the board (which decides how much of the profit shall be given to the shareholders each year) will be largely influenced by the need to retain funds to meet future capital expenditure.
6   Many other board functions could be listed, but perhaps the most important function of all is to maintain the morale of the organisation by effective leadership at all times. *A board of directors must display a manifest harmony, enthusiasm for the firm's products, projects and programmes and a quiet confidence in the firm's future prospects.*

1.4 Functions within an organisation

The term 'function' is widely used to describe almost every type of organisational activity. The pattern of organisations is so diverse and the views of managers in different fields vary so much that it is almost impossible to advance an explanation of the functions within an organisation without laying oneself open to criticism. The difficulty really lies in the alternative wide and narrow definitions of the word 'function'. In its dictionary meaning, the word defines 'the activity proper to anything'. On this broad definition every individual in an organisation has his/her specialist function to perform, so that there are hundreds of functions which could be listed – every job description is a specialist function.

Narrowing the definition of 'function' down, we may take the example of Henri Fayol, one of the early writers on management theory. He divided the functions within an organisation into six major groups. These were as follows:

1 Technical (the production or manufacturing function).
2 Commercial (the function which buys, sells and exchanges).
3 Financial (the function which seeks to achieve the optimum use of capital).
4 Accounting (the record-keeping function).
5 Security (the function which seeks to preserve property and protect important staff).
6 Management (the function which plans, coordinates and controls).

Updating Fayol's list, we should probably today divide the 'commercial' function into two parts – purchasing and marketing – while the greater emphasis placed these days on human resources requires us to add a personnel function. Fayol's classification of management as a separate function refers to the senior level of management only, since the management role operates at all levels to some extent – the factory manager, for example, controlling the work of the factory. Today we might also add a research and development function, and an information technology function.

An even narrower definition of 'function' applies the word to a more specialist type of activity which is super-departmental. F.W. Taylor, the founder of 'scientific management', referred to functional specialists as managers whose specialism required them to act in most, if not all, departments. Thus the personnel officer's function affects all departments; work study is as appropriate to the office as it is to the factory; quality control influences every product made, and so on. Hence these specialist functions were not only departmental, like other functions, but operated throughout the organisation both in an advisory way and with executive authority. Clearly such a function can only operate effectively if pains are taken to ensure cooperation and goodwill from the heads of departments.

Functions and authority

Drawing these ideas together in order to arrive at some acceptable meaning of the term 'function' we may say that the term implies *authority to act with respect to a group of specific activities in the organisation.* If the group of activities is a fundamental part of the organisation, set up to achieve its aims and objectives, it is called a **line function**. Such functions as production, purchasing and marketing are examples. These functions are often referred to as the 'primary group' of activities.

If the function is one which influences all departments, or several departments, like the personnel function, it is called a **staff function**. Even so the personnel officer, for example, will have a line function to perform within his/her own department, where he/she will be superior to other members of the department. The personnel officer's staff function is one of advising, assisting and counselling other line managers in securing personnel of the right type for the posts they have to fill so that the company is never starved of the human resources it requires.

Organisations establish a framework of authority, with successive layers of delegation of authority from higher to lower levels. Such authority is called *de jure* authority, or **legal authority**. Its basis is the agreement between employer and employed, whereby in return for the appointment and the remuneration that goes with it the employed persons agree to obey the authority of those placed over them, and to cooperate in the achievement of the aims of the organisation they are about to join.

Because the process of delegation passes from higher levels to lower levels, a 'line' is established so that *de jure* authority may also be called 'line' authority, or **line management**. Sometimes the lawful nature of the authority is emphasised by giving written statements of the powers conferred upon a manager. These become matters of record maintained by a secretariat, and may require the manager to draw up similar written statements of the powers he/she delegates to others lower down his/her own line of command.

De jure authority will help a manager to achieve recognition from subordinates, but it cannot in fact guarantee that he/she will have authority. *De facto* authority (**real-life authority**) has to be won rather than conferred from above. Many managers give instructions, but if they are to be carried out the social group which receives the instructions has to concede that they must be obeyed. An individual who has superior knowledge, or a reputation for wise decisions, or adequate rapport with employees generally, will get the things he/she wants done put into effect without delay. The informal relationships established with other managers and with staff at all levels will ensure that he/she is conceded *de facto* authority by equals and subordinates, who cooperate in achieving corporate aims. It is not enough that people do as they are told; because in that case they have to be pushed into every little effort. What is wanted is for the manager's authority to be such that others will take up the activity and show initiative and enthusiasm for the work in hand.

The major functions within an organisation are basic subdivisions of the enterprise which take advantage of the division of labour and the use of specialist skills and knowledge. Although they reflect traditional thinking, there are definite advantages to be gained by marshalling expertise along functional lines and it is unlikely that departmental organisation will ever disappear totally from the organisational scene. Let us briefly consider some of these major departments

1 Purchasing department

Before goods can be manufactured or services supplied, raw materials or other requirements must be purchased. This work is of crucial importance, because costing of the final product starts with the price of the raw materials and components purchased for its manufacture, while the overhead costs begin with the purchase of premises, furniture, machinery and other assets, and such items as stationery and documentation. The purchasing department will be responsible for buying the raw materials, machinery, office equipment, stationery and other items needed to produce the firm's products and market them effectively. Purchasing department personnel will evaluate new equipment or business systems to decide whether they should be adopted; they will visit exhibitions, demonstrations or suppliers' premises for the purpose of discussing prices or delivery dates; and they will develop a list of accredited suppliers whose products and terms of trading are acceptable. The purchasing officer may be of board status; he/she will usually be professionally qualified – a member of the Institute of Purchasing and Supply – with a small team of middle management, clerical and secretarial staff.

2 Production department

This is the centre which achieves the firm's production. It is usually called the factory rather than the production department. Its manager will usually be a **production engineer** or **mechanical engineer** and will often have board status. He/she will usually have at least one deputy manager, and a range of middle management staff appropriate to the range of the company's activities. There will also be supervisory grades in most areas and a numerous workforce. Some measure of representation will exist at all levels and industrial relations will be a major concern of the factory manager.

3 Marketing department

The term 'marketing' is applied to a 'super-department' which groups certain functions such as product development, packaging, physical distribution and warehousing, sales, display and advertising under one senior executive, usually of board status. The justification for such a super-department is that modern large-scale business requires such an enormous capital commitment to the production of its products that it is absolutely essential to find customers, or create them if they cannot be found. A product simply cannot be allowed to fail. To ensure the fullest development of the market a strong team is required, and a fully professional approach is essential. The marketing manager and many of his sales managers and area managers will be members of the Institutes of Marketing, Export, Freight Forwarding, and so on.

4 Accounts department

The accounting function is of enormous importance in the modern company since every aspect of a company's activities involves cash flows into or out of the business. The chief accountant or financial director will usually be of board status and responsible directly for all aspects of business finance. This means a heavy workload preparing financial **budgets** to ensure that the company is neither starved of capital nor wasteful of its financial resources. The assistance that can now be given by computerised services enables him/her to watch for trends that are developing in the business and take steps to avoid problems that may be arising. Besides these higher-level functions, the day-to-day bookkeeping and costing activities are of great importance.

5 General administration office

This department is a non-specialist department dealing with all those activities which promote the general organisation of the enterprise. The administrative officer will be a person of wide experience, to whom all other departmental heads can turn for advice on general office procedures. In many enterprises he/she may be in charge of the appointment of staff, the ordering of equipment and stationery, the general supervision of the premises including security, caretaking and cleaning, canteen or refreshment arrangements and many other matters. Very often this office will have the inward and outward mail arrangements under its general control as well as reception and telephone services, safety and first-aid arrangements and, very often, secretarial and word-processing departments. Today computerised systems will be a major interest, especially for larger organisations.

6 Personnel department

The personnel function is to secure for the business such categories of staff as are necessary, with appropriate degrees of skill and knowledge. It advertises for and appoints staff of suitable quality for the various activities of the business, runs induction and training courses and prepares updating lectures, demonstrations and seminars. These serve to bring existing staff to higher levels of efficiency, and to introduce new procedures. The personnel department also preserves records about the performance of individual members of staff; considers candidates for promotion and circularises regular reports for completion by supervisors and departmental heads. It hears complaints from staff and rearranges staffing to avoid conflict where clashes of opinions or principle appear likely to prove troublesome. Finally, it deals with the dismissal of staff, prepares testimonials for personnel leaving employment and handles welfare problems when necessary. The personnel officer will usually be of board status, and a professionally qualified member of the Institute of Personnel and Development or a similar body.

Probably the departments mentioned above are those most likely to have heads of departments who are also directors. The company secretary, who usually has a legal background, attends all meetings of the board of directors, and of the company, and will make accurate minutes of such meetings. His/her main function is to deal with such matters as the transfer of shares and debentures and possibly other legal aspects of the company's activities.

No organisational chart can be more than a guideline, for each organisation has its own appropriate structure. Fig. 1.2 gives one possible scheme.

Other departments may be of equal importance with those shown in certain enterprises. Directly or indirectly the work of every department is subject to the review of the board of directors, and the functioning of every department will appear from time to time (and certainly at times of crisis) as an item on the board's agenda.

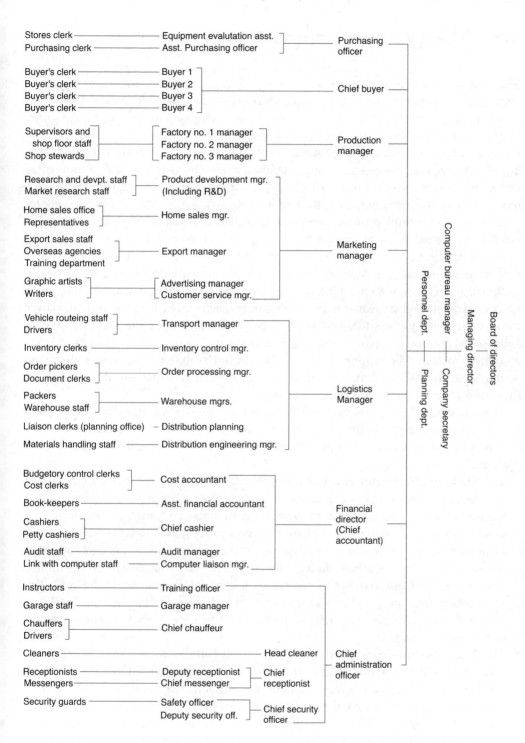

Fig. 1.2   An organisation chart

1.5   The 'systems' approach to organisation

The modern approach to organisation is to regard it as a procedure for setting up a 'system' which will operate successfully in a given environment to achieve the objectives set by top management. A system may be defined as 'an interacting or interdependent group of items forming a unified whole'. Just as a digestive system consists of various organs which are capable of extracting the sugars, proteins and other chemicals in the foods and liquids we ingest, a business system can operate to convert raw materials into finished goods, or to provide services of a particular type, in a given environment. Ultimately at the moment the overall environment is the nation–state, whose laws form the framework for the organisation, though even nation–states these days may be part of a bigger federation (such as the United States of America) or a grouping such as the European Union. Taking the more limited view, that organisations are systems to achieve certain objectives in a national environment, we can work backwards to regard each organisation itself as a collection of subsystems which are interrelated and interacting with one another. Thus the functional departments are hierarchical subsystems each of which tries to fulfil its part of the general plan, but the success of which depends as much upon the activities of other subsystems as upon its own efforts. This is why the formal line authority of the department system has to be reinforced with **informal horizontal arrangements** which cut across departmental divisions and bring in other subsystems to achieve the true aims of the whole system – the aims of the organisation.

The system view of organisations is a dynamic view which takes account of the impacts that decisions in one part of the system make upon other parts of the system.

A number of important concepts illustrate the 'systems' approach to organisations. They are:

1 **The 'chain of effects' concept.** This concept holds that a chain of effects follows from any decision or event that occurs in a system. This chain of effects may be amplified as it reacts with and interacts on other subsystems, or it may be damped down until it has no effect at all. Thus an increase in toolroom wages may ramify into every department or subsystem, and what was originally a limited increase in costs may become a general increase which threatens the viability of the company. The manager who takes a limited view of the implications of his/her decisions, seeing only up and down the 'tunnel' of line management, may do the organisation a great disservice. He/she must be able to foresee the chain of effects that will follow from any decision, in the wider environment of the whole system.

2 **The 'state transition' concept.** This takes the chain of effects concept and uses it to build up a model of the system as it passes from state to state. Every organisation is in a given state, or condition, at any given moment. The influences at work and the decisions taken when it is in one state will produce a chain of effects which will bring it into a new state in due course. When it has arrived in this new state, further outside effects will again create problems which will then be resolved by taking decisions which bring about yet another state of the organisation. *The manager must see problems embedded in decisions and be aware of the likely interactions and interdependencies in the system.* He/she

will then be able to predict the behaviour of complex systems and reduce the disadvantages and maximise the advantages which follow from a decision.

3   **The 'life-cycle' concept.** Certain subsystems in any organisation have a predictable life-cycle which can be anticipated and used. For example, a product has a definite life-cycle – it may be 'fad today and fade tomorrow', it may be more enduring, perhaps following a bulge in the birth rate and lasting several years. If the chain of effects leads the manager to envisage a definite life-cycle for a particular effect he/she must work this into the overall planning. Thus staff likely to be engaged in a particular activity for several years may need to be retrained as the life-cycle of the activity draws to a close. Natural wastage elsewhere might not be replaced so that human factors becoming available at the end of the life-cycle can be transferred to take the places made available. The systems approach enhances the manager's appraisal of his/her own line function by requiring a broader view of the needs of the system as a whole. He/she will be able to evaluate alternative courses of action, budget more economically and realistically, develop control systems with appropriate feedback techniques and raise the team's personal contribution to total efficiency at whatever level it operates.

1.6   Planning control feedback cycles

The coordination and control of the whole organisation's activities start with the framing of general goals and continue until such time as the goals have been achieved. Even then most organisations are continuous, and a new cycle of activities begins. The board must establish procedures which review the work of all departments at regular intervals, and detect unfavourable developments in time for them to be corrected.

Laying down a policy

A major framework for controlling and coordinating the work of any enterprise is the general policy laid down by the board. Policy lays down the principles which guide the firm in its day-to-day activities and is made clear by recording board decisions about matters discussed. When a decision is 'minuted' in this way by the 'minuting secretary' it becomes a part of board policy. It may then, in certain circumstances, be published formally as part of a rule-book of some sort. Thus 'safety policy' or 'pension policy' or 'consumer-relations policy' might be subjects which need to be published so that everyone in the firm knows what the policy is on such matters. Other matters – for example, board procedure – might not need to be published in this way, but could be raised as 'points of order' by board members who felt that the chairman was permitting some departure from normal procedure in the conduct of a particular meeting.

The board, therefore, has a collective duty to lay down policies that will guide staff in their day-to-day activities, in their relationships within the firm and with the general public outside.

Discretion within a policy

However precise a policy may be, cases invariably arise where the matter is neither black nor white, but some shade of grey. The exercise of discretion within a policy is therefore inevitable, and an established procedure will decide who has the right to exercise discretion within the policy. Generally this involves some movement up the chain of command. A asks B (his immediate supervisor) for an afternoon off. B regrets that, while she is authorised to excuse A's attendance on certain grounds, the reason A gives is outside B's discretion. She therefore suggests that A sees C (B's supervisor), who has the power to exercise discretion on the matter. When consulted, C agrees to exercise his discretion and A's request for time off is granted.

Another example might be the granting of credit to a customer. A salesman may be allowed to take orders with an automatic credit period of one month up to a limit of £250. A request by a customer to be supplied with goods worth £1000 would need to be referred to the salesman's area manager, who might have discretion up to £5000. Orders worth more than this figure might need head office approval.

Planning and control

Once policy has been laid down and approval for a particular programme has been given, detailed planning can begin to take place. Planning operates at a range of levels. At the boardroom level it begins to determine the general framework of the organisation. Which departments will be necessary initially and who shall we appoint to lead them? What skills do we require and what induction programmes are necessary for those appointed, to familiarise them with the product or service we are to offer? As progress is made the work extends into more and more areas so that detailed planning of particular aspects can proceed. The layout of the plant, the design of communication systems, the interrelation of activities, the design of systems of work and the familiarisation of all grades of employees with their tasks are not the work of a single day. Endless feedback from each centre of planning activity to management is essential if the difficulties which arise are to be solved; the timing of each activity so as to fit in with other developments may be crucial. This network of activities may appear chaotic to the outsider, but if a proper planning-control feedback cycle is developed the project will eventually secure final approval and full-scale production or operation will be achieved. The general pattern of such a system is illustrated in Fig. 1.3.

Reports

Control systems frequently call for regular reports, either at daily, weekly or monthly intervals. Thus the banking of takings by multiple shop branch managers would be a matter for daily reporting, while stock levels would probably be checked at a monthly stock-taking report. The most common way control is achieved by this reporting system is called **management by exceptions**. A simple example is the teacher's register in any classroom. When the register is marked at the start of each session a series of strokes is inserted for

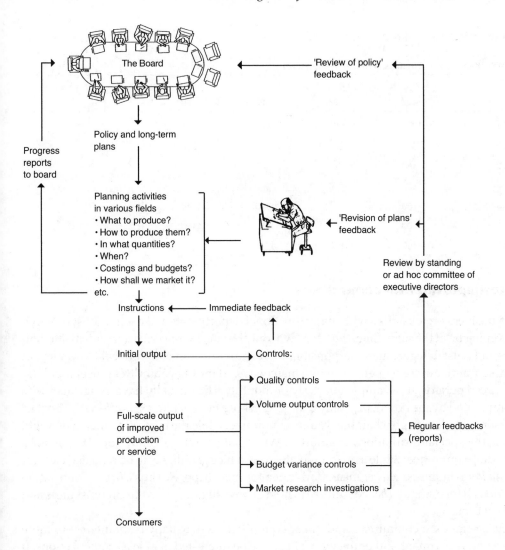

Fig.1.3   A planning-control feedback cycle

each student or pupil present, usually in red ink. An absent pupil is marked by a black circle. The supervisor, usually the head of the school, can see at once the exceptions to the normal rule that every pupil should attend every session. A single black circle may be explained by a dental appointment or some domestic difficulty causing absence, which a note from the parent will justify. Repeated absence calls for investigation, and perhaps some appropriate action – a bunch of grapes for the sick pupil; punishment for the truant; prosecution of the parent who fails to ensure that the pupil attends school regularly. In a similar way, Table 1.1 reveals the outputs achieved by seven pottery kilns designed to produce 1000 units per week. Which of these are exceptional and require investigation?

Table 1.1   Output of kilns

Name of Kiln	Output achieved in weeks shown			
	27	28	29	30
No. 1	850	950	1000	1025
No. 2	950	1000	1000	1000
No. 3	480	520	460	–
No. 4	880	920	940	945
No. 5	750	740	1160	1040
No. 6	1000	1000	1050	1100
No. 7	1760	1840	1580	–

Interdepartmental committees

In a business organisation, with many functional departments and a whole host of activities going on at the same time, the board will only be able to concern itself with major matters and must **delegate** many responsibilities to individuals or committees at lower levels. The committee system operates in two main ways. **Standing committees** meet regularly at agreed periods, for example quarterly or monthly. They usually have a chairman who is appointed by the board, probably a director whose field of interest is affected. Thus the personnel officer might chair the welfare committee, while the marketing manager might chair the special promotions committee. Where an activity is continuous it calls for a standing committee, while a matter which arises which is unlikely to be repeated calls for an ***ad hoc*** committee. *Ad hoc* means 'arranged for this purpose'. Thus a fire at a substation might call for a small *ad hoc* committee to hold an investigation into the circumstances and report back.

Most standing committees and *ad hoc* committees will usually be of interest to more than one department. Either the whole firm will be interested or at least some sections. It will therefore be necessary to appoint, or permit the election of, representatives of each department concerned to the committee so that it is interdepartmental. The committee members then have a dual function. Not only have they to reach conclusions about the matter in hand and prepare a report and recommendations for management, but they also have to inform members of their departments of the developments that have taken place if they are matters for general concern. The reporting back process is of great importance. E-mail helps, but an effective departmental representative has to have access to secretarial help if it is necessary to circulate a report to others in the department.

2 Characteristic features of organisations

2.1 The structure of organisations

Organisations are set up to achieve certain aims, such as the production of goods or services, the preservation of peace and social harmony, the prevention of abject poverty, and so on. These aims have to be achieved by a succession of activities, so that after a time a routine is established, precedents are created, recurring difficulties are met by repeating established procedures previously found to be helpful, and so on. This succession of activities leads in the end to the establishment of an orderly structure for the organisation, with tasks allocated to officials in a fairly complex pattern, with suitable arrangements for supervision and coordination.

Organisations usually start with an initial structural plan, which is modified in the light of experience, particularly as the work to be performed grows or changes. The modifications are made to meet the needs revealed by the work of the organisation and the criticisms it receives from outsiders, particularly clients. Client dissatisfaction can be a powerful influence for change, since it represents strong evidence that the organisation is failing to achieve the objectives for which it was established, or the new objectives which have been revealed by the passage of time. Alterations to the structure of the organisation may prove in the end to meet the needs of the new situation and client dissatisfaction will decrease. A good deal of the evidence for client dissatisfaction will come from business administrators at various levels, and it will be them that seek to reduce dissatisfaction by applying whatever remedy is agreed upon.

Alternatively, such alterations may fail to meet these needs. In some cases client dissatisfaction will be met by indifference or a failure to adjust the working of the organisation for fear of disturbing established routines. Take a 'social security' system which has been established partly to ensure that no-one in a society suffers abject poverty. Over a period of time, to prevent abuse, checks and balances are built into the system so that benefits can only be paid after suitable enquiries, home visits, and so on, have been made. Furthermore, money payments are made by a system of direct credits calculated by a central computer, a system which involves some short delay. The result of these internal arrangements is that an applicant for relief who has sufficient funds to survive a short waiting period can sit back and wait for the machinery to work before receiving his/her relief. The applicant who, for whatever reason, is in desperate circumstances cannot obtain the relief so urgently required. The internal routines have defeated the original objectives, and the 'insecure' client cannot achieve 'social security'. The organisation may even justify the existence of client dissatisfaction on the grounds that to make a special case and grant relief at once to a particular individual is against the principle of 'impartial' social security on which the whole organisation is based. The only solution to such an impasse is a general review of the structure of the organisation by a body having the necessary authority.

Every organisation therefore has a structure appropriate to its aims and objectives, and embodying some centre of authority from which its activities at any given time can be directed.

2.2   The need for authority

Every organisation must have a framework of authority and in modern society the type of authority known as 'legal authority' has become the predominant type. Before considering legal authority in greater detail, let us just refer to the other two types of pure authority: charismatic authority and traditional authority.

Charismatic authority stems from the personality of the person in authority and the personal loyalty and obedience accorded to him/her by virtue of his/her leadership qualities. Such authority may still be found in certain circumstances, such as in times of national peril (in resistance movements during the Second World War, for example). The inventors of new technology, who establish new industries in the face of indifference from financial backers and public scepticism, may similarly achieve authority in their organisations by their charisma (a term meaning 'gift of grace').

Traditional authority is authority based upon established beliefs and the desirability of preserving immemorial traditions. It may have originated in the charismatic qualities of an original leader, the authority devolving upon his/her sons and daughters conferring status upon them. Such 'chieftainship' is met with in monarchies and in small businesses and private companies run on patriarchal lines. The essence of such authority is that it is personal, owed to the individual who occupies the post of authority by virtue of tradition, and his/her activities are bound by those traditions from which the authority stems.

Legal authority. When we compare the above types of authority with what may be termed the normal system of authority for large organisations in modern society, we find that the chief difference is that modern authority is impersonal, rather than personal. The authority belongs to the 'office' and not to the individual. Obedience to the individual stems from his/her elevation to the position of 'office holder' under the rules laid down for the organisation. Everything the official does stems from the authority conferred upon his/her office, and an official who acts outside the scope of the authority of that office will not be obeyed. (Note that the word 'office' here is used in the sense of a particular post or position to which the 'office holder' is appointed – for example, the obedience to which the head of a college is entitled springs from his/her appointment to the office of 'Principal'.)

The great advantage of legal authority as a basis for modern organisations is that it is possible to cater for the complex requirements of modern life. While charismatic authority and traditional authority are based on the personality of individuals, legal authority is impersonal and unaffected by the departure or death of an individual. Loyalty is owed to the office, not to the official occupying the office at any particular moment, so that continuity of loyalty is possible even though individuals change. New offices can be established at will to meet changes in the needs of the organisation or of society. All that is necessary to create a new office is to pass the necessary legal measures. This does not necessarily mean a new Act of Parliament or other legislature, though that does happen at the highest level of rule-making. At lower levels it simply requires the passing of a resolution at the necessary board meeting or committee meeting and the embodiment of this resolution in writing as part of 'standing orders' or a 'book of rules'.

The result is that the organisation is extended to include the new office, which becomes part of a general **bureaucracy**, a term derived from the French word for 'desk'. The term bureaucracy has become a term of abuse, symbolising the existence of a host of petty officials who obstruct action in every possible way. This need not necessarily be the case, for a bureaucratic system is inevitable in the complexities of modern life. It overcomes the limitations of individuals by establishing a system of division of labour. Each office has a sphere of competence within which it is empowered to act. It will in due course achieve efficiency in these activities and perform its functions in an economical way. It is the efficiency and economy of the bureaucratic system which has made it the almost universal solution to organisational problems. However, critics of bureaucracy can also claim with a good deal of justification that some of its malfunctions and inadequacies operate in such a way as to preserve the system even when it is no longer either efficient or economic.

Authority conferred by empowerment

Those who are critical of traditional authority chiefly come from the new type of entrepreneurial organisations which are more fully described later in this chapter (see p. 28). In these organisations a new form of authority is conferred upon the widest possible range of staff by a process known as empowerment. What this means is that everyone is empowered to act in the best interests of the company, and does not need to seek authority from supervisors or higher-level staff. He/she may make decisions and act upon them, and these decisions will be upheld by the company (even if they prove to be wrong). This idea is a very liberating one. It sets people free to do responsible things, but in order to ensure that most of the things done are in the best interests of the company it does call for much wider training, more generally shared knowledge, no secrets from anyone, and 100 percent backup for staff doing their best to promote the company's aims and objectives. A fuller explanation of the advantages and disadvantages of empowerment is given later in this chapter (see p. 31).

2.3   The features of bureaucratic organisation

The features of bureaucratic organisation may be listed as follows:

1 Authority lies, and obedience is paid, to the established impersonal order of offices.
2 Each office is established by rules, which have either been agreed at the outset or laid down over the years as being manifestly necessary.
3 Each official performs his/her functions in conformity with the rules of the office.
4 The rules are applied by the official to any particular problem or case that arises, and after a while as similar cases occur the application of the rules is generalised, that is they are applied in the same way to every similar case that arises.
5 Subordinates who obey the official's instructions are obeying the office as a member of the organisation, and not the individual office holder on a personal basis.
6 The organisation develops a hierarchical structure, with arrangements for appealing to a higher level of the hierarchy, and also the opportunity to state a grievance. The hierarchical structure may also form a part of a **mechanism of compulsion** by which an official who is acting correctly within the rules of his/her office can be upheld if subordinates refuse to obey instructions.
7 The successive layers of organisation permit a considerable division of labour, with each 'office' having its agreed sphere of competence, and an agreed measure of discretion which it can exercise within that sphere of policy. If the circumstances of a particular case or situation require discretion to be exercised outside the agreed measure, it is necessary to move up the hierarchy to seek approval. The system therefore lays down not only what an individual may do, but also what he/she may not do. Loyalty to the system and obedience to superiors become conditions of membership of the bureaucracy.
8 In general the office holder has no right to his/her office, other than the contractual rights in the appointment to it, which may be revoked at will by those with authority. A rare exception to this rule occurs in circumstances where the individual has to display complete independence. Judges under the British constitution have a right to continue in their offices, unless displaced by a very special procedure.

Elements of the bureaucratic system will be found in almost all large-scale organisations, whether they be private sector limited companies, public sector corporations or government departments. Differences in detail will certainly occur and the system permits a wide variety of structures to suit particular needs. The strength of bureaucratic organisation lies in the permanence of an impersonal organisation with formal methods of working. It develops a professional approach, with concepts of duty to be performed dispassionately, treating everyone in the same way.

Its weaknesses are that its very impersonality is inappropriate to some of the aims for which organisations are established. It may lack, in its cold impartiality, the humanity, tenderness or enthusiasm which alone can give client satisfaction in certain circumstances. The large number of rules associated with every office may develop into a defensive mechanism which reduces the service the organisation gives to outsiders and preserves the bureaucracy for its own purposes, as a cosy club for insiders.

These weaknesses alone are sufficient to justify the view held by many top managers that the structure of every organisation needs re-examining at intervals to evaluate its performance and systems of work.

2.4   Non-bureaucratic organisations

While it is true that practically all organisations in advanced societies display features of bureaucracy in their structures, there has been a tendency in recent years for a new system to replace bureaucracy. Bureaucracy operates best in a world which is well ordered and stable, which we may describe as the type of 'world' created by a developed capitalism. Production grows steadily under the general influence of a bureaucratic system based upon the fuller and fuller exploitation of specialisation and the division of labour. More and more people are drawn into the system as technical competence rises, with universal education continued for longer and longer periods. A levelling-up takes place, as the mass of the people attain reasonable levels of economic satisfaction, while a levelling-down process also occurs under the influence of taxation and the extension of 'equal treatment' under the bureaucracy, which reduces class privileges. The result of these trends is that production rises and technology advances under the influence of research and development departments. *Eventually production outstrips demand as a new age of affluence dawns.*

This introduces a new era of uncertainty to which bureaucracy is less well-suited. The original ambition of the industrial revolution, to produce goods independently of human labour, is now about to be achieved. High technology replaces routine labour. A huge reassessment of the social structure needs to be made but it is difficult to reallocate resources against the powerful vested interests surviving from the old system. For example, the new wealth has been created by the high technology, but the rewards for production may be filched by vested interests in the old 'skilled' trades. In the 1960s dockers claimed that work had been stolen from them; printers demanded higher rates of pay for less work on the ground that output was higher; redundancy payments had to be conceded if labour forces were to be reduced and the switch from capital-intensive manufacturing to labour-intensive services required vast retraining programmes. The egalitarian climate in industry does not favour the bureaucratic belief that the person at the top always knows better than the others lower down. Indeed, in an era of galloping technology the person at the bottom may know more than the one at the top, having been trained more recently.

Some recent examples in the former nationalised industries have illustrated how easy it is on privatisation to remove or replace top personnel without the organisation suffering at all. Some major mergers in private sector companies have similarly cast doubts upon the ability of the top level of a bureaucratic system to control an uncertain situation. The activities of specialist workers grouped in separate offices, performing activities in isolation, and without any knowledge of the total requirements of the organisation in the real world, become less and less meaningful.

Organismic structures

What these highly technological industries need to survive in an era of fierce competition where markets have to be created rather than served is an organisation which is lively and active at all levels. This has been called an **'organismic' structure** rather than a 'mechanistic' structure. The features of such a living structure may be listed as follows:

1 Individuals at all levels use their skills and knowledge to *contribute to the common task of the organisation*. This means they must know *the total situation of the firm or organisation in its environment*, and be aware of its aims and objectives. They then undertake activity which will make a real contribution to achieve the aims, or perhaps defeat a difficulty that is interfering with the achievement of the aims.

2 The structure of the organisation takes the form of a network, each individual being joined up to other individuals in a network of communications, control and authority. *Knowledge may lie anywhere in the network, and authority lies temporarily with the individual whose knowledge is most appropriate to the problems currently needing solution.*

3 Communication does not consist, as in a bureaucracy, of reports flowing upwards and instructions flowing downwards, but of information and advice flowing in all directions from centres of knowledge to less informed areas.

4 The rather stultifying and ingrown obedience to the office, which in a bureaucracy requires staff to act within a limited sphere of competence in accordance with established rules, is replaced by a positive requirement for staff to act in accordance with their commitment to the concern as a whole, and the need to promote the general well-being of the enterprise and its material advancement. This makes every contribution by the employee a positive act to achieve the success of the organisation as a whole. The general atmosphere becomes democratic rather than bureaucratic.

Human relations systems

The 'organismic' structure described above introduces into the organisation a large measure of autonomy for the individual. He/she is no longer dominated by a superior, holding the employee's nose in close proximity to the grindstone. Instead he/she is making a contribution to the total achievement of the organisation, in proportion to his/her own ability and knowledge of the particular programme being undertaken.

The 'human relations' movement seeks to ensure that each individual is fitted into the organisation in such a way that he/she identifies with the work in hand, which meets his/her own needs. Thus where the individual is content with merely satisfying economic needs – the part-time working housewife perhaps, whose other needs for self-esteem and self-realisation may be fulfilled domestically – the place assumed in the organisation will be one with a minimum of commitment. Such an individual will be content to clock on and clock off, having performed a fair half-day's work for a fair half-day's pay. Another employee may have quite different needs, and require a position in the organisation which yields not only economic rewards but also psychological rewards in terms of *self-esteem, self-realisation, status and respect from peer groups*.

Almost all organisations will face these types of behavioural differences in their work-forces, and conscious attempts to match the tasks to be performed with the economic and psychological needs of the individuals available will improve operational efficiency. The human relations movement seeks to reconcile the interests of an individual employee with the interests of the firm so that the employee approves of and cooperates with manage-ment policies, through which he/she is able to achieve self-esteem, the esteem of others and a large measure of self-realisation.

2.5 The traditional principles of organisation

We may lay down the traditional principles of organisation as follows:

1 Define the objectives which the organisation is intended to achieve, giving attention to both long-term and short-term objectives.
2 Decide what necessary types of work are involved and group them where possible into areas of responsibility.
3 Designate posts to take care of each area of responsibility and a hierarchy of lesser posi-tions where necessary.
4 Define the responsibilities of each post – and eventually of each position.
5 Accord each post and position an appropriate level of authority by a formal procedure.
6 Draw up and publish statements of policy and codes of conduct so that staff have ref-erence points for all potential problems.

These points require amplification.

1 *Defining the objectives* A new business must start with some sort of business plan and a clear definition of the objectives should be the most important part of this plan. Remember that in the United Kingdom before a company can be founded, a clause known as the 'objects clause' must be drawn up and included in the Memorandum of Association. It is these objects which the company will be allowed to pursue when the registration procedure is completed. Any departure from the objects clause renders the acts of the company *ultra vires* (outside the agreed powers) and illegal. Although it is possible to change the objects of the company by a special resolution there is a proce-dure by which shareholders can object to this. In any case the new 'objects clause' also requires careful consideration.

A new business will usually need financial help and the bank or finance house being asked for assistance will almost always wish to study the business plan. The opportu-nity should not be missed to seek the bank's views on the objects as defined, and this may result in a revision of the stated objectives.

With an existing firm or company where a reappraisal of the organisation is taking place, the objectives may need to be redefined in view of changing circumstances. Perhaps an *ad hoc* committee will have been set up to review the organisation's effec-tiveness and its report will form the basis for a wide-ranging discussion. A good oppor-tunity for a free expression of views should be afforded to all concerned, with reassurances so that morale is not eroded by the uncertainty. In this respect the difference between long-term objectives and short-term objectives may be important. Some reconstructions take several years to put into effect and the areas most remote from change may as well be advised so that nervousness is reduced.

2 *Areas of responsibility* The necessary types of work required will follow fairly easily from the statement of the objectives, but grouping them into areas of responsibility is not so easy. What is needed is a clear representation of the board's ideas to each group of employees and an equally clear channel for reporting back to top management of problems that may arise. Some areas of work fall naturally together, for example sales, exports, packing and dispatch might all quite reasonably come under a marketing director. It is generally recognised that most managers cannot keep control of more than six subordinates and the wider their fields of activity are the more difficult it will be to coordinate their activities and know what is really going on. Where the areas of responsibility are broad, the span of control should be reduced, say, to four, or even three. In designating areas of responsibility, allowances should be made to keep the organisation flexible. Thus absences through ill-health, holidays, retraining and so on are bound to arise and senior staff must be able to cover all areas at all times. The grouping of related activities enables subordinates to be encouraged to broaden their areas of interest and know enough of the next person's work to give cover even if a period of absence is extensive. Nothing gives rise to client dissatisfaction more than to be greeted with the news that Mr A is on leave for three weeks and no-one knows anything about his work. Mutual support *must* be built into the system at every level.

A further aspect of flexibility is that policies, products and markets all change from time to time and it must be possible to move staff about to some extent to meet surges of activity. 'Too many senior staff and too few grass-roots personnel' is a common complaint at times when special campaigns or functions are taking place, and everyone should know that low-level activities are vital to the success of any organisation. They must be prepared to put their shoulders to the wheel if necessary.

3 *Designation of posts and responsibilities* Every job has its job description and although this is well-understood at lower levels of industry and commerce it is sometimes taken for granted at higher levels. There may be some justification for feeling that a person appointed at a professional level to a post such as chief accountant, purchasing officer, export manager, and so on, already knows a great deal about the requirements of the job and there is little point in trying to specify the work involved. On the other hand, every business is unique, with its own special arrangements and difficult areas. It is essential to define clearly:

a The responsibilities attaching to any post.

b Its position in the hierarchy of the firm, with its subordinates clearly specified below it and the person responsible above it, to whom the office holder should report. If the only body above it is the board, this should be made clear. If membership of the board of directors is to apply this should be made clear, and the post holder's agreement to the appointment must be given in writing once a formal resolution of appointment has been passed.

c Any areas where mutual support is looked for between the post holder and other post holders should be specified, so that the appointee is clear that cooperation will be expected.

4 *According levels of authority* Although it might appear that authority arises naturally in many situations, especially where it is charismatic or traditional authority, in fact in most situations it is necessary to confer authority formally on certain posts and positions. This is especially so in a bureaucratic system, especially of a public enterprise, local authority or central government nature. In emergencies staff, particularly young staff, must know to whom to look for a lead, and those who are expected to give a lead must know that they have the authority to act. Of course, necessity always confers authority – the well-known legal position of 'agent of necessity' illustrates the point. If I see a screaming child at the window of a burning house I do not need to ask your permission to borrow a ladder. The law assumes that, as a right-minded citizen, you would give every assistance, and make me your agent of necessity. Not all situations are emergencies and, in general, authority arises from the legal procedures that have been followed in organising the company or institution. This means a board decision in most cases, though this may be no more than conferring upon a director or manager the duty of organising his/her department. The authority of sub-managers and supervisors then proceeds by a sort of 'delegated legislation'. Delegated legislation is a parliamentary term: it means an instrument or order made by a government minister through his department using the powers given by earlier legislation, enacted by the sovereign power.

5 *Statements of policy and codes of conduct* These days summary 'hiring and firing' is not a practical policy in the vast majority of businesses. We must expect to treat employees properly and, in return, may look for equally courteous treatment from the employee. We must induct employees carefully and draw to their attention any health and safety aspects of their work, their conditions of employment, and so on. Copies of any policies and codes of behaviour promulgated by the board should be available and should be delivered to the employee and a signature obtained to acknowledge receipt. These codes are essential points of reference which can be called for judicially in any situation which leads to an inquiry or tribunal.

2.6   Types of organisation

There are many types of organisation and every business is unique, with its own format and hierarchy of command. We may identify the following five main types:

Line organisation

Sometimes called military or direct organisation: every member of staff knows who his/her immediate superior is and who are his/her subordinates. Orders move down the line from top to bottom and reactions to orders (other than passive compliance) move up the line from bottom to top (or as near to the top as they need to go to produce a revised order, or a confirmation of the original order). The relationship between a senior member of staff and his/her subordinates is direct; the managing director gives direct instructions to the departmental managers, for example, and they in turn give direct instructions to the divisional or sectional managers below them.

Line and staff organisation

Taking again a military comparison, a line organisation of the military type may suffer if the general in command has to make decisions on everything under the sun without consultation or advice from specialist advisers in each field. A small staff of specialists may be necessary in the intelligence, legal, strategic and other fields. In industry the planning, legal, personnel and computer staff may be regarded as separate functional organisations acting as bureaux for carrying out and advising on their functional areas. The relationship between such 'staff' organisations and the managing director is known as a functional relationship, with each functional manager drawing his/her authority from his/her appointment to the staff position. However, where the relationship is more personal, as with a managing director and a personal assistant (PA), it is said to be a staff relationship. The PA is only an extension of the managing director, speaking for him/her merely as an extension speaker. The PA's authority is the authority of the managing director, and no separate status exists.

Functional organisations

Here the organisation is centred around the various functions which have to be carried out, as illustrated in Fig. 1.2 (p. 11) and described in section 1.4 (p. 7). The director or manager of each function controls the various aspects of his/her area and coordinates their activities. He/she is responsible for the whole area to the managing director and to the board. The relationship between the managing director and the other directors is functional. At lower levels the relationship between departmental heads and subordinates is partly functional and partly line, and the lower we go in the hierarchy the more it becomes a line relationship of direct orders from superior to inferior.

The multidivisional company

Between 1920 and 1980 the multidivisional company became the universal format for large-scale business organisations. Its introduction signalled the fullest development of capitalism, with the original entrepreneurial interests of the founders of companies transferred to a mature management. Second and third generation descendants of a charismatic founder rarely have his/her leadership qualities; sooner or later the company floats on the stock exchanges of the world. What human inadequacies start, the public sector intensifies by death duties and inheritance taxes; with heirs forced to sell up, new managements take over. In the twentieth century the aim of the new management was to grow in size and diversify far beyond the original dreams of the founders of the companies taken over. The multidivisional company was the medium developed to achieve growth and diversity.

The basic structure of the multidivisional company was as shown in Fig. 2.1. The basic units were the divisions of the company, almost autonomous entrepreneurial units in a single area of business, self-contained as to staffing, premises, the various functions necessary in any major business, and so on, and run by a chief executive whose task was to go after business, pursuing opportunities as they arose. The chief executive had to maintain or, if possible, increase market share by producing new products, revamping old ones, filling niches with subsidiary production centres and providing an increasing profit from these expanding activities.

At the top of the organisation was a group of executives at the corporate headquarters. They had two functions:

a To take a long-term view of the markets and business environments in which the group worked, and to devise strategies for using its capital assets and financial resources in the best possible way.

b To monitor the returns from the divisions, particularly the return on capital employed, to assess each chief executive's success in the use of capital and manpower allocated.

Below this top-level executive group there grew up a layer of specialist management able to advise and supervise the work of the various divisions. Without hampering the entrepreneurial energy of the chief executive and his team, these top-level executives could rein in activities which seemed to be going off course; they could realign activities in a particular field if they conflicted with the work of another division, transferring it to the division that could handle it best. They provided uniform structures of cost accounting, financial accounting, research and development, public relations, and so on. They formed a backbone of interdivisional committees which could ease conflicts between divisions and alert corporate headquarters to grass-roots developments which called for new policies. They thus provided an influential, knowledgeable body for shaping future policy.

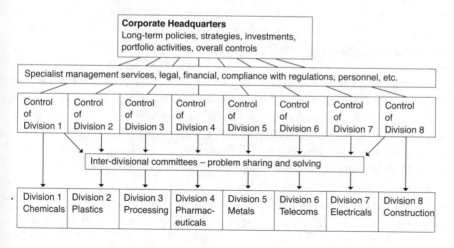

Fig. 2.1 The multidivisional company

Such companies did not depend upon the charismatic leadership of original entrepreneurs. They hired professional production, marketing and logistical staff. They could set up new teams to deal with new activities, and hence could grow profitably in any direction chosen. Above them the various layers of management provided a whole range of expert advisers keeping the general direction of the divisions on course, and ensuring that uniform methods of costing, accounting, personnel management, compliance with regulations and so on, were followed. Above this second tier of management the corporate control exercised by a sophisticated team of top executives laid down long-term policies for future development, devised strategies for expansion and accumulated reserves for future projects. They received reports from all the divisions and reviewed and compared their work. They shuffled their portfolios of investments in subsidiary companies, selling off the less successful ones and always looking for opportunities as other businesses around them developed, expanded or faltered in the competitive free-enterprise world.

Perhaps the best aspect of the multidivisional company from the staff point of view was the security, status and future prospects held out by these enormous organisations. Many people spent their entire lives working in them, displaying tremendous loyalty to them, growing with them as new skills became necessary and moving up the hierarchy, to a secure retirement in the end.

The entrepreneurial corporation

The 1980s was the decade in which it all began to go wrong for the multidivisional company. A shiver ran through one powerful company after another and the solid basis for their organisation with strong teams under a strong central control proved to be a weakness after all. What really happened was that the world proved to be too small a place for a system which believed in limitless expansion. There was a limit, after all. Excess capacity began to appear in industry after industry.

First, the newly industrialised countries (NICs) which developed in the 1960s and 1970s began to eat into the markets of the established multidivisional companies. In the 1920s the whole underdeveloped world was available for expansion. By the 1970s the situation had changed dramatically. Not only were the NICs becoming self-sufficient, they began to undercut the multidivisional companies everywhere in the world – even in their own home countries.

Second, much of the innovation that was going on was taking place in the NICs and not in the multidivisional companies. Part of the trouble was that new industries necessarily start small, and cannot carry big overheads. In the NICs there were no heavy overheads, no bloated corporate structures with tiers of middle management staffs. In the multidivisional companies the bottom line (the final profit made) was everything. Every new venture had to carry its allotted burden of corporate on-costs (overheads), and if it could not it was closed down.

The profitability of multidivisional companies came chiefly from the economies of large-scale operations, with everybody wanting the same thing. When customers became more sophisticated, requiring less bulk and more quality and variety, the multidivisional companies were less well-placed than their NIC competitors.

At first companies tried to hold onto their profit margins by short-term measures. They shut down unprofitable units and 'outsourced' components from their NIC competitors instead. They reduced budgets for acquisitions of small companies. They reduced research and development budgets. Finally they began 'down-sizing', reducing layers of middle management, pruning recruitment, reducing pension schemes, cutting overtime and even demanding wage cuts. Floating off surplus subsidiaries to management buyouts slimmed the company down. All these things helped the survival of the company for a few more years, but what they could not do was recover the entrepreneurial spirit that was essential in the new situation. People need to go to work enthusiastic for the challenges of the day that lies ahead. Generations of a 'They never tell me anything' attitude had stifled the interest and enthusiasm of grass-roots staff. The recruit who told his personnel officer that he hoped to become a small clog in a big machine had inadvertently got it just about right.

The solution to these problems looks like being (for it is still going on) the entrepreneurial corporation.

With the entrepreneurial corporation it is usual to abandon the pyramid diagram of a business organisation with a broad base of low-level staff, with tiers of middle management staff above them and the board at the apex of the pyramid. Instead the diagram is drawn horizontally. Before looking at the entrepreneurial corporation in diagrammatic form let us list the principles involved. These are:

1 No-one is more important than anyone else, because all sorts of talents are required, and all contribute to the pool of talents and energy that eventually provide the goods and services the customers require.

2 The emphasis is on innovation, because only innovation can produce the growth and renewal which are essential in the modern competitive situation.

3 Authority and responsibility should be delegated all the way to the grass-roots level, to create a lean, participative and entrepreneurial organisation. Each individual is responsible for his/her total quality performance and responsiveness to the market.

4 Entrepreneurial drive may be generated from any point in the system, or from any point outside the system. If a new idea is put up to the corporation it will evaluate it quickly and allocate funds and resources to it, if necessary recruiting top-quality staff, rewarded competitively to ensure the success of the idea.

5 Entrepreneurial drive is best structured as a new limited liability company, part of the group and integrated into the group to use the general facilities available, but a separate entity all the same. In this way, if the idea fails it can quickly be phased out and ceases to be part of the group. The assets will be realised and the proceeds returned to the group. If it is a success it is given a further and possibly an increased budget, and its profits are consolidated into the group accounts.

6 With new entrepreneurial initiatives taking place all the time, there has to be some guideline which will act as a reference point for decision-making. This reference point is the 'mission statement' drawn up by the leaders of the whole corporation. A typical mission statement might be as follows:

> *To provide quality and cost-effective paints, plastics and other surfacing materials to domestic and industrial users, and in turn to ensure:*

    a that these end-user products are safe, free of adverse ecological effects, durable and stable

    b that all employees have the opportunity to assist in the development and marketing of such products and realise their full potential in so doing c that the company's shareholders (including staff who wish to participate in share-purchase schemes) receive a satisfactory and growing level of dividend and stock value

d that the quality of life of an increasing number of the world's citizens is improved as a result of the group's activities.

The mission statement would usually be followed by a strategy statement which outlined proposed methods of achieving the mission in the years ahead.

This may seem a very broadly-worded mission statement, but it is just restricted enough to keep the group on course. Any particular proposal can be evaluated against the mission statement. If it appears to be within the guidelines its authors may proceed to draw up detailed plans, costings, and so on. If it is outside the mission statement they may not proceed but, if they choose to do so, may take it elsewhere.

7 It is essential that any new initiative must not just be developed on its own, but must be fully integrated into the work of the group. It is one thing for a bright member of staff to come up with a good idea and draw up initial costings. It is another matter to get everyone in the group interested and cooperative. The 'entrepreneur' is not going to be provided with a full range of equipment and services placed at his/her personal disposal. The aim is to use whatever facilities are already available with the cooperation of all concerned. Dealing with this integration problem is a major task for the 'mentors' (see Fig. 2.2). It is their job to coach, encourage and guide 'entrepreneurs' with a valid idea. They must ensure that a small team of mentors representative of the various areas of expertise needed is brought together to go through the detailed proposals. This will build up an enthusiastic backing for a good idea, and it is more likely to succeed.

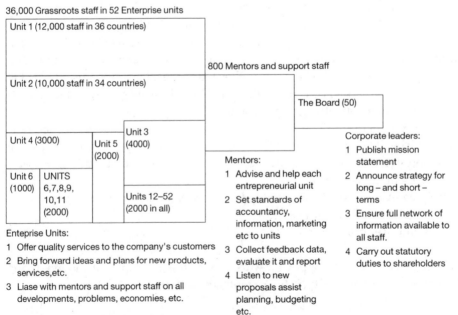

Total staff 36,850 in 41 countries

36,000 Grassroots staff in 52 Enterprise units

Unit 1 (12,000 staff in 36 countries)

800 Mentors and support staff

Unit 2 (10,000 staff in 34 countries)

The Board (50)

Unit 4 (3000)

Unit 3 (4000)

Unit 5 (2000)

Corporate leaders:

1 Publish mission statement

Mentors:

Unit 6 (1000)

UNITS 6,7,8,9, 10,11 (2000)

Units 12–52 (2000 in all)

1 Advise and help each entrepreneurial unit

2 Set standards of accountancy, information, marketing etc to units

3 Collect feedback data, evaluate it and report

4 Listen to new proposals assist planning, budgeting etc.

2 Announce strategy for long – and short – terms

3 Ensure full network of information available to all staff.

4 Carry out statutory duties to shareholders

Enteprise Units:

1 Offer quality services to the company's customers

2 Bring forward ideas and plans for new products, services,etc.

3 Liase with mentors and support staff on all developments, problems, economies, etc.

Fig. 2.2   The entrepreneurial company

8 Part of the whole process is the change made to *empowerment* as the method of conferring authority upon staff. In the more democratic atmosphere of the entrepreneurial company everyone is empowered and encouraged to take decisions on behalf of the company. If the mission statement is clear, and if the coaching of staff by knowledgeable people has been well done, most people will know what the company or the group is trying to do. If they are unsure on a particular point they can easily find out, because everyone is linked through e-mail and voice mail, and anyone can speak to anyone. Therefore everyone can make decisions on behalf of the company, and in most cases their decisions will be wise ones. Faults are tolerated in a number of situations, for example where the decision made was in line with agreed policies and established authority known to all staff. If it was a new situation where we learned something, the fault would be acceptable, but if it was a repetition of a previous error which had been brought to the attention of staff generally, then blame would follow. Also an illegal act could never be countenanced. We do hear from time to time of a currency dealer playing the market in his/her own interest, and unlawfully.

9 Finally, the 'de-layered' nature of the entrepreneurial company is much more conducive to surviving any perils that empowerment may bring. The whole organisation is flatter and more likely to detect an adverse development. There are no secret compartments with people doing their own thing. Communication is better, everyone knows everyone else, the layers of middle management have been reduced and the reins of control are more lightly held and more sensitively exercised. Enterprise is not all, but it is most of what ordinary staff are doing, and in doing so they are acting with initiative and responsibility.

Conclusions about the entrepreneurial company

If we compare Figs 2.1 and 2.2 we see that in some ways the entrepreneurial company is not all that different from the multidivisional company. This seems even more true if we make a detailed study of the annual reports of such companies. This is because, by law, both types of company must report about the same sort of things. The accounting terms used are broadly the same and the statistical results are very similarly laid out. The real differences are that in the entrepreneurial company:

1 The emphasis is on innovation. Companies cannot now just grow by doing more of the same. Customers want better quality, better variety and better value for money today. We have to devise better, more efficient, more attractive goods and services.

2 The route from prototype to public is shorter. Today we have slimmed-down organisations and more personal links with the customer. Today the consumer is king. Everywhere is a buyer's market, not a seller's market. We cannot today say 'We will make ten million of these and you will buy them at £X each.'

3 The emphasis is on the importance of every member of staff. With fewer staff, everyone becomes more vital. They must show initiative, they must believe in the mission, and they must promote the company by quality work, concern for the customer and total responsibility. Everyone is empowered to act on behalf of the company and make decisions which they believe are in the company's interest: to fulfil an order, to meet a customer's requirements, to placate a dissatisfied customer, to reduce an environmental problem, and so on.

The essential elements of empowerment are responsibility, trust, training and support.

Responsibility Every member of staff is deemed to be a responsible person who can be relied on to take decisions in the general interest of the company.

Trust Management believes every employee to be worthy of trust.

Training In order to develop responsibility and justify trust, it is essential for staff to be as widely trained as possible. There should be no 'no go' areas except in special circumstances, for example where there is a legal liability of confidentiality. On routine matters all are entitled to know about the company's mission, policies and organisation.

Support If all are entitled to take decisions they must be supported in the decisions they take. Mistakes may occur, but fault will not be found if they do, provided they were within the power of the person concerned. However, illegal activity will never be countenanced.

2.7 More about systems and subsystems

Every system of organisation, and every subsystem within that organisation, is designed to achieve the overall objectives of the organisation. It may be a rigid authoritarian system or something less authoritarian, with a consultative approach or a participative approach. These permit a reasonable degree of employee cooperation to decide the *manner* in which the objectives are achieved, while reserving policy decisions about *what* is to be achieved for top staff at boardroom level.

A system is a procedure for achieving the objectives of an organisation. It must be devised originally before the start of the organisation concerned and will be developed and re-devised as the business grows and expands. It will inevitably require decisions about many particular tasks which become subsystems of the main system. Each subsystem should be planned, and not allowed to develop piecemeal with everyone doing his/her own thing. If the organisation is a participative one, staff will examine the problem in an *ad hoc* committee and come up with a procedure which works. Each person must know what is to be done, what triggers action on his/her part and how this action triggers the next action.

Designing a procedure, or subsystem, requires:

1 Knowledge of what is to be done – the objective to be achieved.
2 Breaking down of the procedure into individual tasks and processes. Specialisation is the source of wealth because it increases productivity.
3 Decisions about who is to perform each part of the work.
4 Decisions about, and the provision of, specialist labour-saving equipment.
5 Design and production of special forms or electronic signals as required, to route products through the various subsystems as 'work in progress'.
6 The principle of 'management by exceptions' is applied wherever possible. This has already been explained (see section 1.7, p. 14). The exceptional item calls for corrective action – for example, in quality control procedures an exceptional number of 'failed'

items calls for adjustments to machines, or investigation of raw material quality, or retraining of personnel responsible.

7 In designing subsystems, costs must be kept as low as possible consistent with product quality, marketing requirements, and so on. Budgets should be prepared and departures from budget (**variances**) investigated. **Variance analysis** is a specialised technique (part of the study known as costing). We can have raw material variances, labour variances, overhead variances, volume variances, and so on. Thus if costs have risen it may be due to higher prices of raw materials, or higher wages and overhead rates, or due to the fact that output has fallen so that each unit of output has to bear a higher proportion of overhead costs.

Open and closed loop controls

In any system there will be a number of subsystems, each of which may have other subsystems embedded within it. Each part of the system may throw up a problem at any time, for example non-arrival of materials, labour absenteeism, loss of energy resources, adverse environmental effects, the need to press ahead with one aspect or to retard another aspect. We shall need to build in control procedures called 'loops' which can (perhaps automatically) deal with a problem. Such a loop control may be a closed loop – where the discovery of a quality defect, for example, is corrected by alterations to the system, adjustment of temperatures, pressures, machine settings, and so on. Many computerised controls take effect with this sort of loop. Other closed loops can be more sophisticated and may change the goals to be attained to take advantage of a changed situation. Thus a strike at one form of transport might generate different routings in the dispatch department, with different packaging material, documentation, labelling and markings, and so on. The system has to be devised to achieve the optimum results in various situations.

Other loops may be 'open' in that they cannot automatically institute a correction procedure but call for a revision of the decision-making process and a chain of modifications to the systems devised earlier. Thus an adverse environmental effect or consumer dissatisfaction may lead to modification or recall of a product. Demand may leap ahead, calling for the switching of resources from less popular goods and services, or it may fall off dramatically, calling for cessation of production of a particular product. These situations call for a review by the board or other decision-making body to revise the system or subsystem in the light of the changed situation. They mean that the present system no longer operates as a unified whole, and needs to be revised to restore its integrity as a system.

A diagrammatic representation of a system is shown in Fig. 2.3.

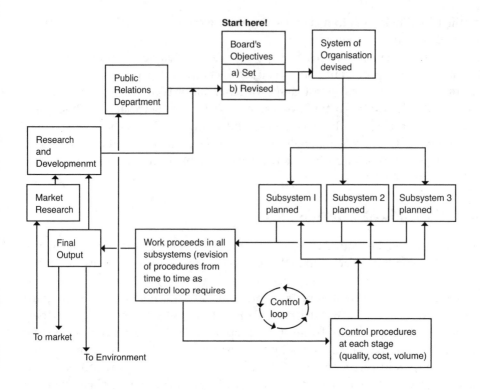

Fig. 2.3   A system and subsystems to achieve objectives

Notes:

i   The Board's objectives are set out and a system of organisation is devised.

ii   The product is produced or the service is made available.

iii The control loop tests the product or the service and an immediate feedback adjusts for any problems.

iv Final output is made available and the product or service is marketed.

v The complaints, responses, etc are investigated by Public Relations Department, R&D, etc and lead to a resolution of any problems and revised procedures approved at Board Room level.

3 The structure of business enterprises

3.1 The pattern of organisations

The entrepreneur is an individual who steps out of the mass of humanity and undertakes the organisation of production. The word actually means 'undertaker' – one who undertakes to create goods or services needed by humankind. The simplest type of organisation is therefore that set up by a **sole trader**, who takes upon himself/herself the task of combining the factors of production to create some useful good or service. Where two or more people combine we have an arrangement called a **partnership**. A partnership is often referred to as a firm. In earlier times it became common to save time in the name of a partnership by only naming one of the partners and calling the rest his 'company'. So Jones & Co. meant Jones and his other partners, whoever they might be. Later still the word company developed a special meaning, and today is generally taken to mean a **limited liability company** set up by registration under the regulatory rules of the country concerned. In the United Kingdom, for example, these are contained in the Companies Acts 1985–9. The significant difference between partnerships and companies as we use the word today is that companies have a separate legal status conferred upon them by a statutory process known as 'incorporation'. This means 'becoming a body'. In the eyes of the law an incorporation enjoys the same legal rights as any other body (i.e. legal person). It may own land, collect capital, employ factors of production, distribute profits, sue and be sued in the courts, and so on. Of course it cannot do really personal things like getting married, having children or dying. When a company comes to the end of its useful life it is 'wound up', a process which sells off the company's assets and distributes the proceeds to those entitled to the money, usually the creditors and the shareholders.

These three types of unit – sole traders, partnerships and limited companies – are the chief units in the private sector of the economy, though another type of organisation – the non-profit-making club – may be very important. The cooperative societies are a good example.

Where the manifest weaknesses of the private enterprise system made it clear that some sort of social control of production was necessary, new types of organisation were devised. In the United Kingdom, as in all countries, there had, of course, since time immemorial been a small **civil service**. As recently as the nineteenth century the Board of Trade consisted of only two people, the president and his clerk. The civil service began to expand after social measures in the 1870s introduced a Board of Education and a Department of Health. This civil service was joined by local government services in the 1880s, and many local government bodies set up municipal undertakings to run water, gas and other supply services under the powers obtained by private Acts of Parliament.

Another type of organisation which began to appear was the **autonomous public corporation** such as the former Port of London Authority. As with companies, such corporations have legal status and personality conferred upon them by Act of Parliament. Unlike the civil service they are not subject to day-to-day parliamentary control by the House of Commons question-time procedure. This type of organisation was deemed to be the most appropriate for nationalisation of such industries as coal, gas, electricity, transport, and so on. Similar institutions will be found in most countries.

The distinctions between the groupings centre around ownership and entitlement to profits. In the private enterprises it is clear where the ownership lies in each case: with the proprietor, proprietors or shareholders. They are also entitled either to the whole profit or to an agreed share of it. With the non-profit-making units the ownership rests rather loosely on the membership of the club or society. Strictly speaking there are no profits, only surpluses. A surplus means that the members have paid more for the club services than the cost of these services, and are entitled to a refund (or dividend). In many cases the refund is not made but the surpluses are used to extend club facilities and build up reserve funds. With public enterprises the ownership rests with some corporation created by Act of Parliament or other law-making body. Funds are made available either officially or by the sale of stock such as the former Port of London stock. Interest payments on this are honoured out of the profits, any surplus either being used for developments or for reserves, or perhaps in the case of nationalised industries passing back into public funds. The privatisation of many nationalised industries in the United Kingdom has reduced the number of autonomous corporations in recent years.

A short description of each type of business unit is now appropriate.

3.2   Sole-trader enterprises

A sole trader is a person who enters business on his/her own account; selects a site appropriate to the activities he/she has in mind; labours in the business with or without the assistance of employees; contributes the original capital by personal saving or borrowing on his/her own responsibility; and finally receives as a reward the proceeds (if any) of the venture. The **advantages** of sole trading are:

1 No formal procedures are required to start except that licences are needed for certain types of business activity. The name of the business is important. In the UK if the name to be used is not the proprietor's own, then this true name must be revealed on all invoices, letterheads and so on. It must also be displayed in a notice on the premises in a set form which is laid down in the Business Names Act 1985. Some care is necessary in choosing a name since it is the responsibility of the trader to choose one which does not conflict with any other name chosen by anyone else. Thus 'Beautiful Gardens' may be a nice name for a garden centre, but 'Beautiful Gardens of Ilford' is safer because there is less chance of being confused with any other firm. More than one trader has had

all his/her credit cut off by suppliers and all credit cards taken away because a trader somewhere else in the country using the same name has been declared bankrupt. (A leaflet about the choice of business names is available from the Guidance Notes Section, Department of Trade and Industry, at Cardiff. Telephone them on 02920 388588 for a single copy of the notes on business names.)

2   The sole trader is able to put his/her plans into effect at once, having no-one with whom to consult or agree procedures. Such businesses are adaptable to suit the opportunities that arise.

3   Personal control gives effective direct management with no communication problems. The customer is known to the proprietor, who caters for the customer's expressed wishes and personally sanctions credit to avoid bad debts. Staff are similarly personally controlled, so that waste is avoided, lost time is minimised and effort is rewarded.

4   For many small businesses expansion need only be pressed to the point where the market is adequately supplied. This often proves to be economic and to yield non-monetary satisfaction in a sense of service to the community.

5   Having no-one to consult, the self-employed person is entitled to the full profits of the business, apart from tax liabilities to the Inland Revenue.

6   Business administration problems are entirely a matter for the proprietor, without interference from any other person. The enterprise stands or falls by the success of the proprietor in overcoming them.

The **disadvantages** include the following:

1   Long working hours.

2   Difficulties over holidays – the business must either shut down or be left in the care of someone who has only an indirect interest in it.

3   Ill-health may present problems.

4   The proprietor tends to become a 'jack of all trades', needing to be his/her own buyer, stock-keeper, salesman, packer, delivery driver, and so on.

5   The proprietor is fully liable for all the debts of the business. This includes, if necessary, the sale of all personal possessions, the home, furniture, car, and so on, to realise money to pay the debts. The proprietor is said to have **unlimited liability**.

6   Growth can only take place if the entrepreneur ploughs back the profits into the business, and consequently expansion may be a slow process. If money is borrowed for expansion purposes for the business, not only will the bank or other lender cream off a good slice of the profit in interest on the loan, but it will usually require security in the form of a mortgage. This may mean that the proprietor loses control of the assets should the expansion prove less profitable than hoped.

7   The business is part of the estate of the proprietor, whose death will make it subject to **inheritance tax**. This tax replaced the earlier death duties in 1987. This may mean, if the value of the business is greater than the permitted limit (£250 000 at the time of writing) and no other funds are available, that the business might need to be sold to pay the amount of tax levied. It is possible to take out life assurance to provide a sum of money which can be used to pay the tax.

8   Like many small-scale enterprises, the sole trader's business may be a high cost business, because the level of specialisation will be small.

Unfortunately today in almost all types of business the atmosphere is highly competitive. Many large-scale firms generate so much capital that they are constantly on the look-out for the nodal points (points where growth appears to be taking place) in the economy. The inclination of such firms to buy into what appear to be prosperous small businesses places the sole trader under severe pressure to take the easy way out and allow the business he has started to be absorbed by one of the larger units. To resist the pressure, a sole trader may turn instead to seek faster growth by taking a partner.

3.3   Partnerships

When a partnership is formed the partners agree to join together to pursue a particular type of activity with a view to profit. There need not be any formal arrangements, but it is best if a **deed of partnership** is drawn up at the start. A good lawyer will often suggest many points that the partners should agree on from the beginning, and if these are put in writing and witnessed many later difficulties may be avoided. There is no limit to the arrangements that may be made, but in the UnitedKingdom there is a Partnership Act of 1890 which controls partnerships on all matters where the partners did not reach agreement. It is an excellent example of an Act of Parliament, and the reader is advised to obtain a copy from Her Majesty's Stationery Office and study its 50 sections.

The **advantages** of taking a partner include:

1 Increased capital, permitting the business to expand more rapidly than is possible by the ploughing back of profits earned.
2 The responsibility of control no longer rests with one person. This makes possible holidays and free weekends, and reduces the worry the sole trader experiences in times of ill-health.
3 Wider experience is brought to the firm, and some degree of specialisation is possible; this is particularly true of professional partnerships. A physician and a surgeon may form a partnership, or lawyers with experience in different fields – divorce, criminal law, commercial law – may combine to offer a more comprehensive service to the public.
4 Very often a young person teams up with an older person. The young person has his/her health and strength; the older partner has the capital and the experience. Together they make a satisfactory team.
5 The affairs of the business are still private.

The **disadvantages** may be listed as follows:

1 The partners must both be supported from the business. It follows that the business must earn as much profit *pro rata* now two of them are working as it did before with only the sole trader at work, if the original trader is to be as well off as he/she was before they formed the partnership.
2 They still have unlimited liability for the debts of the business. Since they are also liable for one another's actions, an unwise or uncontrolled act by one partner can seriously affect the other, or others.

3 Consultation with, and securing agreement of, the partner may be a tedious business to a partner who has formerly made his/her own decisions and acted at once.

4 The partnership is adversely affected by the death of a partner, whose share may be withdrawn to pay both the inheritance tax and the beneficiaries. It is therefore desirable for each partner to take out life assurance to provide a lump sum benefit in the event of the other partner's death. The lump sum will be for the benefit of the surviving partner, who uses it to pay up the beneficiaries and so on, and then becomes owner of the business in his/her own right.

The partnership type of organisation is particularly suitable for professional people, such as doctors, lawyers and accountants. It is also appropriate to most small-scale businesses in retail trade, road haulage, manufacturing, agriculture, horticulture, and so on.

3.4   Limited Liability Partnerships (LLP)

One essential feature of partnerships is the unlimited liability of the partners. They are liable jointly and severally for the debts of the firm, and also for any wrongs done by the firm, for which damages or fines are imposed (such wrongs as negligence, nuisance, dangerous premises, and so on). Unlimited liability means that the partner is liable to the limit of his/her personal wealth – home, car, most furniture etc must be sold to pay the creditors. Since many professional partnerships may have 60–100 partners, scattered around the world, it is clearly unfair to make them all liable to the limit of their personal wealth for losses suffered elsewhere, which are are no fault of their own. A system of limited liability would be fairer. How can it be achieved? The history of companies helps us here.

The principle of limited liability

Where a person has funds available for the promotion of business activity, but does not wish personally to take any part in the conduct of the business or the management of the firm, it seems unfair to require him/her to carry the burden of unlimited liability which attaches to sole traders or partners. The principle of limited liability holds that such a person should be liable to the extent of the capital contributed, but no further than this. The limitation of liability in this way unlocks savings which would otherwise merely be hoarded by their owners, and releases them to play a productive part in the industrial and commercial fields.

In the early days of the industrial revolution people who contributed capital to industrial firms were held to be full partners, and many had to sell their homes and other possessions when speculative projects collapsed and the partners were required to contribute to pay the debts of the firms concerned. Only in 1855, when the increasing demands for capital met resistance from savers who had already seen others suffer hardship through no fault of their own, did Parliament sanction limited liability for the shareholders of companies. Shareholders were liable for the losses of a company to the extent that they had invested capital in the business, but no further.

The Limited Liability Partnerships Act, 2000, allows partnerships to be set up as Limited Liability Partnerships. The name has to end in LLP (for example Smith and Jones LLP). This is a warning to those who deal with the partnership that they are dealing with an incorporation (a legal person created by law to run this business). They are not contracting with the partners personally, though they may still sue a partner who has been negligent.

The LLP comes into existence when at least two people who are in business to make profits subscribe their names to a document called an 'Incorporation document' and send it to the Registrar of Companies, who has been ordered in the Act (section 18) to undertake the new registration procedure. If any change occurs in the names of the partners as partners leave or join, these changes must be registered within 14 days.

It remains to be seen to what extent the business community will adopt this new format of activity.

3.5   The limited liability company

In the United Kingdom limited liability companies are of three types: chartered companies, statutory companies and registered companies. **Chartered companies** are set up by the granting of a royal charter, and the classic examples were the East India Company, the Hudson Bay Company, and certain universities. Today charters are usually reserved for professional organisations such as the Chartered Institute of Transport. **Statutory companies** were set up by the passing of an Act of Parliament. This method was used for most of the early companies, such as canal and railway companies. The Act embodied the safeguards Parliament deemed necessary, and accorded the powers to purchase land compulsorily, and so on. As the number of such enterprises grew, a simpler system was required. The **registered company** system enabled companies to be set up by a simple procedure of registration with the Registrar of Companies. The first Companies Act also accorded limited liability to the shareholders. Today the effective acts are the Companies Acts 1985–9. Studying these Acts is an essential study for any student of organisations, demonstrating how Parliament empowers companies to operate in a framework of restrictions which it deems desirable to safeguard the public interest. Readers from other countries are urged to study the methods used in their own countries for setting up limited liability companies.

The formation of a company

To form a company under the 'registered company' procedure, the promoter of the company must find one more person prepared to join him/her in signing a **Memorandum of Association.** This memorandum is a formal statement that they wish to be associated with one another for the purpose of carrying on a business of a certain type (stated in the **'objects' clause**). The seven clauses are:

1　The *name* of the company, with 'Limited' as the last word. This word tells anyone who does business with the company that the shareholders have limited liability. It is a warning to them not to deal with the company unless they are quite sure they can afford the risk. Many people think a company is more reliable to deal with than a sole trader or partnership, but this is not necessarily so, since creditors can only claim against the capital contributed. This may be as low as the members like, and in practice £100 companies are often formed to be available at any time they are required. These are called 'off-the-shelf' companies. If you consult your local *Yellow Pages* telephone directory under the heading 'company formation agents' you will see such companies offered for sale. At the time of writing the cost is about £150 and the companies are usually £100 companies, that is their registered capital is £100. A business person wishing to set up a company saves time and trouble by purchasing one ready made. The objects of the company can be varied by a simple procedure, and so can the authorised capital, and the name. So a company which has been set up by a specialist company promoter can be taken over for a nominal sum and altered to suit the needs of any business. Whether a company is taken over in this way or set up in the way being described, the word 'Limited' at the end of the name tells everyone dealing with it that they can only look to the £100, or any authorised increased sum, for satisfaction in the event of difficulties.

　　Small companies like this are called private companies, but if a company's shares are to be bought and sold on the stock exchange the name has to end in the words 'public limited company' (PLC). As the minimum capital has to be £50 000, such companies cannot be purchased off-the-shelf.

2　The *address* of its registered office.

3　The *objects* of the company. This states what the company will do when it is established, and forms the legal basis for its activities within the fields specified. Other objects are *ultra vires* (outside its powers). This is a protection to the shareholders. Suppose I invested £500 in a company that was to develop a revolutionary type of aero engine, which I believed had a great future. I suddenly discover that the directors are using my money to buy sugar, which happens to be rising on world markets. I would naturally feel that this was not the purpose for which I had subscribed my capital, and would be able to obtain an injunction restraining the directors from using my money in an *ultra vires* way. In recent years, to prevent the hands of directors being tied by very restrictive objects clauses, it has become fashionable to word the objects clause more loosely. For example: 'to trade in a wide range of products and services in such geographical areas as the directors may decide.' This obviously reduces the control any shareholder has over the actions of the company – but of course if the investor does not like the clause he/she will invest elsewhere.

4　A statement that the *liability* of the members is *limited*.

5　The amount of *share capital* to be issued, and the types of share.

6　An undertaking by the signatories that they desire to be formed into a company registered under the Acts, and that they undertake to purchase the number of shares against their names.

7　This rule requires that the names and addresses of the first director (or directors) and the first company secretary shall be stated in a prescribed form. This statement must be signed by the other members and contain the consents of the director(s) and secretary to their appointments.

Having drawn up and signed the Memorandum of Association, the directors usually then draw up detailed **Articles of Association**, which control the internal affairs of the company. Such matters as the procedure to be followed at meetings, the duties of the managing director, the borrowing powers that may be exercised, and so on, are considered and agreed. A set of model articles, called **Table A**, is printed as a statutory instrument (S.I. 1984 No. 1717). These articles will be effective and binding on all companies issuing shares, unless the company's own articles specifically invalidate them on some point.

Registration of the company

The promoters of the company may now proceed to register the company under the Acts. They present to the Registrar of Companies the Memorandum of Association; the Articles of Association; a statement of the nominal capital, on which a tax of £1.00 per cent is payable; a list of directors and their written consents and promises to take up shares; and a statutory declaration that the Companies Acts have been complied with.

If all is in order, the Registrar will issue a **certificate of incorporation**, which bestows upon the company a separate legal personality. The company can now do all the legal things that an ordinary person can do, for example, it may own land and property, employ people, sue and be sued in the courts, and so on. Before it may begin trading, however, it must secure the capital it needs. With a private company this will largely be contributed by the founders so there is no difficulty. With a public company it must be obtained from the public, either directly, or indirectly through institutional investors. In order to do this the company issues a **prospectus** which tells members of the public about the company and invites them to subscribe for shares in the enterprise.

Classes of shares

People with savings to spare have to be tempted to invest in an enterprise, hence the wide variety of shares and bonds offered to them. Some people want a high return on their capital, and to obtain it are prepared to run some risk. Others want security for their savings, even though the rate of interest is lower. Security is particularly difficult to ensure in inflationary times. For example, savings in government securities are absolutely secure; if you leave them in for 50 years you will receive £1 for every £1 invested, but if that £1 will then only buy goods worth 20p because of inflation over the years, you have really lost money on the investment. We say that the **nominal value** (nominal means 'in name only') has remained the same, but the **real value** (in terms of what it will purchase) has declined.

A full explanation of the various types of share is not necessary here, but readers unfamiliar with the main points should refer to Table 3.1.

Table 3.1 Comparison of different types of share

Types of investment	Reward earned	Degree of risk	Who buys them	Who issues them
Ordinary shares	Equal share of profits, hence nickname 'equity shares'	Carry the main risk	(a) Well-to-do investors who want big returns; (b) institutional investors, for a balanced portfolio; (c) people interested in capital gains, rather than revenue profits	Private and public companies
Deferred ordinary shares (founder's shares)	Share of profits after ordinary shares have had some (say 10%) profit	Same as ordinary shares	They are taken by the vendor of a business when he/she sells it to a company, to show he/she has confidence in the new company	Public companies chiefly, but also private companies
Preference shares	Definite rate of dividend (say 7%), but only if profits are made	Less than ordinary shares as they *usually* have a prior right to repayment	Investors seeking security rather than large dividends	Public and private companies
Cumulative preference shares	As above, but if profits are not earned in one year the dividend accumulates and is not lost	As above	As above	As above
Participating preference shares	After taking the fixed rate (say 7%) these shares earn extra dividend if the ordinary shares get more than 7%	As above	As above	As above
Debentures (loans to companies; debentures are not really shares)	Fixed rate of interest (say 6%), payable whether profits are made or not	Very small	Timid people wanting a secure investment, and institutional investors building balanced portfolios	Public and private companies, if permitted by their Articles

Table 3.2   Comparison of profit-making private enterprise units

	Aspect	Sole trader	Partnership	LLP partnership
1	Name of firm	Any name provided it is either the proprietor's true name or their names, or a notice has been displayed as required by the Business Names Act 1985	Any name provided it is either the proprietor's true name or their names, or a notice has been displayed as required by the Business Names Act 1985 (UK)	The Limited Liability Partnership Act, 2000 permits partners to set up as LLP partnerships (for example, Box and Cox LLP). See the Act for detailed rules
2	How formed	By commencing business without formality except (1) above	By agreement, which may be oral or written; limited partnerships must be registered with the Registrar ofLimited Companies	By agreement, intending partners having subscribed their names to an 'incorporation document' and sent it to the registrar
3	Control of the firm	Proprietor has full control	Every partner is entitled to manage	Every partner is entitled to manage the business
4	Liability for debts	Liable to the limits of personal wealth	Jointly and severally liable for debts; and for torts (civil wrongs) to the limits of personal wealth	Clients of the partnership contract with the LLP and the partners have no personal liability except in tort (for negligence)
5	Relationship between owner and business	The business is the owner, and has no separate legal existence	The business is the owner, or owners, and has no separate legal existence	The business is an incorporation with separate legal personality
6	Membership of firm	One	Two or more	Two or more
7	General powers	At will	At will, subject to agreement; if no agreement, Partnership Act 1890 applies	At will, subject to agreement. If there is no agreement regulatory rules already laid down under the Act apply
8	Transfer of ownership	By sale of 'goodwill'	Only with unanimous consent	Changes of partners must be registered withing 14 days
9	Controlling Acts (UK)	None	Partnership Act 1890 (UK)	Limited Liab. Partnership Act, 2000
10	Disbanding of firm	At will or by bankruptcy	Firm may go bankrupt or be dissolved by notice, by mutual consent or by death of a partner	The Secretary of State will publish rules about these matters
11	Advantages	Independence; personal control of staff and granting of credit; decisions acted upon at once	Increased capital; days off and holidays possible; wider experience of partners; privacy of affairs	The Act gives limited liability to partners who are no longer liable to the limit of their personal wealth, except for negligence
12	Disadvantages	Long hours, no holidays; illness affects conduct of business; unlimited liability; small capital	Unlimited liability; death or retirement ends firm; profits must be shared	Clients dealing with the LLP can only look to the LLP for compensation if they suffer loss due to breach of contract

Limited companies

LTD **Private limited companies**	PLC **Public limited companies**
The registered name, registered under the Companies Acts 1985–9, ending in the word 'Limited' as a warning to future creditors	The registered name, registered under the Companies Acts (1985–9) ending in the abbreviation PLC (Public Limited Company) as a warning to future creditors
By registration under the Companies Acts, with due legal formality	As for private limited companies
Directors control the company. Members have no control at all, but may elect a new board at the annual general meeting, or at an extraordinary general meeting if they wish to do so	As for private limited companies *The control of the company is in the hand of the shareholder.*
Limited liability for all members – only liable to the limit of capital contributed	As for private limited companies
The business is a separate legal personality from the members	As for private limited companies
Minimum two. No maximum under the 1985–9 Acts	As for private limited companies
As laid down in the Memorandum of Association and Articles of Association	As for private limited companies
Shares may only be transferred with consent of fellow shareholders	Shares are freely transferable
Companies Acts 1985–9	Companies Acts 1985–9
Company may go into voluntary or compulsory liquidation	As for private limited companies
Limited liability Death of shareholders does not affect the firm Capital can be found from many members Privacy to some extent on affairs	Limited liability Death of shareholders does not affect the firm Very large capital can be collected
Publication now required, but since 1985 there are special rules for small and medium-sized companies to prevent large companies targeting them for takeover purposes	Full public knowledge of the company's affairs

Trading certificate

Before a public company can begin to trade it must secure a **trading certificate**. This is issued by the Registrar of Companies when registration is finally completed by lodging with him/her the following documents:

1 A statement that the minimum capital has been subscribed.
2 A statement that the directors have paid for their shares.
3 A statutory declaration that the Companies Acts have been complied with.

The minimum capital is that amount of capital stated in the prospectus as being the minimum which, in the directors' opinion, is necessary for the success of the enterprise. If this minimum is not reached all the capital collected must be returned to the shareholders. Directors can ensure a successful commencement of trading if they have the issue **underwritten** by financiers prepared to buy the shares should the public not do so.

Holding companies

The vast majority of companies in existence today have been set up as registered companies under the Companies Acts 1985–9. Most companies start as private (that is, unquoted) limited companies, and then 'go public' by making an application to the Stock Exchange Council to be quoted on the stock exchange, where shares are bought and sold publicly. The term **holding company** is applied to any company which 'holds' other companies by holding 51 percent of their voting shares. The companies held are called **subsidiaries**.

Parliament was anxious, in the years before 1948, to establish firmer rules for the conduct of holding companies. For example, switching of funds from one company to another used to occur. The 1948 Companies Act laid down that a holding company should produce final accounts which consolidated the accounts of the whole group (the holding company and its subsidiaries). These 'group accounts' eliminated any hidden movements of funds which concealed malpractices. For example, it was quite common to lend cash to a subsidiary on the last day of the financial year – to make its financial position seem healthy – and to take it back again on the first day of the next year. Group accounts, and other measures, improved the standard of behaviour of large companies very considerably in the years after 1948.

Holding companies are therefore companies with subsidiaries. The reader is urged to write to one or two major companies and ask for copies of their final accounts, which list the subsidiary companies. Since they are often companies which trade abroad they are frequently multinational, and the term **multinational** is commonly used to describe holding companies with foreign subsidiaries.

3.6   Non-profit-making units (clubs and societies)

A certain number of business units are non-profit-making clubs and societies. They are formed to confer on their members certain benefits in the way of club facilities, discount trading, or value for money. Such clubs and societies often make profits on the year's trading, but these are not profits in the normal commercial meaning of the word. They really represent over-payments by the members for the services they have received, and are usually called surpluses. Examples of such business units are the working men's clubs in the north of England and the cooperative societies.

Cooperative retail societies

The first successful 'Co-op' store was founded in 1844 in Toad Lane, Rochdale, by 28 weavers nowadays remembered as the 'Rochdale pioneers'. The idea was to buy foodstuffs at wholesale prices and sell them (to members only) at market price. Profits were divided among members in proportion to the value of their purchases. The share-out (dividend) took place twice a year. By 1845 there were 74 members, the turnover was £710 and the profit £22.

The cooperative movement spread rapidly. Societies were set up in towns all over the United Kingdom. In 1862 the members voted to set up a wholesale organisation, the Cooperative Wholesale Society. This society not only supplied the retail societies like any ordinary wholesaler but also ran factories, farms, transport services, and even tea gardens to provide everything the retail societies needed. The chief aim in this activity was to ease the serious unemployment of those days. The retail societies joined the wholesale society in exactly the same way as the ordinary members joined the retail society. All the profits of the Cooperative Wholesale Society were shared among the member retail societies, and all the profits of the retail societies were shared among the members. Thus in the end all the profits returned to the members of the retail societies, whose purchasing power kept the cooperative movement going.

Agricultural cooperatives

These are very common in many countries and enable the small-scale farmer to achieve some of the economies of large-scale organisation. They may be marketing cooperatives, which grade, pack and distribute farmers' produce, or purchasing cooperatives, which buy seed, fertiliser and equipment at discount prices, supplying or hiring these items to farmers.

Producer cooperatives

In recent years a new type of cooperative has been developed in which those wishing to supply goods and services on a cooperative basis set up either as companies limited by guarantee (not shares) or as 'friendly societies' registered under the Friendly Societies Act. There is no transferable equity capital; the members act as both directors and employees and contribute their labour for a relatively low reward in the initial stages (a procedure known as contributing a 'sweat equity'). An unusual feature is that if the society is disbanded the members do not receive back any share of the assets, which are made available either to the cooperative movement or to a charity.

A Cooperative Development Association (CDA) operates at a national level to promote cooperation in all areas, and to train and educate those interested in the development of cooperation, for idealistic reasons.

3.7   Public enterprises

Here the reader will note that the United Kingdom is chiefly referred to, but readers are urged to consider the history of public enterprises in his/her own country. In the United Kingdom, from 1946 to the start of the 1990s, the economy was divided into two roughly equal parts, the private sector and the public sector. The private sector comprised all those firms described earlier – sole traders, partnerships and limited companies. The public sector comprised during those years not only all those institutions traditionally run by the state (the army, the forces of law and order, the Post Office and public education) but many nationalised industries which had been brought into the public sector for idealistic reasons.

Socialist doctrines favoured public ownership of the means of production, distribution and exchange, and after the end of the Second World War a large number of Acts of Parliament were passed to put these ideas into effect. We need not go into the details here of why these industries were largely denationalised in the 1980s and early 1990s but, to give one example, the nationalisation of transport brought not only trains, canals, coastal shipping and long-haul road transport under control but also every road vehicle over 30 cwt (that is, light vans). The resultant nationalised industry had 934 000 employees. The nation could not really find anyone to head such a massive organisation and by 1953 denationalisation of some road transport had begun. Today the public sector is much reduced by the denationalisation (privatisation) of such major industries as gas, electricity, water, coal mining, road haulage, the railways, the steel industry, and so on.

A full discussion of these developments need not concern us here. We will only consider a few of the more interesting aspects. The reasons for bringing a particular activity or resource endowment within the public ownership may be listed as follows:
1 Natural right
2 Security
3 Fundamental importance
4 Social necessity

5 Natural monopoly
6 Heavy capital cost
7 Bad labour relations

A few lines of explanation are helpful here.

1 *Natural right* There is a body of opinion which holds that certain things ought to belong collectively to the entire nation, and be used and preserved in the general public interest. The most obvious example, which has not been as publicly pressed as perhaps it should have been in the United Kingdom, is the land itself. The case for the expropriation of landowners is very strong in some countries, where abuses by the landlord class are particularly blatant. In the United Kingdom abuses either took place so long ago that they have ceased to draw attention, or are adroitly managed. The nationalisation of coal, undertaken largely for other reasons, was certainly influenced by the feeling that such an obvious gift of nature should be nationally owned, and the opportunity was taken in the same Act to nationalise the other hydrocarbon fuels, oil and natural gas. Although unimportant at the time, these resources are now of great importance, yet their nationalisation has to a great extent been reversed by current privatisation programmes.

There are not many other natural resources which could be regarded as every citizen's birthright but there might be, in an environment increasingly designated 'a concrete jungle', a case for nationalising sand and gravel, for example. Salt is also mined in large quantities. The principle also applies to one or two other things. Ancient monuments and museum collections are usually preserved in the public interest. Since time immemorial roads and other rights of way, and the right to travel up rivers, have been regarded as inviolate, though a good many statutory procedures for interfering with these rights (in a greater public interest) exist. The number and variety of bridges over our motorway network illustrate the preservation of these ancient rights by the motorway engineers.

2 *Security* The general security can only be ensured by communal activity. Private enterprise is inappropriate in the police and armed services, and in early days the mails were regarded as of such importance that the Post Office was run as a public department. This was abandoned in 1968 when the Post Office Corporation was set up. The inadequacy of private enterprise for safety services is well illustrated by the early fire insurance arrangements. Fire brigades operated by insurance companies frequently refused to put out a fire at premises which did not bear a 'fire mark' from their own company, but stood by to hose down premises nearby that were insured but not yet alight. They even, on occasions, deliberately interfered with rival fire brigades, preventing them from putting out a fire, in the hopes that the manifest inefficiency of the rival brigade would bring their own company more business.

3 *Fundamental importance* Some industries are of basic importance to the whole economy. Electricity, gas and water supplies are the chief examples. Although all of these can easily be supplied by private enterprise, their basic importance is a strong reason for operating them as nationalised industries or public corporations. Where other aspects in our list also apply, such as points (5) and (6) below, the case for including such industries in the public sector is reinforced.

4 *Social necessity* Many goods and services are part of the social needs of an advanced sophisticated society. Education, drainage and sewerage systems, public health controls, the National Health Service, ambulance services, recreation facilities and adequate housing standards are examples. Provision must be made, in some cases for all citizens, in other cases at least for lower income groups. The tendency is to run these as local government or national government activities.

5 *Natural monopolies* A monopoly occurs where the supply of a particular good or service is in the hands of a single organisation. In some cases, by the very nature of things, it would be absurd to have any competition at all. We do not want three taps on each sink supplying Smith's, Brown's or Jones's water, nor three electric light switches in each room so that we can choose our electricity supplier. It would be pointless to run trains on parallel lines from Glasgow to London, competing for the trade available. Where a product or service is a natural monopoly it is usual for Parliament to insert clauses protecting the public interest in statutes which confer powers on private firms. This was done with the early railway companies, for example. Most natural monopolies – gas, water, electricity and railway transport – were nationalised at some time in the last fifty years, but most have now been returned to private ownership.

6 *Heavy capital cost* Some industries have such heavy capital costs that duplication in the interests of competition is wasteful. The heavy costs may be in the development, as well as in the industry itself. Thus the research and development costs in the nuclear energy field are burdensome, although of course a security aspect also influenced the decision to set up the Atomic Energy Authority (now partially privatised as AEA Technology, PLC). Airlines have heavy capital costs to bear, and so do airport authorities. Some people think it would be a good idea to nationalise the cement industry, which it is almost impossible to enter because of the high capital cost. Had the cement industry abused its near-monopoly position it is highly likely it would already have been nationalised, but an investigation found that no abuse had occurred.

7 *Bad labour relations* In the case of coal the bad industrial history of coal mining was largely responsible for nationalisation. The bitter experience of miners over generations led to an impassioned call for the socialisation of this means of production, which seemed to many to be an obvious example of a gift of nature that ought to be socially owned.

A full discussion of the merits or demerits of nationalisation is inappropriate here. We are mainly concerned with the organisations themselves.

3.8   Autonomous public corporations

Autonomous public corporations are corporations established by statute to perform a particular function with the exercise of only limited parliamentary control. The usual arrangement is that an activity which has been badly managed by private operators is taken over under the authority of Parliament and a suitably qualified and experienced team is appointed to run it. Since interference by politicians on day-to-day matters is undesirable, the corporations are autonomous – they control their own affairs – but Parliament debates the state of the industry on one day of the year. These are called 'supply days'. By tradition what is discussed on a supply day is decided by the opposition party. Therefore, if the state of the industry to be debated is considered excellent, the opposition could choose some other topic to discuss. Widely used in the years when major industries were nationalised, there are now very few major public corporations.

3.9 Nationalised industries

As explained above, most nationalised industries in the UK have now been returned to private ownership, but students overseas in countries which still have nationalised industries might like to know the UK experience in this area. The initial drive to nationalise was ideological – part of the socialist programme – but in certain cases it was supported by other motives. In the coal industry there was a long history of industrial unrest, and in railway transport there had been more than a century of abuse of the railways' natural monopoly. This abuse had been largely controlled by the end of the nineteenth century, but by then the increased competition from the roads was eating into the railways' privileged position anyway. The result was that the railways found it difficult to make sufficient profits to maintain their huge network with all the social responsibilities Parliament had heaped on them in earlier times. There was strong trade union pressure for nationalisation in these industries.

The objectives of nationalised industries

One problem with nationalised industries is the difficulty of defining their objectives. Members of Parliament are jacks-of-all-trades rather than experts. They are often not agreed about the objectives to be achieved by nationalisation, or farsighted enough to anticipate the difficulties. If nationalisation is proposed because of the unsatisfactory state of an industry, presumably the new enterprise must offer a better service to the public, with fair treatment of employees and a due regard to public safety, and so on. How extensive should the service be? Is it to be at the whim of the newly appointed management? If it is excessive it may draw capital away from other more essential projects in quite different fields. Is it to manipulate its requirements to assist other parts of the economy, or buy in the world markets at competitive prices? This type of decision – to buy a British aircraft, for example, when it would have been cheaper and perhaps better to buy a foreign equivalent – has often arisen.

The general financial objective when nationalisation began was that public corporations should – taking one year with another – avoid losses. The phrase 'taking one year with another' was understood to mean that an odd loss in one year should be made up the next year whenever possible. Some industries – the railways, for example – proved quite unable to do this. Others managed to break even on current account but did not earn a fair return on capital invested. In some years the manipulation of the economy by government had prevented the original policy being carried out. Thus a period of price control may have been reinforced by an official brake on price rises by nationalised industries even though the price increase was essential if the financial requirements laid down in the Act concerned were to be realised. *What is clear is that nationalised industries cannot be expected to behave like private sector industries and just make profits. They are brought into existence to achieve political and economic solutions which could not be achieved by private sector firms, and they must therefore be judged by their success in achieving these solutions.*

Criticisms of nationalisation

Those who criticise the achievements of nationalised industries usually do so on the following grounds:

1 Most nationalised industries are run as statutory monopolies. The consumer cannot obtain supplies from any other source. Inevitably such organisations have a tendency to develop a 'take it or leave it' attitude, and there is no incentive to produce an improved product or give an improved service.

2 The industries are nearly all basic to the nation's industrial needs, and therefore cannot be allowed to fail. This must mean that any losses incurred will be borne by the taxpayer. This makes it more likely that unjustified wage increases will be conceded by management, and that marginal projects (those where it is doubtful whether the income will cover the cost) are more likely to be proceeded with than in private industry, since the taxpayer will cover the unprofitable projects in the end.

3 Since the provision of a service is more important than making a profit there must be a tendency to extend the service as fully as possible. Strong trade union organisations have often resisted any attempts to cut labour forces or restrict capital expenditure even where it has become clear that new technology in other fields justifies the phasing out of old methods.

The result has been a good deal of industrial and social unrest, and only a determined reversal of nationalisation policies and a privatisation programme has been able to permit the expansion of new technology and methods of work. Practically all nationalised industries were therefore sold off to private buyers.

3.10 Local government institutions

In every economy an important part of the services required is local in character. Education, health services, drainage and sewerage works are required all over the country and are inappropriate to control by the central government. A lower order of government, which reaches out to every locality, is required. In the UK a comprehensive restructuring of local government took place following the Radcliffe-Maude report. The number of local authorities was reduced in 1974 from over 1200 to 421. As the year 2000 dawns there are about 350.

Subsequent restructuring has meant that from 1996 there are 36 metropolitan districts or councils, 32 London boroughs, 47 English shire unitary authorities, 34 county councils and 238 district councils in England. This makes a total of 388 local authorities in England. In Scotland there are now 29 unitary councils, and three Island councils. In Wales there are 22 unitary councils.

Functions of the new authorities

The chief functions of the new authorities include major responsibilities in town and country planning, education, housing, police and fire services, traffic and highways, consumer protection, personal social services and many more.

Municipal undertakings

This type of organisation used to be much more important than it is today, because many water companies, electricity supply companies and gas companies were municipally owned. The nationalisation of such public utility services reduced the scale of local enterprise but it is still common to find such institutions as swimming pools, leisure centres, and so on, run as municipal enterprises.

3.11 Central government departments

In recent years a certain amount of experimentation (with super-ministries, for example) has caused frequent changes in the running and responsibility of government departments, so that any list is subject to change at the whim of the government in charge. In general there are about 20 ministries, with about two-thirds of them sufficiently important for the minister in charge to be of Cabinet rank. The major ministries are the Treasury, the Foreign Office, the Home Office, and those of Defence, Social Services, Employment, Education and Science, the Environment, Wales, Scotland, Agriculture, and the Department of Trade, Energy and Industry. All departments have considerable sums of money to spend in pursuing their activities and are therefore influential in the economy.

Besides these official departments, there are a large number of small bodies set up under a variety of Acts of Parliament to administer certain aspects of official policy with an unbiased attitude which views the matter concerned from the point of view of the national good. They are called quangos (quasi-autonomous non-governmental organisations): a slight misnomer in that, though they are reputed to be non-governmental, they are in fact the creatures of government, and membership of them depends on patronage from one government department or another to a considerable extent. One MP has identified a total of 3068 quangos spending over £2000 million annually, so that their influence is considerable. Some reduction in numbers has taken place in recent years since Philip Holland's report, but they do perform in many cases a useful function. The objection to them is that they are often not fully accountable to the public for the decisions they make and the expenditure they incur. The various tourist boards, the Forestry Commission and similar bodies are typical quangos.

Part Two

Functions within organisations

4   The production function

4.1   The production process

The purpose of business activity is to create goods and services required by humankind. Production is chiefly concerned with the supply of goods of various sorts, but since many services depend upon the use of tools and equipment (dentistry and surgery, for example) even they have some interest in production.

Production requires us to take the natural products of the world, which are the sole source of wealth (defined as an abundance of goods and services) and operate on them with human skills to turn them into improved natural products, which can satisfy our wants. Economists call these things that can satisfy 'wants' **utilities**, so we may say that the purpose of production is to create utilities which satisfy wants. The place where this is done is called by the general name '**factory**', a building where manufacturing takes place.

Just how we manufacture and what we manufacture depends upon the 'want' we are trying to satisfy. Every manufacturer has a particular field of interest, for 'a jack-of-all-trades is a master of none' says an old proverb. The factory's size and layout vary with the product, the processes required, the plant and machinery that can be developed and the techniques that can be devised. In general, the following considerations enter into the production policy of a firm:

1 The nature of the product, its design, marketing, packaging, storage and eventual distribution.
2 The volume of output to meet the market's needs.
3 The techniques necessary, which often may impose limits on the production process – for example, cement-making plants have to be of a certain size if the process is to be efficient.
4 The resource requirements: raw materials, components, labour and capital equipment of every type.
5 Controls, including quality, volume and price controls, but also progress-chasing of individual orders.

4.2   Types of production

There are four main types of production, which have an impact upon the design and layout of factories. They are:

1 Job production (or unit production)
2 Batch production
3 Flow production
4 Process production

1 *Job production* Job production or unit production is the specialised production of 'one-off' orders for a particular customer or client. A ship, or a bridge, or a ball-gown or a bespoke-tailored suit would be examples. In general this type of product calls for a wider variety of skills and a wider variety of materials than other forms of production where repetition means that materials will be standardised and machines will be used more intensively. We cannot usually design and plan the job until the order is placed, though a certain amount of pre-contract planning might take place. There is a great need to look for work in this type of production, since machines and employees can be idle much of the time if a reasonable series of one-off orders is not obtained. In practice, subcontracting work for some other firm may be a solution to the 'idle-time' problem, so long as it is of such a type that the main contracts are not delayed. Job costing is used to allocate the costs incurred to particular jobs, with a generous allocation of overheads if the contract will bear it.

2 *Batch production* Batch production is used in a variety of situations, particularly where a product is required as a component for other manufacturers, but can be made more quickly than the product for which it is intended. Thus volume control knobs can be made quite quickly – say hundreds per hour – but the television sets for which they are destined take longer to produce. It is usual to produce a batch of such parts, and take them into stock, say 10 000 at a time. They are then controlled by the usual stock-taking methods and a new batch is requisitioned in time so that an out-of-stock position is avoided.

   Another example of batch production is where more than one customer uses a particular part or machine so that a one-off order might as well be turned into a batch, with the extra items being taken into stock for future orders. Certain economies can be achieved by this type of batch production. What makes an economic batch size is debatable, for example the amount of storage space might be a controlling influence.

3 *Flow production* This is the stereotype of mass production where there is a steady demand for the product and an endless, repetitive sequence of events permits the division of labour, the use of special machine tools and high levels of power. Henry Ford defined it as follows: '*Mass production is the focusing upon a manufacturing project of the principles of power, accuracy, economy, system, continuity, speed and repetition.*' The difficulty is that the work is broken down into mere operations, each performed by a different operative. Productivity is high, but boredom soon sets in with the repetitive nature of the work. The use of robots may become possible to reduce these problems. The difficulty is for the worker to realise self-esteem and the respect of peer groups in such a system of production, and the tendency is for those who earn their living in such flow-production systems to realise their true personalities in the non-working situation: the family or leisure – pleasure activities when work is over.

4 *Process production* Process production is a special type of flow production where the product passes through a succession of processes, the output of each becoming the

input of the next process, and so on. A number of by-products may result as partial products of each process. Costs accumulate as the product moves through the system and quality controls will be implemented at each stage to determine the results of each process. The separate processes are distinct technically and, while the resulting collection of technology and skill is convenient and economical (all the equipment for a process being gathered together in one place), it may mean more material handling, with the product having to be brought in and processed and then taken on to its next destination. Progress chasing may become an important activity, and routeing of parts has to be systematic and controlled.

4.3 Site selection and factory planning

From start to finish, the building and equipment of any factory is a lengthy process and a whole range of problems has to be solved. We may distinguish:
1 *The selection of the site* This will be influenced by the following factors:
   a Where are the raw materials to come from? We may locate near the source of raw materials, or near the port of importation if they are to come from overseas.
   b What power and other facilities are to be used? We may locate near a coalfield or near a hydro-electric dam or, if electric power is to be used in relatively small quantities, we may locate almost anywhere. Some organisations (oil refineries, for example) often generate their own electricity and even sell their surplus power to the electricity supply companies. Closeness to water may be important for some industries.
   c Transport facilities may be important. Railway, motorway and airport facilities may be required and riverside or seaside locations may be advantageous, especially in countries with poorly developed land transport facilities.
   d The supply of labour may be important, as may local authority cooperation in housing provision.
   e The site must be large enough for the purpose, and the possibility of expansion at some future date may be important. The subsoil must be appropriate and any local restrictions (planning permission, and so on) must be investigated.
   f Sometimes official aid may be important in location, for examples in areas designated as development areas, or regions entitled to support from the Regional Fund of the European Union.
   g Closeness to the market may be important for goods which are easily damaged, such as furniture.
2 *The building* The chief considerations here are:
   a The type of work involved and the weight of machinery to be used. Heavy industry is best housed in single-storey buildings, where ground-based floors can be made adequate for the weight they are to bear. Light industrial work can be housed in multistorey buildings, which make more effective use of land and give economies in heating, power supply, communications, and so on.

b Ancillary buildings, such as washrooms, toilets, canteens, research facilities, and so on, may be separated from industrial buildings if this is preferable from a cleanliness point of view, or to avoid vibration or noise.

c The eventual layout may dictate certain features of the building, especially with flow or process production where materials or components may need to access the production lines at convenient points. The aim is to use the floor space in as intensive a way as possible while at the same time giving regard to safety, efficiency, and economy of operations. Part of the layout planning must include plans for clearing the production lines to storage and warehousing areas.

d End-user departments must be considered when planning layout. For example, some processes have to be isolated for health and safety reasons. Goods inwards department must be located near the arrival bay and the materials stores, which should be convenient for the main factory areas where the raw materials will be used. Inspection departments may be situated near the end of processes, so that sampling the product at each stage is convenient and random (that is, every unit of output has an equally good chance of being selected for testing). If batch production of sub-assemblies is used, the finished parts stores should be convenient to the point in the assembly line where the parts are used and packing materials should similarly be conveniently placed for the dispatch department. The latter department should also be conveniently placed for road, rail, or river haulage.

4.4 Plant and equipment

Many items of plant and equipment are large, costly, require to be built into position and have a long life once installed. Choice of the correct item is important. Careful shopping around for the best buy may be necessary, and the importance of clear specifications, modern design, reliability and servicing contracts cannot be over-emphasised. Many machines are in strong demand; they must be ordered well in advance and clear delivery dates should be specified.

4.5 Materials and materials handling

Although the procedures for ordering materials are part of the purchasing function and are dealt with more fully in Chapter 5, the closest liaison between the factory manager and the purchasing officer is required. We cannot always get materials to the exact specification we require at the price we can afford, and there can be a conflict of interest. A purchasing officer who always buys the cheapest material may not understand the technological processes. The cheapest crude oil, for example, may yield the wrong quality products in the refining process, or incur extra costs in distillation. We cannot make silk purses out of sows' ears. Price is always a major consideration, but so are quality and suitability for the purpose intended.

Other aspects are:

1 *Certainty of supply* We must receive supplies in such a way that we are never starved of resources but also do not waste working capital by over-ordering or incur heavy storage costs or stock losses by holding larger stocks than necessary. Where supplies are seasonal it may be necessary to have suppliers in several parts of the world, each sending produce at the optimum time.

2 *Procedures on delivery* This is again a function of the purchasing department rather than the production department but, where direct deliveries are made to the factory, checks on quantity and quality must precede signature on delivery notes. Quantities must be taken into stock before issue against requisitions (though the latter may be replaced by automatic measuring of usage in many processes). Some deliveries, called just-in-time deliveries (JIT) are made daily, at the actual site of production in the production line. Next day's deliveries are ordered daily by phone or fax.

3 *Materials handling* Materials handling is expensive, and can be dangerous. An appropriate range of handling devices (stillages, pallets, lift-trucks, turret trucks, and so on) should be provided and proper training in safety aspects should be given to all staff. The system for bringing resources to the point where they are needed, and removing the finished parts or final products, must be considered as an integral part of the production process. Double handling should be avoided. 'Don't put it down, it costs money to pick it up again' is an old maxim. Gravity feeds on static rollers, and powered rollers may be used, while elevators, hoists and conveyors may be needed to speed handling and save labour. These physical distribution problems are referred to in more detail elsewhere in this book (see p. 125).

4.6   Production administration

Production administration involves three main areas: production engineering, production planning and production control.

Production engineering

Let us presume we have a range of products in a particular specialist area, a plant already on stream with a known capacity, an adequate supply of materials of various sorts and a staff who know their jobs and can be expected to pull together. At any given moment there is a range of problems presenting themselves which need to be reviewed. They include:

1 The need to keep in touch with customers, competitors and developments in our whole general field so that we are aware of all the trends in customer requirements, product usage, new materials, new markets, and so on. We must ensure that our products do not stand still, but are updated, renewed and revamped as required. Production department is vitally interested in these matters and considerable liaison will develop

between the factory, the research and development department and the design department. Various names are in fact used for this area.

Research goes on at several levels, for example scientific work in the general field of theoretical knowledge related to the firm's products, raw materials, and so on; troubleshooting research aimed at solving a problem, for example testing alternative materials where a supply problem has developed with existing ones; finding alternative uses for waste resources from an existing production line, and so on. The results of research may then be handed on to the design department for development into new or improved products.

Every product has design problems, not only for the product itself but for the jigs and tools which will enable its production to take place. Few people realise the skills required in the tool-making department, where even a simple press to stamp out plastic products may cost tens of thousands of pounds. The tool has to be polished to a mirror finish, so that after each pressing the product falls out of the press with a similar polish, immaculate in its appearance. It is the skill of the production engineer which makes the product itself a success, as those who have assembled even a simple product like a pre-packaged bookcase or coffee table will appreciate.

The new products must be clearly visualised, and it is usual to draw up a specification for the product, its purpose, general nature, suggested composition, component parts, and so on. This leads to the preparation of drawings, with dimensions, tolerances, and the materials to be used. At this stage, scale models or full-size models and eventually prototypes may be made, and will usually result in modifications to the proposed product. Final drawings will then be made, patents will be applied for and production planning can begin.

All these matters require considerable engineering skill, with a team of people bringing particular skills to the general field of endeavour, supervised by the factory manager.

2   The need to keep plant and equipment not only working, but renewed as necessary so that methods of production, rates of production, product quality and delivery deadlines are constantly met and are competitive with other firms in the industry. A new product may require special processes and operations which have to be incorporated into the existing framework of production. We must decide how the work is to be done, who is to do it, whether they need specialist training, whether they need special jigs or tools or power sources, and so on. The company's personnel policy may need to be adapted. Work study, which is referred to later, enters into these arrangements at every stage.

3   *Estimating and quoting* Many orders have to be secured by preparing estimates of the costs likely to be incurred and quoting a price for the job. There is a legal difference between an estimate (which is an approximate price and may subsequently be revised) and a quotation which is a firm offer capable of being accepted and making a binding contract. Even so, in inflationary times it is usual to insert clauses into quotations which permit the price to be increased if the offer is not accepted within a very short period, and if the work is prevented from proceeding with reasonable speed.

Wherever possible in estimating, it is necessary to build up part-estimates which are on file and known, so that requests for a price for a job can be expeditiously handled.

Thus the costs of using various quantities of each class and quality of material should be tabulated so that a price which recovers the costs and yields a profit can be built up quickly. At the same time costs for some jobs will bear little relation to the actual work done, because in some trades it is usual to charge what the job will bear, irrespective of the cost actually incurred, so that a job which can support a heavy charge can subsidise other jobs which are more competitively priced. Like the surgeon who charges an orphan nothing and a millionaire's child a high price for the same operation, cross-subsidies are frequently a feature of costing activities.

Production planning

Production planning is a range of activities which seeks to make the best use of available capacity in a factory while at the same time meeting the marketing requirements. Our aim is to fulfil the orders placed to customers' satisfaction while at the same time making the most economical use of machines, operators and materials. The work involves:

1 Turning marketing requirements into schedules of activities in the various cost centres of the factory, so that technicians and operatives are gainfully employed using the available machines, without excessive 'dead' time in any particular area.
2 The schedules and works orders must be arranged in such a way that the various processes are balanced to avoid bottlenecks in production. The flow of materials and parts must be adequate to ensure that the utilisation of personnel and machines is up to standard. The costing of orders has been based on standard levels of achievement, and failure to reach these levels will result in **costing variances** which will be the subject of enquiries later (see 4.7 below). Where under-utilisation seems likely to occur it may be possible to fit in a batch production of some component to fill the time usefully.
3 Close liaison between marketing and production should be a feature of production planning, so that the odd rush-order can be accepted and fulfilled by rescheduling work which is safely within its allotted time-span.

Taking an enquiry received for a particular one-off job, we can follow the chain of events:

a *Should we quote for the job or not?* This requires us to consider whether we have the necessary capacity to do the job, the machines, labour and material. If we have no excess capacity, can we make it available by rescheduling current commitments? Have we the time to order and take delivery of materials which are not in stock at present?
b *What exactly is required?* If the conclusion to (a) above is that we should quote for the job, the very considerable work of preparing a quotation can now proceed. The product must be analysed and broken down into its material components; the operations required to turn raw materials into finished parts; the machine loadings that will result; the jigs and tools required and costs involved. Documents such as materials schedules, operational sequence schedules, route cards, lists of parts, and so on, will be roughed out and a full specification drawn up.
c *The quotation* A formal quotation must then be prepared, indicating the extent of the work to be performed and either supplying detailed costings or an overall global figure. When this quotation is accepted the production planning can proceed.

d Drawings will be prepared, specifications for parts will be drawn up, detailed descriptions of each part prepared, and so on.

e Materials schedules will be prepared, showing the various types and qualities of material needed and the quantity of each.

f Sequence schedules (route cards) will be drawn up, giving the operations to be performed, the time allowance, and so on.

g The sequence schedules will now be allocated in detail to a master production schedule, the timescale for the total operation will be devised and loading programmes for various cost centres will be prepared so that supervisory staff are aware of the programme as it affects their cost centre.

h Works orders will now be prepared to authorise supervisors to proceed with the manufacture of various components and the control and progress-chasing activities will begin.

Such a complex series of planning activities calls for careful control and a number of commercial planning boards are available with various magnetic or other devices for signalling the completion of various stages. One of the best and most comprehensive ranges is the LegaMASTER range of planners, available from Edding Lega International BV, Kwinkweerd, 62 NL–7240 AC Blochen, Holland (telephone 0031 573 257 433). An example of a LegaMASTER production control board is illustrated in Fig. 4.1.

Fig. 4.1 Example of LegaMASTER Proline Channel Planner

Notes:
i The control board has a pre-printed grid under a vitreous enamelled surface and will accept magnetic symbols and tapes. It can also be written on with LegaMASTER water-based pens and wiped clean with a damp cloth or with dry-wipe markers which are cleaned off using a dry paper tissue.
ii It is wall mounted and comes complete with wall fixings.
iii LegaMASTER offer a wide range of planning facilities and are always pleased to discuss specific planning problems.
iv Planning can be based on one month, three months, six months or a year ahead.

Production control

Production control has three elements: progress control, material control and quality control. For some activities a technique called **critical path analysis** may also be required.
1 *Progress control* This is concerned with the progress of an order through its sequence of operations, expediting parts which appear unlikely to meet their deadlines, resolving difficulties due to non-arrival of materials or components, feeding back information about the progress (or hold-up) of production to areas likely to be affected. The progress chaser, who is of assistant-supervisory grade, needs to be cooperative, well-liked, firm yet friendly and able to get on with all sorts of people. The role is essentially one of keeping everything 'cool' in the best interests of the company and the workforce. Each cost area may have its progress chaser, and each product or job may also have a progress chaser who follows the job through the various cost areas. No hard and fast system can be laid down, and with priorities changing from time to time a good relationship between progress staff and workshop supervisors is essential. The most vital areas to control are those on the critical path because they have no leeway in the production schedule and must be completed on time, but any activity may come into this category if it was started late, all the leeway having been used up before the start of the activity. (Critical path is explained on pp. 67–8.)

The **supervisor** is an important person in any system of production because he/she is the final link between management and the shopfloor. Much of the production effort begins when the supervisor allocates particular jobs to particular individuals or groups of workers. The drive to get production started comes largely from the supervisory grades, and much of the training of young staff is in their hands although courses may be run before a new technique is used or a new product is introduced. A good deal of the paperwork – recording of machine times, job completion times and units completed – is carried out by supervisors. They also have the difficult task of motivating staff, ensuring fair play between employees, solving minor disputes and dealing with difficult employees. They must understand and be able to carry out personally all the different sorts of processes they are supervising if they are to keep the respect of the shopfloor staff, yet they must not do the work themselves but get others to do it. Clearly these are not easy tasks, and call for skill, diplomacy, tact and energy.
2 *Materials control* This is dealt with more fully elsewhere in this book (see Chapter 5) but once materials have been issued by stores and their routeing about the factory begins,

the progress chaser will play some part in tracing any supply which fails to reach its intended use-point. The movement of raw materials through the factory is called work-in-progress and it will normally flow through the various cost centres without delay as each stage is completed. Problems arise when a breakdown or power failure at some point holds up a process, and leaves other cost centres ahead with idle time. Other jobs may have to be brought forward to fill the gap, and reports may need to be made to explain the costs involved – for example, machines may need to be reset and then reset again when the original work finally arrives.

3 *Quality control* Quality control is a specialised function, which seeks to preserve product quality by examination at intervals of a sample product to discover whether it meets the standards laid down by the design engineer. There are innumerable aspects to quality control, and methods vary from product to product. The classic example tells of the head of a certain world-famous pottery who exercised quality control at the end of each day by hitting with a hammer every pot that failed to reach his high aesthetic standard. Not all product qualities are so easily detected, for example the lengths and diameters of nails and screws cannot be evaluated at a glance and some more systematic method of investigation is called for. The principles are:

a Select samples for inspection by random methods (which means that every unit of production has as good a chance as any other unit of being selected).

b Draw up a quality control chart which shows the standard to be aimed at (the specified dimension, breaking point, and so on) as a horizontal line.

c Plot on this chart the actual results achieved from measuring the dimension, breaking point, and so on, of the samples chosen. The points plotted will rarely be exactly standard, but will appear above or below the standard line.

d If the results appear to be too far from the standard to be acceptable, call for a revision of machine settings, and so on, to correct the error.

Such a chart is shown in Figure 4.2.

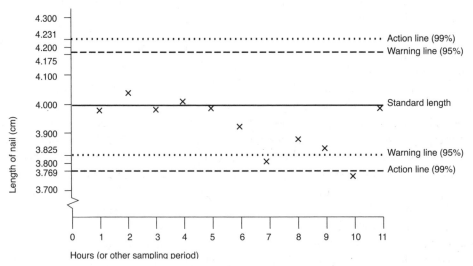

Fig. 4.2 A quality control chart (for the length of nails)

(Reproduced by permission from *Pitman's Statistics for Business*)

Notes:

i   The standard length of the nails is 4.000 cm.

ii A sample is selected every hour, and measured.

iii At first the samples are fairly close to the required standard but after about 5 hours they become more variable – they are shorter.

iv The machine should be reset, certainly by the time we get to the 10th hourly sample.

Critical path analysis

In many major contracts and production activities certain basic activities have to be performed first, for example we cannot build a factory until we have cleared the site. A technique that may be useful at this point is that of critical path analysis. Other names for the same general approach are network analysis and Pert (programme evaluation and review technique). The problem is to devise the most economical method of working so that each part of the work is begun at the optimum moment and is ready for use when it is required in the overall plan. This will ensure that the work is approached in the most direct way so that the journey to final completion is as short as possible – *made along the critical path*.

The technique depends upon three ideas which arise in every project: events, activities and duration times.

An *event* is a starting point or a finishing point, or an intermediate point where some sort of partial completion stage can be clearly identified. Thus the purchase of premises, or the arrival of a crane, or the redecoration of a room might be an event.

An *activity* is a period of effort which leads to an event. Thus the arrival of a crane (an event) may permit the start of an activity (loading or unloading) that leads to a further event (the departure of a vehicle or the opening of a site store for the issue of materials).

A *duration time* is the time required for a particular activity.

Critical paths are arrived at by drawing a diagram called a network. By convention a network is drawn from the left-hand side of the page, where the events and activities start, to the right-hand side of the page, where they finish. Each event is numbered, and each activity is indicated by a line with an arrowhead at the right-hand end where the activity finishes. Against each activity line the expected duration of that activity is shown. The general idea is best understood by looking at a simple network, such as Fig. 4.3.

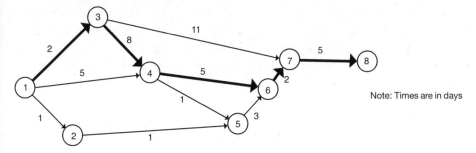

Note: Times are in days

Fig. 4.3   A simple network showing the critical path

Notes:

i   Each event is shown by a circle and they are numbered from left to right of the page, in the time sequence in which they occur.

ii An event is not reached until all the activities leading into it have been completed. The only event that has no activities leading into it is the starting event 1.

iii Activities are shown as arrows. They are clearly identifiable tasks to be performed, usually by one person or one team of persons. The length of the arrow has no connection with the duration of the job, it merely helps to join up the network. The duration of the activity is marked alongside the arrow in agreed units, such as hours or days.

iv An activity cannot begin until the event it starts from (the tail event) has been reached (see (ii) above).

v   An activity is described by naming its tail event and its head event. Thus activity 1–2 takes 1 day and activity 1–3 takes 2 days.

The critical path is that series of essential events which has the longest time-path; in other words, the project cannot be completed in less time than the critical path indicates. Thus event numbers 3, 4, 6, 7 and 8 are the ones that decide the critical path in Fig. 4.3. The project will take 22 days to complete. Activities on the critical path have to be carried out in the time stated. Activities which are not on the critical path can be allowed to 'float'; we can get activity 1–4 done at any time during the 10 days that 1–3 and 3–4 are being completed, so long as we start it by day 6 so that it gets done in time.

Clearly, critical path analysis is an art which has to be learned. The stages in planning a project may be listed as follows:

1   State clearly what has to be done.
2   Break this down into events, activities and duration times.
3   Draw the network.
4   Analyse the network and decide how to schedule the activities.
5   Check the schedule against the network.
6   Institute progress controls over the project as it moves through to completion.

4.7   Costing aspects of production

Costing is a very important aspect of production. Unfortunately it is also a subject in its own right which can only be touched upon here. The reader who is particularly interested must refer to a major text on costing, such as *Costing* by Lucey, published by Letts. The process of estimating and quoting for jobs has already been referred to, and may be illustrated by the step diagram given in Fig. 4.4. The elements of cost are as follows:

1   Materials.
2   Labour.
3   Direct expenses – by which we mean overhead expenses directly related to the product concerned, such as the design costs for a jig to hold the product during a drilling operation.

4 Indirect expenses – by which we mean overhead expenses not directly attributable to a particular job, but shared among all jobs on a *pro rata* basis. Examples are rent (charged out on a 'floor space occupied' basis) and light and heat (charged out on a ratio basis to the value of the job compared with the total value of jobs done).
5 Selling costs (for example, packaging, postage, and so on).
6 Profit. This can hardly be described as a cost, but in economic terms it is a cost we have to pay for the use of the capital and the risk being run by the proprietor.

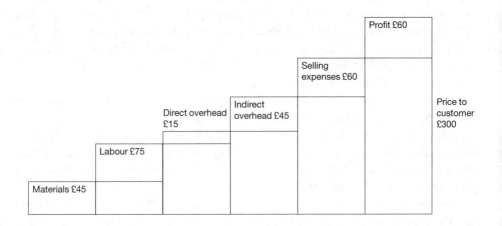

Fig. 4.4 How costs are built up

There are a number of different methods of costing. They include job costing, batch costing and contract costing, which are known by the general name of **specific order costing**. Another group is operation costing, which includes process costing and service costing. We do not place specific orders for petrol and similar chemicals; they are made by complex chemical processes and once the product is available anyone can be supplied, but the price must cover the costs of the various processes. Applied to these groups of costing activities are certain well-known principles and costing techniques: **absorption costing**, which seeks to absorb overhead costs by spreading them over all the products of a firm, and **marginal costing**, which differentiates between fixed and variable costs and studies the effects on profits of changes in the volume of output (which causes variable costs to change while fixed costs are unaffected). **Standard costing** is a method of pricing jobs in such a way that any variation from standard is revealed and can be investigated to detect inefficiency or adverse movements of cost. Such variances include price variances, usage of materials variances, volume variances and overhead variances.

'Make or buy' decisions

'Make or buy' decisions are a special case of costing appraisal in which we decide whether to make a product ourselves or buy it in from another supplier, adding a profit margin before selling it on to the customer. There are many situations where this type of decision has to be made. For example, if we have plenty of spare capacity and a job can be done easily in our own workshops using existing facilities we shall take the job, make the product required and use our spare capacity in a sensible way. If the job requires raw materials we do not have, or a class of labour we shall have to employ specially, or machinery we must buy in for the purpose, it is much more likely we shall buy the product in. The thing that is in short supply is called the **limiting factor** – the thing that limits our ability to take the job without any worries. It is this limiting factor, whatever it is, which requires the decision. Shall we buy the extra machine, or the specialist materials required, or shall we find someone from whom we can 'buy in' the product? If repeat orders are a possibility, this will be an incentive to make the product – a one-off job is more likely to be bought in.

The concept of marginal costing is important in 'make or buy' decisions. Marginal costing is only concerned with the extra costs that will be incurred if we decide to make the product. We need not charge any overheads to this extra job, except direct overheads incurred particularly for this job. Since we have paid our other overheads already, there is no need to burden this job with a share of them. If we buy the product in, it will cost the supplier's price. If we make the job ourselves, it will only cost us the marginal cost. So, unless the supplier's price is less than the marginal costs, we should make the thing ourselves. If we cannot make the item without incurring expenses which will take the marginal costs up over the price of the bought-in item, then we should buy it.

Other non-cost elements do creep into the decision. Will we have to reveal our know-how to the supplier if we buy the product in, with the chance that he/she will eat into our future markets? Will he/she repeat the order at the same price should we need to repeat the process, or will the supplier opt out and take some more lucrative contract?

4.8   Work study

Work study is the detailed appraisal of what has to be done, and the way that we do it, so that we achieve the greatest possible output of added value from the least possible input of effort and resources. Every industry is adding value to the resources made available by nature. This is the process of wealth creation, by which we mean the creation of an abundance of goods and services. It is this increase in value that makes possible the rewards paid to the factors of production, the chief of which is labour (so that in a sense work study is a way of raising wages), and the other rewards to factors: rent, interest and profit. This is putting the case for work study in economic terms. It is sometimes difficult for employees to see that improved working necessarily benefits them; but in recent years it has become crystal clear that the survival of firms depends upon efficient working, and unemployment will be the only end of any attempt to hold back efficient methods of work.

Work study is conducted in two ways, **method study** and **work measurement**.

Method study

This is the scientific approach to the study of working methods. It may take the form of a scientific appraisal of the methods to be used in a new development, so that the factory layout will be logical, the delivery of materials and parts will be efficient and economical, the array of powered tools, presses, and so on, will give every operative an appropriate level of support and so on. With an existing system it will mean the reappraisal of the methods in use at present; the design and construction of such improvements in layout as seem appropriate; the introduction of new computerised systems where current methods are manifestly obsolete; the introduction of more powerful, faster machines where appropriate, and so on.

Once a new method has been introduced, or an old method has been modernised, it must be supervised for a time to ensure that unexpected snags do not develop, or that a new method is not bypassed by traditionalist employees who disapprove of it. The results under the new method as against an earlier method should be compared and evaluated to ensure that the intended aims are being achieved.

Work measurement

Work is infinitely varied, and not all work can be measured accurately though it can usually be evaluated in some way. The purpose of work measurement is to arrive at some idea of what can be achieved in a given period of time by a reasonably conscientious worker. This is easier with a simple repetitive type of work, for example drilling a sub-assembly in an engine component, than work of a one-off nature, such as the design of a jig for holding the sub-assembly while it is being drilled. The jig may take two or three weeks to make, while the sub-assemblies can be put in, drilled and removed every 30 seconds.

Work measurement only becomes possible when method study has resolved how the work is to be performed. The movements made by an operator performing the approved method can then be studied and timed. Allowances may need to be made for personal needs, and for fatigue. From the evidence collected, some sensible unit of work can be arrived at – say drilling 50 sub-assemblies – and a time for this unit can then be calculated as **the time allowed**. This time allowed may be used to calculate wages and bonuses under one or other of the bonus systems familiar to cost accountants. Some sort of standard labour cost can then be used which will assist in pricing components, jobs and products.

Fig. 4.5 shows these two aspects of work study in diagrammatic form.

4.9   Maintenance and production

It stands to reason that production facilities will not keep going for ever, and regular maintenance is essential, while prompt attention to breakdowns that occur is vital. Breakdowns cause serious losses, waste of operator time, delays which may result in failure to meet deadlines, loss of contracts, and so on. Maintenance department will often be a specialist function under the general control of the production manager or works manager. It has a number of functions, but its overall purpose is to ensure that breakdowns are avoided by a wide regime of preventive maintenance. As its name implies, preventive maintenance is

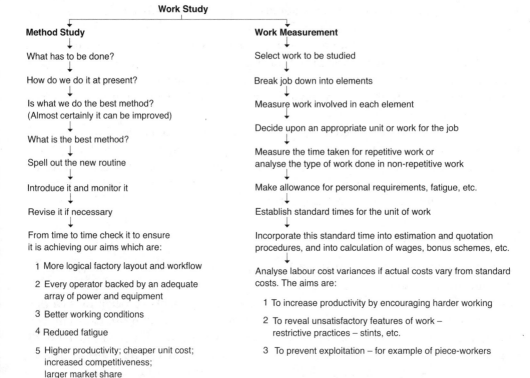

Fig. 4.5 Method study and work measurement

regular maintenance which anticipates failures and breakdowns by replacing parts that are wearing out before they break down. To take a simple example, if it is known that electric light bulbs last on average 500 hours, then a regular maintenance programme to replace them after 400 hours of use will avoid them burning out. There is quite a lot of work involved in changing light bulbs, and a system which replaces all the lamps in a room at the same time will probably be cheaper than changing them individually when they burn out.

There are many aspects to maintenance, and specialist technicians in each area must be employed, for example mechanics, electricians, painters, decorators, and so on. The aim is to keep a plant running without breakdowns, and to deal promptly with breakdowns that do occur. If maintenance requires some section of the plant to be out of use temporarily, this can be done with a minimum of dislocation – for example, in known slack periods, or by arranging deadlines to avoid the period when maintenance is taking place.

The chief features of maintenance work are:

1 The preparation and maintenance of plant inventories, furniture and fitting inventories, building records, and so on.
2 The preparation of maintenance schedules for each type of asset, and the supervision of these schedules to check that routine procedures are being carried out, inspection schedules are being followed, and that adequate supplies of lubricants, solvents, cleaning materials, vulnerable spare parts, and so on, are available.
3 The maintenance of services at all times – gas, electricity, water, compressed air, fuels for motor vehicles, sanitary arrangements, and so on.
4 The regular maintenance of buildings, especially from the health and safety aspects, regular inspection of storage and access areas, displays of notices about dangerous aspects of premises, and so on.
5 Liaison with other departments about programmes of maintenance work, closure of areas due for overhaul, and so on.
6 Induction procedures for new staff, training in safety procedures, adequate systems for reporting and actioning faults, and so on.
7 Costing and budgeting for maintenance expenses to ensure an adequate supply of tools and equipment, and the proper recognition of maintenance costs as an element in total cost which must be charged out to jobs and contracts.

4.10 CAD, CAM and CIM

This is not a specialist book on production, which is only one element in the general subject of business administration, but the use of computers at every level in production must be referred to. It began as **computer-aided design** (CAD) where the ability of the computer to draw from coordinates enabled it to create lines on a television screen. The computer instructs dots of light to form lines on the screen, each point on the line being measured from X and Y axes as on an ordinary graph. If the points have been fixed on the screen the computer can be instructed to join them. If a full and detailed list of instructions is fed in about a particular component, the resulting drawing will be a complete technical description of the component, or assembly. Associated with the drawing will be other useful information, such as material specifications, parts required, costings and many other details which the computer will sort, shuffle and retrieve from memory as required. It can enlarge or reduce parts of a drawing if this is helpful. Of course there is a great deal of work to do to feed into the computer's memory a whole range of standard parts – screws, nuts, bolts, sheet metals, and so on – but once done such a library of information can be used again and again. The result is that most of the boring, repetitive work of technical drawing is eliminated. There is no need to erase wrong lines, they can be removed without difficulty, adjusted as required and after final checking the diagram can be printed off.

From computer-aided design grew **computer-aided manufacturing** (CAM). The dimensional data stored in the computer can be used to manufacture the component and the whole machining procedure can be simulated on a VDU (visual display unit) to ensure that the procedure is foolproof. The whole cycle of manufacturing can be tried out in theory before the real activity takes place. Snags which, using traditional methods, would not have been discovered until the manufacturing process was under way – with consequent delays to the production line and down-time for machines – are now discovered by simulation, and adjustments made before the cycle of production begins.

These ideas led to the performance of repetitive manufacturing processes by computerised instructions to particular machines. An endless belt of paper tape in the early machines took the machine through a sequence of activities to produce a particular part or component. Later, as computerisation developed, **computer-integrated manufacture** (CIM) became possible, with all the movements of materials and work-in-progress, and eventually finished components being decided, executed and inspected by computer.

Such manufacturing systems are expensive to set up, and are most economic for long production runs where the costs can be spread over a large number of units. However, where a particular package of programs can be purchased economically to achieve some sections of a complex activity, even small runs of production may be economic.

5 The purchasing function

5.1 The nature of purchasing

The function of the purchasing department is to obtain for the firm or company everything it needs to carry on its activities, except labour, which is obtained by the personnel department. The items to be purchased are of four main types. These are:

1 *Capital assets* These are purchases of plant, machinery, motor vehicles, office equipment, tools and appliances of every kind. They last a long time – longer than a year – and are distinguished from items that last less than a year, which are called consumables. Capital assets are often extremely expensive – a single crane may cost as much as £500 000, for example – and the purchasing officer has much to do to ensure that such items are properly approved before ordering, after a period of careful evaluation by staff who know all about the asset concerned. Often particular members of staff are appointed to supervise the purchase of assets in particular fields (for example, office equipment), and no requisition will be considered that does not bear the signature of the appropriate official.

2 *Consumable items* These are items used in the course of business, such as letterheads, envelopes, paper clips and so on, for office use; and lubricants, cleaning materials, greases and so on, for factory activities. Much of the ordering of this type of good is routine – it is simply a case of ordering when stocks are running low – but all such items are valuable and easily pilfered, so their use should be monitored. Staff should know that management views misappropriation of such items as a serious offence.

3 *Goods for resale* Firms in wholesale and retail trade buy goods to sell again at a profit, after perhaps performing such useful services as breaking bulk, distribution, display, and so on. So widespread is this sort of business activity that the word 'purchases' has come to mean 'items bought for resale at a profit', even though the purchasing department may buy many other items. So the purchase of a machine or of typing paper for office use is not 'purchases' in the usual meaning of that word, which is reserved for goods that are to be resold.

   Some goods which are purchased for resale are invoiced at 'recommended retail price', say bicycles at £120 each. The buyer is given a discount called trade discount which reduces the price to the buying firm, so that when it resells at the recommended retail price it will make a profit equal to the trade discount. Trade discounts are usually between 25 and 55 percent; anything less is insufficient for the trader to cover his/her overhead expenses.

4 *Raw materials and components for manufacturing activities* If we are manufacturers there is another kind of purchase, the purchase of raw materials and components that are

embodied in the product during the manufacturing process. We have to convert the raw materials and components into a finished product. The purchasing officer will need detailed **specifications** of the materials required, and of the components to be bought in from subcontractors or suppliers. It will usually be a matter of serious concern that the quality of materials or parts meets the specification, and to this end it will be usual to deal only with approved suppliers who have proved over the years that they can meet our requirements.

The work of securing supplies of these four types of requirement is important and requires sound control by qualified staff. Usually the purchasing officer will be a senior memebr of staff, though not necessarily of boardroom level. He/she will certainly be asked to sit in at board meetings where agenda items affecting the Purchasing Department are to be discussed. A purchasing officer is usually a member of the Chartered Institute of Purchasing and Supply, one of the most important professional bodies. Their address for students interested in securing membership is Easton House, Easton on the Hill, Stamford, Lincs. PE9 3NZ (telephone 01780 756 777).

5.2   Role of the purchasing officer

The purchasing office is sometimes called the buying department, and the purchasing officer may be called the buyer. However, today the term buyer is often used for lower-level staff who have authority to buy particular lines in particular areas of merchandise, and have a budget which they can spend in the approved area. They may be given a monthly 'open to buy' figure which limits the buyer's ability to spend in line with the availability of funds in the general cash budget of the whole business.

The purchasing officer has the following functions:

1   To assemble specifications of requirements for all departments with a view to purchasing the required quantities and qualities of goods of all kinds.
2   To investigate sources of supplies and assemble data on each source and the variety of supplies it might produce.
3   To evaluate potential suppliers and draw up an **index of suppliers**.
4   To negotiate contracts and the management of projects to obtain the best value at the most economical price.
5   To acquire the goods and services needed by placing orders with approved suppliers.
6   To inspect goods and services to ensure they are of adequate quality and according to contract.
7   To supervise inventory control, and lay down a regime of stock limits, re-order levels, and so on.
8   To supervise handling, storage and physical distribution of raw materials, components and finished goods until they are transferred to the marketing department (or other sales function).
9   Disposal of waste, or goods surplus to requirement, at the best price possible.

These various duties need a fuller explanation.

Specifications of requirements

We cannot allow anyone to go out and buy the items a business requires, for if we do they may select goods without careful consideration of the quality required, or they might not negotiate the best price possible. With any major area of activity or with any new project, the purchasing officer will call for specifications of the exact items required, the exact qualities of materials and so on, to be ordered. This requires departments and project leaders to consider all aspects of their resource responsibilities carefully, so that they have thought the whole project through and given serious thought to each type of resource.

Having done so they will draw up specifications which are clear and correctly expressed in terms of the trade concerned, so that the purchasing officer can either approach existing approved suppliers for tenders or quotations, or can find new sources if similar materials or parts have not previously been ordered.

Sources of supplies

Even if a purchasing officer has an established index of suppliers, he/she is bound to be approached from time to time by new suppliers. Such enquiries may often come from official bodies, embassies, state trading organisations and so on, trying to break into the market with new sources of supply. The officer will examine all such requests, and may perhaps attend meetings to inspect supplies on offer, or briefings about new sources and suppliers. Purchasing is a long-term activity and, even if the purchasing officer only places small orders to test out the quality and delivery record of a new supplier, these will be welcome and may lead to bigger orders. We do not usually tie ourselves too closely to a single supplier, for a breakdown, strike, local riot or war may interrupt crucial supplies. It is usual to have two or three regular suppliers, who consequently are solicitous of our welfare and keep their prices competitive.

Index of suppliers

To prepare for all future purchasing activities by the organisation the purchasing officer builds up an index of suppliers, with whom proper consultation has taken place about the supply of the type of goods likely to be required, the quantities likely to be needed and the prices likely to be charged. This will call for close links between the supplier, the purchasing officer and the end-user within the company so that a sound business relationship is established. It may call for the submission of samples or prototype components by the supplier, or for tenders (in which the supplier agrees to supply either a specified item or quantities as and when required, at a known price). Over the years a succession of orders will be placed with the approved supplier, who naturally becomes amenable to suggestions about the ways in which our regular custom may be encouraged. For example, a supplier might agree to package the supplies in a particular way, or to deliver them at unseasonable hours.

The index of suppliers lists all the details needed for efficient operations, such as name, address, telephone numbers, names of contacts at various levels, types and quantities of goods usually supplied, delays likely to occur so that orders can be placed in good time for delivery as required, and so on. This type of index brings order into the purchasing of goods, and avoids the delays and disappointments which would arise if staff in need of goods merely contacted an unknown supplier with an enquiry for goods which later proved to be sub-standard or failed to arrive. Formecon Services Ltd provide a useful 'supplier profile' (address at the end of this chapter).

Negotiating contracts

The purchasing officer will place countless orders during the year, and each order constitutes a separate contract with the supplier concerned, but it would be tedious if a full contractual agreement had to be negotiated for each order placed, and the purchasing officer will negotiate a proper contract between his/her organisation and each supplier, with terms acceptable to both parties. These terms will usually be based upon a **set of Standard Terms and Conditions** but some negotiation may be necessary on particular points if the supplier is in a strong position (for example, a monopoly supplier of a particular machine).

Such negotiations require a good knowledge of contract law and the set of Standard Terms and Conditions on which they are based should always be the subject of legal advice, preferably given by the legal department of the trading organisation for the industry concerned. The aim of the contract is to ensure sound standards of supply by the supplier, who will be deemed to know the quality of materials, components, and so on that we require and will have a duty to supply goods of the quality required, fit for the purpose intended. This will ensure adequate redress of any grievance over a particular order, even if when the order was placed no special contractual arrangements were made, it being assumed by both parties that the supply would be governed by the terms laid down in the normal course of business between us.

Such contracts would be renewable at appropriate intervals, say annually, to give both parties a chance to review the terms agreed in the light of changing circumstances. In inflationary times it might be sensible to arrange some indexation of prices to take account during the lifetime of a particular contract of rises in the prices of raw materials, overhead expenses, and so on.

Acquisition and inspection of goods

One of the basic ideas of a purchasing department is centralised buying, the advantages of which are as follows:
1 No-one but the properly authorised buyer may place orders on behalf of the firm or company.
2 All requisitions from departments will be fulfilled from central stocks and when stocks need to be replenished new bulk orders will be placed with authorised suppliers so that advantage can be taken of quantity discounts, extended credit periods, and so on.
3 On delivery, goods will be inspected before a clean signature is given on the delivery note, and immediate notice will be given both on the note and in writing separately of any shortage, breakage, wrong goods, and so on.

4 Goods will be taken into stock in a proper manner, with stock levels being raised in accordance with the delivery, and a goods received note being made out for the purchasing department, with copies to the requisitioning department, the costing department and the accounts department. Statements arriving later will not be paid unless the goods received notes indicate that all items charged for have in fact arrived.

This gives excellent control over the ordering, inspection and recording of purchases.

Physical distribution management (logistics)

Although this is a big subject and may not entirely be the responsibility of the purchasing officer, it remains a fact that goods of all sorts which have been ordered and received are eminently pilferable and may also be the object of burglaries, hijackings, and so on. The purchasing officer has a general interest in seeing that goods ordered actually reach the requisitioning department without damage, pilfering or theft. Damage is less likely if goods are properly packed or stored in bins, crates, and so on, and moved by handling equipment which is adequate for the work in hand. Vehicles should be in good condition and secure, and movements should be controlled so that driver malpractices are reduced or detected. For example, tachograph records will reveal unauthorised stoppages; all complaints of shortages should be rigorously investigated and blame attached to the responsible party.

Disposal of waste and goods surplus to requirements

Waste is a common feature of many manufacturing processes and there are many situations where goods, machinery and so on become obsolete or unfashionable. All such accumulations should be disposed of as quickly as possible and sooner, rather than later. The fact is that waste and redundant items go on costing money if they are not disposed of. They take up valuable space and they may deteriorate and become hazards of one sort or another. It is the neglected and overlooked areas which often accumulate rubbish which eventually catches fire. Most waste has some value and should be disposed of at the best price possible. If it has no value, pay someone to clear it and make the space it is occupying available for other purposes. Since it is the purchasing department that is always looking for space, and which has these redundant items cluttering up its stores, it is usually the purchasing officer who disposes of them.

5.3   Purchasing department procedures

Much has already been said about preliminary arrangements to build an index of suppliers. We must now go through the procedure to list the various activities connected with ordering, and mention a few points on each.

Requisitions

The general rule is that a department requiring an item will put in a requisition for it, and if available in stock the purchasing department will deliver it to the requisitioning department as soon as convenient, adjusting the stock records accordingly. If the stock level of any item approaches the re-order level as a result, an order will be put in hand to replenish stock.

If the item requisitioned is not in stock it will go through the ordering procedure.

Ordering

Before we can order we must check:

1 That the requisition comes from a duly authorised person.
2 That the request is similar to previous requests and within usual arrangements for that class of good.
3 If it is a new item, that prior arrangements have been made about it and that there is a duly authorised supplier.
4 If this is not the case and the item is required urgently there may have been a *prima facie* breach of arrangements – someone responsible has overlooked the item or not anticipated a need. This should be taken up to reduce the frequency of such events in the future, while at the same time the order procedure goes ahead as best it can.
5 The order should be dispatched and a copy retained for our records. If a written or computerised record of orders is kept, this should be updated to include the order placed.
6 The order should be monitored to see whether it arrived by the agreed date; some sort of progress-chasing procedure should be instituted either by the purchasing department or by production control department.

Note that an order, like other business documents, should have the names and addresses of both parties to the transaction and an exact description of the goods required: the quality, quantity, size, colour, unit price and so on. It should begin with the words 'Please supply' since it is a formal offer to purchase which, when accepted by the seller, makes a binding contract between the two parties. The date should be clearly stated, and if delivery is required by a specific date, this must be stated, for example 'Delivery required by 31 July 20…'. This makes the delivery date part of the essence of the contract, and failure to comply with it would be breach of contract.

Sometimes suppliers supply order forms which simplify ordering as they list all the products, with boxes which only have to be completed by inserting the number required. There are advantages for the supplier, in that the goods listed on the form are usually in the same order as they are stacked in the warehouse, and an order-picking lift-truck can move around the warehouse systematically collecting items required in the correct sequence.

Goods received notes

The purchasing department will usually lay down a procedure for receiving goods. The chief points are:

1 Drivers should not be given clean signatures on delivery notes unless goods have been examined for signs of damage. This does not mean they have to be opened and inspected, but examined for an appearance of damage. The phrase usually used is 'Received in apparent good order and condition', but if this is not the case the delivery note should be claused 'Goods damaged on arrival' or 'Goods appear wet – internal damage suspected', and so on. Notice on the delivery note is not enough, however, and must be followed up, preferably the same day, with notice in writing on letterhead.

   Sometimes a particular employee (perhaps with a deputy) is the only person entitled to sign for goods on delivery notes, and notices to that effect are put up in the delivery bay. This makes it less likely that a clean signature will be given for goods which have not been properly checked.

2 The goods should be examined without delay, the contents being compared with the advice note which is packed with them or attached to them in a polythene (or other) envelope.

3 A **goods received note** should be made out, with particulars of the goods received and details of any shortages or damage. Copies should be sent to the purchasing department, which will relate them to the order, and either close the order if full delivery has been made or indicate the balance to follow.

Suppliers' invoices

Suppliers' invoices are sometimes the document on which we shall pay for the supplies, but with regular suppliers a monthly statement may be sent at a later date. In any case we shall not pay until we know all the goods have arrived safely (which will be apparent on the goods received note). We shall also check all extensions, calculations, and so on; ensure that proper discounts have been deducted; claim any credit that is due for returns, and so on. When this is all satisfactory we shall pass the invoice to the accounts department for payment (or retention until the statement arrives later in the month).

5.4 Inventory control

The purchasing department may not have control of stores and depots directly, since they may be more easily managed physically by the factory manager or depot manager concerned. The purchasing officer will lay down principles for exercising control over stocks, and will specify maximum and minimum stock levels. The aim in controlling stocks is to be in a situation where all requisitions from user departments can be fulfilled so that production is not held up, but at the same time stocks are not excessive. Excessive stocks waste capital, which is tied up in slow-moving items unnecessarily acquired, while at the same time deterioration sets in. Those who have requisitioned rubber bands, which on arrival prove to have perished because they have been in stock for years, will appreciate the problem.

Some idea of the procedure is given in Fig. 5.1 and the notes below it.

STOCK LEDGER CARD

Description *Flow valve*   Maximum stock *750*   Charging system *FIFO*
Code No. *F2134*   Minimum stock *200*   Delivery time *1 week*
Location *17.21.3*   Supplier *Plumbing specialities*   Re-order point *250*
                                                          EOQ *500*

Receipts				Issues (Needed in the company)					Balance		
Date	Ref. Qty	Price £	Value £	Date	Ref.	Qty	Price £	Value £	Qty	Price £	Value £
20..	*FIFO*			20..							
				Jan 1					200	4.00	800.00
Jan 5	GRN12 500	5.50	2750.00						700	various	3550.00
				Jan 10	R107	550	200 x 4.00 350 x 5.50	2725.00	150	5.50	825.00
Jan 19	GRN27 500	7.20	3600.00						650	various	4425.00
				Jan 26	R157	400	150 x 5.50 250 x 7.20	2625.00			
									250	7.20	1800.00

Fig. 5.1   A stock control card

Notes:

i   The maximum stock of flow valves is 750 (which is in fact the sum of the re-order point (250) and the EOQ – the economic order quantity – of 500). If stock falls to 250 units so that we re-order, and no more flow valves are requisitioned, the order of 500 will arrive and give us a maximum stock. The re-order point takes account of the time lag before an order can be received, and the average consumption in that period.

ii   The EOQ is the best order to place, since at 500 units costs are at a minimum. An expla-nation of EOQ is given at section 5.6 below. Each time we order we ask for 500 units, and these are recorded on the GRN (goods received note) and on the stock ledger card.

iii The charging system is FIFO (first in, first out). Thus the 550 units issued on 10 January are charged as being 200 of the £4.00 valves and 350 of the £5.50 valves. This leaves 150 valves in stock, worth £5.50 each. As stocks have now fallen below 250 (the re-order point) and also below the minimum stock, we must re-order at once.

Work through the rest of the card to make sure you follow the system.

Stock-taking procedures

The purposes of stock-taking are three, as follows:

1 To discover the value of stock in hand at the end of the year. This is an important figure when doing final accounts since it is used in the Trading Account to find the gross profit of the business. The basis of this calculation is:

Gross profit = Selling price (net turnover) – Cost price (cost of stock sold)

The figure 'cost of stock sold' is made up as follows:

Stock at the start of the year + Purchases (less returns) during the year – Stock at the close of the year

The whole calculation is illustrated in Fig. 5.2.

Trading Account for year ending 31 December 20....

	£	£		£
Opening stock		17 295	Sales	127 500
Add Purchases	42 500		**Less** Sales returns	1 500
Less Purchases Returns	850		Net turnover	126 000
		41 650		
		58 945		
Less Closing stock		18 945		
Cost of stock sold		40 000		
Gross profit		86 000		
		£126 000		£126 000

Profit and Loss Account for year ending 31 December 20....

	£
Gross Profit	86 000

Fig. 5.2   How closing stock is used to find the gross profit

The point to note here is that any false figure in the closing stock will affect the profits of the business. If the stock is overstated the 'cost of stock sold' will be reduced, and the profits will be overstated. If the stock is understated the cost of stock sold will be increased and the profits will be reduced. It follows that the accounting bodies have laid down a rule which says: **stock must be valued at cost price, or at net realisable value, whichever is lower**.

If we value stock in this way we value it at cost price normally, but if for some reason it has deteriorated while in stock and is now worth less than cost price, we value it at the price we would get for it now after paying any expenses of disposal (that is why it says *net* realisable value). In this way we take the loss on deteriorated stock now, because the stock has suffered this loss in the year just ending.

2 The second reason for valuing stock is to detect bad buying, which is revealed by an appraisal of the stock to discover which lines are slow-moving. It may be found that one particular buyer purchases excessive quantities of stock, determined to keep his/her section well supplied even though turnover does not justify it. Buying items which are

not popular or have passed the peak of public interest, where they are 'fad today and fade tomorrow' items, is always bad. Buyers have to know the trends and must hesitate to buy further stocks when the trend has peaked.

3 Ordinary stock-taking does not directly detect theft of stock either by staff or by shoplifters, though it can do so indirectly through a ratio called the gross profit percentage (see below). However, in one class of retail trade it can be detected directly. Where head offices do all the purchasing and send goods out to branches for sale, they usually charge the branches at selling price. There is no need for a branch manager to know what the goods cost. Head office adds on its mark-up of profit and invoices the branch for the goods at selling price. An example best illustrates the system. Suppose branch A has £10 000 of stock (at selling price) on its shelves on the first day of June and is sent £50 000 of stock (at selling price) during the month. At stock-taking on 30 June it is found to have £8500 of stock (at selling price) still on the shelves. It follows that the manager should have paid into the local bank as takings:

   £10 000 + £50 000 − £8500 = £51 500

He/she should either have the stock or the money, and if the figures do not agree the difference must be losses due either to shoplifting or to staff theft (of cash or stock).

Of course such a method of stock-taking at selling price does not give us the correct figure for the 'closing stock' on the Trading Account. The £8500 must be reduced to cost price for head office purposes by deducting the profit mark-up added originally.

One way for a branch manager to cheat on such a system is to put the goods on the shelves at a higher selling price than head office has specified, the extra cash thus obtained being pocketed (or perhaps used to cover stock misappropriated). It is usual, therefore, when doing the stock-taking, to compare the marked prices with the head office prices, and ensure that this type of malpractice is not taking place.

The arrangements for checking stock may be as follows:

1 *Annual stock-taking* This is for the purpose of valuing stock for the preparation of the final accounts of the business and the determination of the profit for the financial year. The procedure is:

   a Count the stock physically (disposing of all damaged stock at the same time).
   b Value each type of stock using the rule laid down by the accounting bodies, mentioned above.
   c Multiply this value by the number of items in stock.
   d Add up the grand total.

2 *Spot-check or audit* This is designed to detect losses due to pilfering, waste, and so on. It should be done without warning by a team of investigators and the number of units should be compared with the stock records.

3 *Perpetual inventory* This system is the usual system described in Fig. 5.1 where the stock ledger card or bin card is updated each time stock is received or issued. The number of items and the value of stock is known all the time, according to the stock records, but of course a spot-check may reveal that some stock has been stolen or issued without being recorded.

Stock ratios

A ratio is a figure which brings out the relative importance of one factor compared with another. Two ratios about stock are helpful:

1 Rate of stock-turn (rate of stock turnover)
2 Gross profit percentage

1 *Rate of stock-turn* To find this we use the formula:

$$\text{Rate of stock turn} = \frac{\text{Cost of stock sold}}{\text{Average stock at cost price}}$$

Average stock at cost price is found by taking the sum of the opening and closing stocks and dividing by 2. Thus in Fig. 5.2 above we have:

Opening stock (£17 295) + Closing stock (£18 945) / 2 = £18 120

Using this figure to find the rate of stock-turn we have:

$$\text{Rate of stock turn} = \frac{\text{Cost of stock sold}}{\text{Average stock at cost price}}$$

$$= \frac{£40\,000}{£18\,120}$$

$$= 2.2 \text{ times}$$

As a trading business makes a profit at the time of sale, the rate of stock turnover tells us how many times a year we make our profit margin on the average stock held. If we can increase the rate of stock turnover, we shall increase profit. For example, a rate of stock turnover of 4.4 will mean double the profit that has been earned in this example, provided we can get the increased sales without cutting our prices.

The average stock has turned over 2.2 times in the year. Is this a satisfactory rate of stock-turn? We cannot say until we know the type of stock concerned. It would not do for fresh fish or new-laid eggs, but it might be all right for slow-moving items like grand pianos or combine harvesters.

We can extend our understanding by turning this rate of stock-turn into a figure which shows how long an average item is in stock. The answer can be in months, weeks or days. The calculation is:

$$\frac{12 \text{ months}}{2.2} \quad \text{or} \quad \frac{52 \text{ weeks}}{2.2} \quad \text{or} \quad \frac{365 \text{ days}}{2.2}$$

$$= 5.5 \text{ months} \quad \text{or} \quad = 23.6 \text{ weeks} \quad \text{or} \quad = 165.9 \text{ days}$$

Such ratios detect the buyer who has too many slow-moving items in stock.

2 *Gross profit percentage* Strictly speaking, this ratio is not just about stock, but it can lead to investigations which reveal stock losses. To find the gross profit percentage we use the formula:

$$\frac{\text{Gross profit}}{\text{Turnover}} \times 100$$

In Fig. 5.2 this gives us:

$$\frac{\text{Gross profit}}{\text{Turnover}} \times 100 \qquad \frac{86\,000}{126\,000} \times 100$$

$$= 68.25\%$$

This seems to be a very high percentage of gross profit, but it is in fact not at all unusual since we have to deduct all the overhead expenses of the business before we can find the net profit, or clean profit.

The point about the gross profit percentage is that it should be a constant from year to year if our business is being conducted in the same way. For example, even if we double sales we shall have to double our purchases, so that in terms of the ratio of profits to turnover it will be the same ratio, even though the actual figures are double those of last year.

Assuming that our gross profit percentage should be constant, if last year's figure was 74 percent and this year's is only 68.25 percent, what has happened? It could mean:

a The manager is stealing the money.

b The staff are stealing the money.

c The manager or staff are stealing the stock.

d The public are stealing the stock.

e Bad buying has meant loss of perishable stock – too many tomatoes, fruit and so on, going into the dustbin because of deterioration.

f It could mean a number of other sorts of inefficiency as well, but these need not concern us here.

5.5   Stores control

The purchasing officer has a major interest in stores and store-keeping, since all purchases finish up in store somewhere, and their good management and supervision is of crucial importance. Ideally, stores have to be located where both delivery and accessibility to the end-user are easily arranged. This is not always a straightforward matter. The type and variety of stores is important. Some goods can be stored in plastic work-boxes ranged in racks and are easily accessible; other items are stored in bins while large items must be allocated a bay. It follows that the layout of the building is very important and keeping track of items is not at all easy. For example, we can rarely store items alphabetically, because the arrival of a new item would require us to move everything up one place to make room for it. As businesses grow, the large central store tends to give way to smaller store units close to the various production departments and supplying the items used by a particular department. For example, we may have a raw materials store for metals, timber and similar materials and a components store for bought-in or batch-produced items.

Goods received, having gone through the reception procedure, have to be taken to the appropriate location, are entered on the bin card or other stock record and are then available to production departments against official requisitions signed by an appropriate foreman, supervisor or progress chaser. The requisition forms will be used to reduce stock levels on the bin cards before being sent to costing department which will allocate the cost of the items issued to the job record named on the requisition.

Findings items in store quickly is vital if production is not to be held up. Adequate signposting and floor plans at several points should be available, and in many cases computerised records will be used to reveal the location of all items. Bar coding of all stored items helps computerised records of the location of items in the store. Safety, ease of access by fork-lift trucks if required, fire prevention and security are major aspects of importance in the design and layout of stores.

From the business administration point of view, the following aspects of store-keeping are the most important:

1 The system that is introduced to run the stores, once implemented, can only be changed at enormous cost. It is therefore important to think the whole operation through at the very start, and consider location, access, layout, staffing, documentation and stock control very carefully.

2 Stores must be classified and if required it may be necessary to allocate a separate store to each class of goods, in the best location for that particular field of activity. Thus direct materials, components, tools, spare parts, maintenance requirements and finished goods may be allocated different storage areas.

3 The link between requisitions from stores and the costing of orders should be considered, and decisions made about form design so that the link is clear. Generally speaking, every material and each component used must be charged to the job or contract concerned, and so must any charges for the use of plant, tools, compressed air, and so on. A typical cost sheet illustrated in Fig. 5.3 shows the detailed nature of these records and the recovery of overhead as an on-cost for each costing area. Obviously such records require a great deal of routine work, and copies of the documents used to draw items from stores must flow through to the costing department for recording on the cost sheets. Computerised stock systems are widely used.

4 With regard to the costing activities referred to above, decisions have to be taken about the way in which goods are charged out to jobs and contracts. The possible methods are:

   a FIFO (first in, first out)
   b LIFO (last in, first out)
   c simple average cost
   d AVCO (weighted average cost)
   e standard cost
   f replacement cost
   g base stock price.

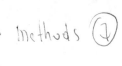

This is not a costing book, but – briefly – in inflationary times prices rise month by month. Suppose we have 10 square metres of a particular material in stock, 4 of which cost £4 per square metre and 6 cost £5 per square metre. A requisition arrives for 6 units. Shall we cost this at FIFO (4 x £4 + 2 x £5) or LIFO (6 x £5) or at simple average price (6 x £4.50) or at AVCO (6 x £4.60), and so on. Clearly there is a strong argument in favour of costing the item at the replacement price of – say – 6 x £7.50 since as soon as we issue the 6 square metres we shall have to replace the stock and pay the new price. We must have all such matters clearly agreed if the costing clerks are to know how to keep their records correct.

5 *Stores control and audits* This has already been discussed to some extent but a few further points are worth consideration.

a *Audits* Audits are usually required annually as far as companies are concerned and are certainly desirable for all other organisations. The stores should be subject to regular audits, more frequently than once a year, and it is best to use a team of full-time auditors in a large organisation. They need not necessarily check everything at the same time, but checking should be on a random basis, which means that all areas of the stores have an equally good chance of being selected for audit. These areas selected should then be thoroughly checked, including any evaluation of redundant stock, slow-moving items, deteriorated stock, issue against proper requisitions only, and so on.

b *Holidays for stores staff* A common practice of staff who are misappropriating stock is to avoid taking their holidays, and to arrive early and leave late – just in case earlier misappropriations become obvious to their replacements. This aspect should be watched. Serious losses have often been discovered by accident, as where a storekeeper who rides a motorbike and is injured on the way to work is found to have covered up serious disparities between the stock records and the actual stock in hand.

c *Gate copies* The use of a 'gate copy' of invoices issued to customers collecting goods from store is useful in some businesses, since it gives the gatekeeper a chance to check the vehicles leaving through the gate to ensure that only items invoiced are being taken away.

d *Returned materials* When materials are issued and costed out to a particular job it is often the case that when the job is completed there are surplus materials to be returned to stock. This sort of material is easily pilfered and it should be a requirement that supervisors see that it is returned to stock, with a special form which can be treated like a credit note to reduce the charges on the cost sheet since the material was not used. A similar treatment for scrap material should be followed. It will then be sold for the best price obtainable.

Customer's Name & Address:								Job description:				Contact's Name:				Serial No.			
Telephone number:				Job number:															
Materials used	F	£	p	Components used	F	£	p	Drawing Office	F	£	p	Machine shop charges	F	£	p	Cost summary	F	£	p
																Materials			
																Components			
																Drawing Office			
																Machine shop			
																Fabrication Shop			
																Packing Dept.			
Total				Total				Total				Total				Transport Dept.			
Add on cost at 50%				Add on cost at 50%				Add on cost at 200%				Add on cost at 150%				Other charges			
Total to summary				Total to summary				Total to summary				Total to summary				Total costs			
																Add profit			
Fabrication Shop	F	£	p	Packing dept.	F	£	p	Transport dept.	F	£	p	Other charges	F	£	p	Invoice total			
																Final Report: Note here any problems connected with this order			
Total				Total				Total				Total							
Add on cost at 100%				Add on cost at 75%				Add on cost at 100%				Add on cost at 200%							
Total to summary				Total to summary				Total to summary				Total to summary							

Fig 5.3 A costing sheet

5.6   Economic order quantity

Students may be interested to see what lies behind the fixing of EOQs (economic order quantities). The word 'economic' implies that 'least cost' is involved. When holding stocks there are two costs involved: acquisition costs (often called re-order costs) and holding costs. Re-order costs are high when the re-order quantity is small, and cheapest when we place large orders and get volume discounts. Holding costs are low when the re-order quantity is small, and high when the volumes we buy are large, because we have to provide storage space, run the risk of deterioration, and so on. When these two costs are added together to give the total cost, the economic order quantity is revealed. It is that quantity where total costs are lowest. The illustration in Fig. 5.4 shows the point clearly.

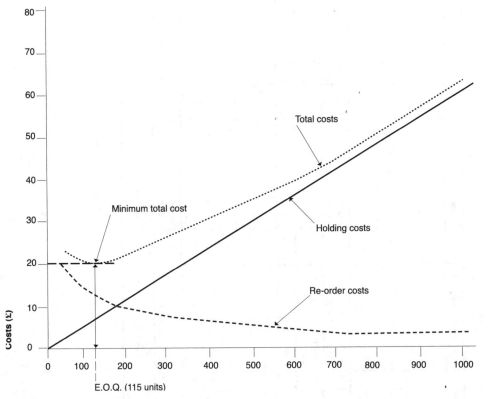

Fig. 5.4   Economic order quantity

Note: Those interested in seeing Formecon Services Ltd's 'supplier profile' should write to them at Gateway, Crewe, CW1 6YN, Tel 01270 500 800.

6 The research and development function

6.1 The functions of the research and development department

Most organisations will have some sort of research and development department (R&D), though in many cases in small firms it will perhaps be a fairly rudimentary part of the organisation. In larger firms it will be a subsystem with its own departmental organisation but within the span of control of a senior member of staff, perhaps the marketing director or the factory manager. It will have links with most departments, partly because it will usually be engaged to some extent in problem-solving for them, and partly because its raw materials are ideas generated within the firm, or introduced from outside, and these may be fed through from any department as they are sparked off.

The chief areas of research are as follows:

1 Basic research, which is concerned with advancing knowledge and techniques in the whole general area of activity in which a firm operates.
2 Problem-based research, which is aimed at solving problems which arise in the course of business, perhaps problems associated with products, or projects, or in packaging or distribution, or posed by new legislative requirements.
3 Applied research, which may be concerned with changing an idea into a marketable product or service. Equally it may be concerned with improving existing methods or organisation, the use of new materials, cost-cutting, and so on.
4 Development work is the design and planning of production methods to bring a new product into production so that it can be added to our marketing portfolio and offered to customers. This may call for models and prototypes, testing and evaluation, cost analyses, and so on, to ensure an acceptable and viable product at a price consumers can afford. More recently, the employment of computer-aided design (CAD) has streamlined this process and saved both time and money when developing products for introduction or modification. Further details on this subject were covered in section 4.11, p. 73.

6.2   Basic research

Basic research leads to an extension of knowledge in a particular field. It may be carried on within a firm or company or it may be cooperative research carried out by a trade association or an industry-wide research team to which all firms are invited to contribute. Matters of national importance may be sponsored officially by bodies such as NERC (the Natural Environment Research Council) which, besides official funds, may seek to obtain funds from other sources by undertaking research projects on behalf of other bodies such as the European Union, foreign governments, United Nations bodies, and so on.

Basic research is expensive, the experts required to carry it out do not come cheap, the facilities they require are expensive and back-up teams in such fields as computerised research are essential. Just how these costs are to be recovered is dealt with later in the chapter (see section 6.7 below).

6.3   Problem-based research

Much research is problem-based. The work is infinitely varied. The sequence of activities is:

1 What is the nature of the problem drawn to R&D's attention?
2 How should the problem be tackled? There may be an outside research foundation which can be commissioned to tackle the project, but it is often more satisfactory to choose a member of staff who is knowledgeable in the field to act as project leader. He/she will then build a small team to solve the problem, possibly with one member who has been seconded from an outside research organisation where this seems likely to be helpful.
3 Whatever the nature of the problem it will be necessary to provide an appropriate working space for the team, capital equipment, computer facilities, materials, and so on. Costings will need to be drawn up and budgets approved. The work may be of an emergency nature and staff on other projects may have to be drafted in to complete it quickly to avoid loss of markets or interruption of production.

6.4   Ideas generation

Ideas are the basis for most R&D work. We have to be alert to developments in our industry and prepared to consider ideas coming in from outside, and willing to generate ideas 'in-house'. Obviously the head of department cannot be expected to produce all the new ideas; they can be generated at every level. The sources of new ideas may be listed as follows:

1 *Outsiders* Some of these are eccentric inventors who submit ideas, machines, technical processes, and so on. These people may have a higher success rate in their suggestions than less dedicated outsiders. Many customers may draw our attention to defects or improvements in existing products, and some may suggest new devices which they wish they had. All such enquiries and suggestions should be sympathetically considered, perhaps by a small standing committee of R&D staff who would evaluate them and perhaps commission a feasibility study. In any case, all likely future projects should be pigeon-holed for consideration later if the present climate of activity does not offer an immediate opportunity.

2 *Suggestion boxes* Insiders are often in the best position to suggest a new idea, whether it concerns a new product, or a variation on an existing project, or a new method of working. They are meeting the day-to-day problems and doing the day-to-day work. If they suggest a change to the foreman, he/she may scorn it or even resent the new idea because one of the lower ranks thought of it. If, instead, there is an open invitation to put new ideas in a suggestion box, with cash prizes for successful ones, the suggestions go to an independent open-minded panel who will consider them on their merits. One car worker whose job included sticking down a rubber floor mat in the boot purchased one of the range for his own use and found in due course that a snag developed in a tank below the rubber mat. Struggling to remove the mat, he realised that it was a waste of time and a great nuisance to stick the mat down. The cost savings achieved were such that the award for his idea paid for the car he was buying. Usually the award is geared to the value of the savings, say 50 percent made over the first 12 months of use.

Not everyone is equally good at putting forward suggestions – some may consist of a mere idea, totally undeveloped. Others may be presented in a fully developed form, with detailed suggestions of the materials necessary, the plant or equipment required, ways in which present excess capacity could be utilised, the likely market, and so on. In this way new talent may be discovered and a recruit to one of the design teams found in-house, previously unsuspected of having this type of talent.

3 *Brainstorming* A 'brainstorm' session is a communal effort to produce new ideas in which a group of staff of all ranks is brought together to hold a general discussion in which new ideas and new products are discussed. No idea is too crazy to be put forward (for a limited period, say 5 minutes). The idea is then discussed and worthwhile ones become the subject of more detailed consideration. The idea is that no-one should inhibit anyone else from putting forward a proposal. In practice, senior members of staff may well inhibit younger members from even offering suggestions, and a general invitation to all staff to contribute ideas – in a fully developed form – for circulation in writing to the panel members may be more productive. The panel then acts as a 'think tank' considering well thought-out proposals.

6.5   Applied research and development

Applied research tries to create a marketable product or a marketable service from an idea. Equally, it may take a new idea about management, documentation, and so on, and seek to implement it as a new method of working which will achieve cost savings, or find a new use for former waste products, and so on. Remember that every product has a life-cycle in which it moves through a sequence of situations. First it is a new and unique product which is highly profitable. Later it begins to lose appeal at the same time as imitators come in with their own, newer versions. To resist this competition, the product must be renewed, or revamped to maintain its appeal and its market share. Applied research may have a part to play in devising these renewals of appeal, changing shape, colours, style, and so on.

Development work is concerned with the conversion of an accepted idea into a fully established product or service. It may involve the making of prototypes; their evaluation and testing; the solving of production problems by the making of special jigs, tools, and so on; the training of servicing staff and so on.

The full range of activities may be listed as follows:

1   The initial idea
2   The evaluation of the idea, followed, if considered to have potential, by a feasibility study which may include some element of market research.
3   The economic justification of the project in terms of its cost, possible selling price and estimated market. This leads to adoption of the project or its rejection.
4   If accepted, a prototype is developed, or a pilot plant is built. This is tested fully and test marketed. If successful a patent will be applied for. Where CAD is employed, this process may be enhanced by the ability to reduce the number of modified prototypes produced. Instead the computer can discover defects and make necessary modifications, resulting in the need for only one prototype. The benefit of this is shorter lead times and reduced development costs.
5   If agreed, the project goes into production and a launch date leads to its marketing.

6.6   Patents, trade marks and service marks

A patent is a government grant of exclusive privilege in making or selling a new invention. Governments vary, but in the United Kindgdom a patent may be granted for an invention which is new, involves an inventive step and is capable of industrial application. A 'new' invention is one that is not part of 'the state of the art' as generally known before the date of filing the application. An inventive step is one that is not obvious to those skilled in the art as at present known. There must be some change of the known art which leads to a new use or application. An industrial application is one that can be used in any kind of industry or in agriculture. Once a patent is granted it becomes the personal property of the grantee and may be assigned, licensed, mortgaged or simply used without competition for a period, at present 20 years (Patents Act 1977).

Research and development often results in new products, processes, and so on, and these belong to the employer of the staff in the R&D department, and not to the individual inventor, so long as they were made in the course of research on behalf of the employer, as part of the furtherance of the interests of the employer's undertaking. If an employee makes an outstanding contribution to a project which is beneficial to the employer, the Act does permit some special compensation.

At any time a proprietor may ask the Comptroller of the Patent Office to make an entry on the register that licences are to be as of right – which means anyone can have one who comes to an agreement with the proprietor. Where a patent is not fully exploited and three years have passed since registration, anyone may apply to the Comptroller for a declaration that licences should be as of right, and if the case is proved the Comptroller will issue a licence on suitable terms so that the proprietor is fairly rewarded – but such a licence may be delayed if the proprietor can claim that full exploitation could not be achieved in three years because a greater time was necessary.

A **trade mark** is a mark, such as a device, brand, heading, label, name, signature, word, letter or number, or any combination thereof, which is used for the purpose of connecting goods in the course of trade with some person having the right to use the trade mark, as proprietor or registered user. Once registered, the registrar will refuse to register similar marks for any other purpose (Trade Marks Act 1983). A similar position with regard to the registration of service marks also applies to marks associated with the offering of a particular service. Help with registering trade marks and service marks can be obtained in most countries from official sources. In the UK help comes from the Trade Mark Protection Society, 289 High Holborn, London, WC1V 7HU (telephone 0207 405 2677). Such marks may be of interest to R&D departments wishing to safeguard brand names and similar devices. The right lasts for seven years, which may then be renewed for a 14-year period, and then for further 14-year periods, indefinitely.

6.7 R&D in the business organisation

In Fig. 2.3 (p. 34) we saw the research and development department as an element in the system designed to achieve management objectives. To prevent too complex a diagram this situation was not fully developed, but we can now look at the department's place in the system rather more fully.

There is a popular belief that experts should be 'always on tap, but never on top'. The R&D department will necessarily be staffed by experts in their particular fields, who will have much to contribute to both the theory and the practice of the 'state of the art' in any industry. What they may not be – and certainly this is the popular belief – is practical, down-to-earth management material who can put into practice the clever ideas they have generated. This popular belief no doubt maligns some R&D staff, who are as practical as the next man or woman, but the idea that they should not be allowed to wield too great a power in the practical affairs of everyday life is very prevalent.

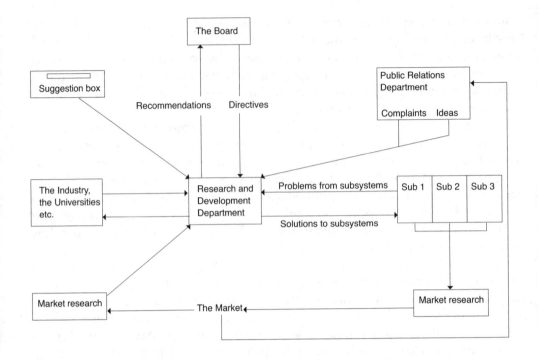

Fig. 6.1 Research and development as a subsystem of the business organisation

Just what the link is between the R&D function and the board of the company concerned varies widely. The head of R&D will be a senior person, but perhaps a scientist with nothing to contribute to the management of the company except advice about problems and products. In that case the most likely use top management will make of research staff services is to call the head of department in, on an *ad hoc* basis, when an agenda item dealing with a problem or a product makes the R&D opinion worth hearing. An annual review of R&D will probably be held, when the whole field will be looked at. The chief features of such a review will be:

1 A report on the past year's work, with an account of the main advances made, the projects undertaken, the products that have resulted, the learned papers published, and so on.

2 An evaluation of future programmes. Some work may have to be abandoned; some may have suggested new areas which should be opened up; the department may wish to bid for official projects which will provide funds, and so on.

3 Individual projects may be featured to bring out the costs involved, labour hours, capital budgets, technician support costs, and so on.

4 An evaluation of funding will be an important aspect of this work. Research is rarely allowed to become a bottomless pit into which funds are poured. The biggest problem is to justify the expenditure and recoup it. Where there is an end-product – a new drug, for example, in the pharmaceutical industry – the costs can be recovered eventually, out of the sale of the product. Where there is an improved organisation, such as the mark-

ing of vehicles to promote safety in road accidents, it may be possible to recoup the costs out of a licensing system payable by the users of the warning plates prescribed. Consultancy services for other bodies are a major source of revenue, as are grants from official bodies seeking a solution to general problems. Thus the Institute of Hydrology at Wallingford may recoup some of its costs from consultancy services to foreign governments investigating ground-water problems, dam construction, flood relief programmes, acid rain, and so on. Sometimes experts can earn fees for their department as expert witnesses at trials and arbitration hearings.

One other way of recovering research costs is to include a percentage of research costs in overhead added to every invoice (without specifically stating the breakdown of costs). Thus research would be an element in every price quoted. While this is a useful way of recovering costs, it may make us uncompetitive in some contracts. This may mean we have to turn to charging what the contract will bear. Thus a competitive contract might not carry any of the research burden, but another contract which was not competitive would be loaded with more than its fair share.

Where an organisation has employed CAD, it will benefit from reduced costs and lead times. In addition, where it has restructured to create a 'flatter' organisation, the organisation may also benefit from more committed and motivated R&D staff, who are well qualified to show enterprise and initiative.

7 The marketing function

7.1 Introduction to marketing

Marketing is a complex activity, which increased in importance in the second half of the twentieth century. It seeks to understand consumer needs and meet them by a general supervision of production, distribution and selling activities. To some extent it is a logical development made necessary by the mass production of goods which reached such perfection in that century. If the difficulties of production have been overcome to such an extent that there need never again be any shortage of goods, it follows that the marketing side of business activity must grow to ensure that this vast quantity of resources reaches those who require them, the consumers seeking to satisfy their wants. That some of the problems of ensuring world-wide consumer satisfaction are in fact political and depend upon the management of prosperity around the world cannot be denied, but marketing cannot go as far as that. What marketing tries to do is ensure that the whole organisation of a firm or company is pulling together to:

1 produce the things that people really do want;
2 package them as attractively as possible;
3 bridge the gap between producers and consumers as efficiently as possible, which means bridging the **time gap** by adequate protection and preservation of the product, and bridging the **geographical gap** by sound physical distribution arrangements;
4 finally sell the products, at prices which yield a profit, by an efficient wholesaling and retailing system.

We therefore have the marketing department as a super-department with a marketing director exercising a wide span of control over a number of other departments. Formerly viewed as autonomous departments, these are now grouped under, and represented on the board by, this senior director with a wide, co-ordinating brief to achieve the objectives listed in 1 to 4 above. It is helpful to study this span of control in diagrammatic form as shown in Fig. 7.1.

Each of these general areas is discussed more fully below. First we must examine the general marketing philosophy which marketing directors seek to establish and which serves as the reference point for all marketing activities.

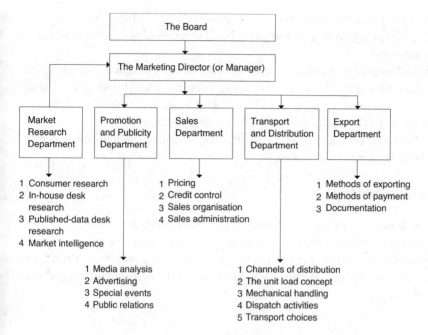

Fig. 7.1 The marketing function in a large company

7.2 The marketing philosophy

Generally speaking, the key feature of a marketing philosophy is that the company is consumer orientated, not production orientated. In former times, when production was the difficult thing and technology was king, it was quite common for customers to add their names to waiting lists and wait until they were informed that the product was ready for them. Henry Ford's early dictum that 'You can have any colour car you like so long as it is black' may be said to epitomise the production-orientated attitude. When Ford started to offer cars of other colours you could say the day of the marketing man/woman had arrived – the automobile industry had had to become consumer orientated.

A marketing philosophy may be summed up as follows:

1 We need to establish a public image which presents the company in the best possible light, as a public-spirited, ecology-conscious, quality producer of eminently desirable goods and services.
2 Within that public image we have to achieve certain objectives, including turnover objectives, market share objectives and return-on-capital-invested objectives (which implies profitability).
3 These objectives are to be achieved uniformly, in every corner of the land, and even of the world. We are not chasing 'a fast buck', or interested in making a sale irrespective of the consequences, or engaging in cut-throat competition. We are working to sell our products in such a way that goodwill is optimised, and the customers return again and

again for the same types of products in the same places. All staff must know the philosophy, and be in sympathy with it and apply it in all their relations with wholesalers, retailers and customers.

4 Since the relationship between ourselves and the customer is crucial to the achievement of repeat business during the 'lifetime' of the customer it is not to be regarded lightly. Customers are not easily won, and once a relationship has been established it must be nurtured just like any other valuable part of our enterprise. Customer relations management (CRM) should be a designated duty of a key person in the marketing department. More of this later (see page 105).

A definition of marketing

Marketing may be defined as an activity that moves finished goods from the point of production, across the time gaps and the geographical gaps which separate producers from consumers, into the possession of another party – a wholesaler, a retailer or a final consumer – in such a way that a profit is achieved as a reward for the manufacturing and marketing effort involved.

7.3   Market analysis and research

A marketing manager must know everything he/she can about the market at which the company's products are directed. The size of the market does not only involve the numbers of people who want a particular product but also their affluence. A small market with a high average income may be more attractive than a large market of relatively poor people – economists tell us that 'want' and 'demand' are not the same thing. Market research is concerned with finding out, as accurately as possible, the present and future requirements of the market, but we do not view the market passively, but envisage active stimulation of it. If people in the market do not know about the product, how can they be informed about it? Whose product is taking the lion's share of the market at present? Can we compete with them better and, if so, will it be by price, or quality, or attractive packaging, or better servicing?

Some of the essential elements in market research are as follows:

1 *Consumer research* In the last analysis it is the final consumer we are trying to satisfy and whose opinion about a particular product we need to know. Stimulation of consumer interest which generates enquiries for our product at the retail level will lead to increased enquiries from wholesalers and consequently increased orders. We may get right into the consumer's home with television or radio advertising, but both are expensive and we may not be able o afford them. Before this stage we may research the consumer field with questionnaires or interviewers, seeking opinions about the use made of this type of product; how much they would be prepared to pay, and so on.
   This type of research is usually carried out either by postal questionnaire or by a team of interviewers who conduct a sample survey. The whole exercise is a statistical prob-

MARCH 2007

BUSINESS MANAGEMENT & ADMINISTRATION

Instructions to candidates:

a) Time allowed: Three hours (plus an extra ten minutes' reading time at the start - do not write anything during this time)

b) Answer any FIVE questions

c) All questions carry equal marks. Marks for each question are shown in [ ]

1. a) Explain under what circumstances a business owner might also be a business manager. [10]

   b) Describe the main functions of the board of directors. [10]

2. With the aid of organisation charts, explain the types of authority most suitable for the following:

   a) the human resources department of a large plc
   b) a doctors' partnership
   c) a small family-run company
   d) a local convenience store [5 each]

3. a) Identify the traditional principles of organisations. [10]

   b) Briefly describe TWO of these principles. [5 each]

4. In a memorandum to your Office Supervisor, explain:

   a) how you would introduce work study into your organisation
   b) the likely benefits which might result [9 each + 2 for format of memorandum]

5. There are various sources that a Purchasing Officer can use to identify potential suppliers.

   a) List the main sources. [6]
   b) Explain the benefits of EACH source. [7]
   c) Explain the disadvantages of EACH source. [7]

continued overleaf

6.	The company you work for produces MP3 players and the Marketing Department has asked you to assist them in deciding on the most appropriate media for advertising a new more powerful generation of players. Reply to the Marketing Manager in a suitable format, providing this information and giving reasons for your choice.		[16 + 4 for format]

7.	Explain, with examples, under what circumstances you would use the following:
	a)	internet
	b)	intranet
	c)	extranet
	d)	email		[5 each]

8.	'An effective manager delegates his/her authority to his/her subordinates.'
	a)	Define the term **delegation**.		[8]
	b)	Describe how it should be undertaken.		[12]

lem, which cannot be studied here, but everyone engaged in conducting market research needs a basic knowledge of statistics, a subject which every aspiring business administrator should study.

2 *Desk research* As its name implies, desk research is done in-house, or possibly at the local library. We may be able to use past records in one area to give a guide to likely demand in a new area. We may be able to pinpoint areas which would be more appropriate because records show that it is more densely populated, or on average more affluent, or on average has more children than other areas (if this is an important aspect for us), and so on.

   Besides 'in-house' data there is a wealth of official publications which can be used to discover keys to the market, for instance the published *Family Expenditure Surveys* show how much income average families spend on the various items they buy and this enables us to estimate the total market expenditure in which our products can hope to share. Similarly a wealth of data about export markets is made available by such bodies as the European Union and the United Nations, while some of the big banks make available (at a price) surveys of market prospects in most foreign countries. *The Economist* and *Euromonitor* similarly publish economic reports on many countries around the world.

3 *Market intelligence* There is a wide variety of official and private market intelligence organisations collecting and analysing intelligence data on a minute-to-minute basis about both home and overseas markets. With advancing tele-processing networks available, it is possible to link up with computers, where data is stored, and extract it for a fee which will be invoiced later. Other services such as the Export Intelligence Service automatically match the categories of products registered by a subscriber with tenders invited and contracts offered by overseas countries. A subscriber is alerted immediately to any marketing opportunity that presents itself in any of over 200 overseas territories. Much market intelligence work, however, is an in-company activity rather than a mere listening in to outside organisations. Reports coming back from representatives, agents and wholesalers in the field should generate a wealth of information, continually updated, on the size of markets, the affluence of markets, and the growth potential within a market. For example, demand for a particular product rolls like a wave through a nation and these trends should be watched for and anticipated. Today's baby boom for the nappy manufacturer produces in a few years a toy boom, then a school textbook bonanza, good business for the jewellers in twenty years' time as diamond engagement rings are in strong demand and within a year or two we are back to the baby boom and a further cycle of activity. The marketing director must plan ahead for five, ten or even fifteen years, with a rolling programme of product renewal and diversification.

Market assessment is a continuing activity for market-orientated firms. The marketing manager must reassess at regular intervals the whole environment in which his/her firm's products or services are being offered to the general public. It is helpful to list some of the elements in any market assessment. They should be looked at objectively, from the viewpoint of an outsider making an unbiased judgement of the current situation. Matters of interest include:

1   What is the total 'population' interested in this product, or service? Are any influences at work to reduce this population and, if so, how can the firm adjust to meet them?

2   How affluent are they, and has there been any change in their *per capita* incomes recently? Can any change in affluence be envisaged?

3   What motivates a customer in choosing our product? Can we do anything to increase his/her motivation? Is there any reason for this motivation to decline in the future?

4   Are there likely to be any changes in the end-user market? Can we adapt the product to cater for a group at present only marginally interested? What changes will be needed and how shall we test-market it with this new group?

5   Is the market static or is it expanding or contracting? If it is expanding, is our present growth rate keeping up with the growth of the market? If we are growing at 10 per cent per annum but the market is expanding at 20 per cent per annum our actual market share is declining. By contrast, if the market is declining and we are maintaining sales we may become the dominant firm in a collapsing field. Are more astute competitors getting out by diversifying into other areas?

6   Do we dominate the market? If so, how vulnerable are we to competition? A firm with 80 per cent of the market is very vulnerable to competition. Even 10 or 15 per cent of sales lost to a rival with an astute marketing idea may cream off all the profit element in our activities. Similarly, with all our eggs in one basket we may be vulnerable to a change of taste or fashion. Even a change in taxation may hit our firm more than proportionately, as many firms have found with changes in VAT rates in recent years.

7   Are there any new products we should be looking at? Have new materials a potential development in our own field? If so, we should try to adopt them before competitors have the same idea. We must not be complacent, just because our products have always been made in a particular way. Remember that in any given year 20 per cent of production is using materials not even invented a quarter of a century before. Even last year's failure by a competitor may become this year's success if he/she is working on the problems and smoothing out the difficulties. Do we know what he/she is up to? Is our programme of test purchases comprehensive enough to evaluate the work of competitors?

8   Are we monitoring the trade and technical literature adequately? What products in our field are new around the world? Have we seen and assessed them? Could we obtain a licence to produce them and improve our product mix?

9   What criticisms have been levied at our products recently? What criticisms could we levy at our present range? Would we buy them and, if not, why not?

10 Are there any marketing techniques we are neglecting which would extend sales, perhaps into new fields? Have we examined non-traditional (for us) techniques? Who knows about such methods and can give inexpensive advice?

Clearly, the list is almost endless. A stern reappraisal of our current situation must be helpful in avoiding pitfalls and charting a new course in the enduring search for customers prepared to demand our products.

Conclusion about market research

Market knowledge is an extremely important aspect of success in business. The more we know about the market the more likely we are to be able to keep ahead of public demand in the areas for which we seek to cater. We may identify new product areas or new versions of existing products. We should certainly identify what is best about each of our products and ensure that these aspects are retained and improved. We shall find within our markets some segments of the market with particular needs and can direct attention to these needs in our future work.

7.4 Promotion, publicity and public relations

Every aspect of promotion and publicity comes under the general supervision of the marketing director and it is a complex field. Various types of events feature in the general promotion programme, for example shows and exhibitions, sponsored events, product launches, discussions, seminars, conferences, television and radio presentations as well as the many different aspects of advertising, which are discussed below. Enormous sums of money can be dissipated in these activities, while the return attributable to them is difficult to quantify (or even identify in some cases). By contrast, the old advertising adage is still true: 'If you don't advertise you certainly know what you're doing – but you are the only one who does!' Promotion is absolutely essential for all businesses and especially for marketing-orientated companies, but the problem is to know which is the best buy in the various media outlets available. Promotion is not cheap. About 40 per cent of the cost of most heavily advertised products goes in promotion costs and has to be recouped in the price charged. A customer who wants the product is forced to pay the cost, even though most of the advertising is irrelevant to him/her.

Coupled with this general problem of promoting both the organisation and its products, there is a related problem of public relations. The term PR is to some extent suspect in the minds of the public since it is often associated with cover-up and whitewashing activities when a company has a problem. This suspicious attitude to PR is often unjustified, because public knowledge is often less than complete and media staff who pick up public concern and air it in newspapers, and on the radio and television, are not always known for their scrupulous behaviour. The fact is that bad news is good copy for the media man, and good news is of little interest to anyone. The PR representative who defends a company or a product by putting the full facts before the public is not engaged in a cover-up but in the rebuttal of unjustified criticism.

Public relations

Not all firms can afford a public relations department or the fees of a specialist PR consultancy, but they should appoint an individual who is authorised to handle such matters on the firm's behalf and assumes responsibility for doing what can be done to promote the firm through sound public relations policies. Sometimes such a person is designated 'press officer'. He/she must be reasonably high up in the firm, and as literate as possible since press releases and public appearances are likely to be fairly frequent occurrences. A clear PR policy should be discussed at the highest level and set down in writing as a point of reference for the press officer in the resolution of any problem. The essential parts of such a PR policy are:

1   We should know what the board or other top-level panel conceives to be the desired impression the organisation wishes to make. Thus a specialist manufacturer of high-level, top-quality products and a mass-production manufacturer of cheap utensils may seek entirely different images.

2   How wide is the impact the board wishes to make? Some companies promote a world-wide image for such things as popular drinks, fine wines, brands of whisky, and so on. Others are content with a national image or a local image. Even in that smaller field the firm may only wish to win the good opinion of customers, for example, young people likely to attend the concerts or use the facilities or products offered. They may be reconciled to a permanently disinterested or antagonistic view from some sectors of the public, but will make it clear to staff which sectors they do appeal to and hope to influence in the firm's favour.

3   A major concern will be the correction of any wrongful impressions or adverse criticisms of the company's products, behaviour, working conditions, and so on. To rebut these the press officer or other official must:
    a   be knowledgeable about all the company's products
    b   be knowledgeable about all aspects of working conditions, pay, and so on
    c   have the full support of (and be told the true facts by) any departmental head whose department is being criticised: such people must be regarded as available at any time for liaison purposes should a problem develop.

4   Two more limited, but very important, sections of the 'public' are the trading partners of any company. These are our suppliers and our customers, which usually means wholesalers, though we may supply retailers direct. These two groups will be concerned with our general impact and impression on the whole community, but more directly concerned with such matters as our financial standing, trading probity, technical expertise, servicing record, and so on. The word soon gets around if any weakness develops in these fields, and such rumours require immediate responses at the very highest level in the form of press releases, press conferences, telephone calls to key people and firm rebuttal (and threat of legal action against the source) of any untrue statements.

5   Finally there is a positive side to this public relations activity. The cheapest advertisement is a 'news' story. The big order, the successful completion of a contract, the Queen's Award, the 'top apprentice award', the 'star prize' for a lucky customer, the one millionth book by a best-selling author – all these make news. The press officer must keep in with local journalists and feed them stories which will be of use to them and keep the company before the public in an interesting way. The journalist knows he/she is being 'used' but in return will expect to be given the true facts when a major news story breaks and a real scoop can be provided. A scrap book should be kept of all 'news' stories, with a note of the date, the journal or trade magazine, and the journalist responsible for it.

In this section the other aspect of public relations work – responding to dissatisfied customers, problem-solving, and so on – is not dealt with, since it has been referred to earlier under the research and development function.

Customer relations management

A narrower sector of public relations work is customer relations management, which is concerned with the building of a large database of customers, carefully profiled to record their individual tastes and interests, their past record of orders, their payment history, and so on. This activity is only narrower in the sense that the topics for concern will not be as widely spread, but the actual activity may be much greater, and more directly related to the success of the company. We may list the following activities as some of those which should be pursued if we are to retain our customer base:

1　Every piece of publicity, advertising, mail-shot, and so on, which produces a response, should be monitored by the customer relations manager. A procedure should be implemented for feeding every enquiry to him/her, with any details that can be gleaned about the customer – for example, type of business, number of employees, annual turnover, and so on. The gleaning of such information should be borne in mind when designing response slips to be filled in by interested parties.

2　A follow-up system should be devised for those that fail to respond to literature after requesting it, so that they can be turned into first-time customers and eventually regular customers.

3　Dissatisfied customers should be given special attention, to overcome their discontent and retain them in the clientele.

4　Consideration should be given to the establishment of a 'loyalty' card system where customers earn some cash dividend or gift for loyalty to the supplier. Of course such rewards have to come out of the profits from the extra business, but the total cost can be very small (say, 1 per cent of the order value). One feature of the loyalty card system is that customers have a limited capacity for loyalty cards – there are only so many slots in a wallet or purse. Therefore they are unlikely to sign up with everyone and their loyalty to the few firms they do support is self-reinforcing.

5　The profiling of the customers can yield a number of marketable products. For example, a list of people who do *not* have video recorders may be of great interest to a company launching a new product in this particular area, because the literature will have more chance of being read. Such lists are saleable.

Clearly there are many advantages to be gained by an understanding of our customer base. We have today a customer-centred business environment. Growth and profitability depend on the acquisition of an increasing body of customers. The costs incurred are a substantial investment which can only be supported if we retain customers for repeat orders, spreading the costs of acquisition over a lifetime of customer loyalty.

The publicity department

The publicity department is concerned with all aspects of promotion and publicity, of which advertising, sales promotion and display in showrooms, shop fronts, and so on are the chief activities. A piece of research carried out a few years ago for the British Business Press, called *How British Business Advertises*, showed the breakdown as in Table 7.1.

Table 7.1   Percentage of budget spent on various media

Business press	34.5 *(Magazines) business*
Brochures	14.4
Exhibitions	14.1
Direct mail	8.1
PR	6.0
Directories	5.5
Newspapers	5.7
Videos/AV	2.8
Premiums	2.1
Point-of-sale	1.5
Posters	1.4
Sponsorship	1.0
TV	1.2
Radio	0.5
Others	1.2
	100.0

Source: MIL Research Ltd, for the British Business Press

When one remembers the enormous sums spent on television advertising and then notices that this only constitutes 1.2 per cent of the advertising budget of British businesses, it brings home the enormous marketing activities taking place every day in all the various fields listed.

The head of publicity has a wide variety of duties to perform. Briefly, we may list the following:

1 To draw up a programme of publicity which is balanced between the various types of media available and most appropriate to the products to be sold and the customers who should be aware of them and using them.
2 To build up a team of staff, with the necessary skills and expertise, and co-ordinate their activities. This may include the temporary loan of staff from other departments when a large function like an exhibition is to be staged. Advertising departments can rarely command enough personnel for major activities and the biggest cause of failure of such events is a shortage of individuals on the actual day or days, to keep the visitors and customers happy and answer their many queries.
3 To decide upon an appropriation figure for the advertising expenditure and then allocate it between the various activities and exercise budgetary control over its use. This is never an easy exercise, since it is difficult to strike a balance between what we can afford and what would be ideal for promoting our product. There are many suggested bases

for judging what is the correct figure but the best one probably is the 'job-to-be-done' method. One estimates what the job to be done is at this particular time and costs it up, taking account of current prices. Thus we may have to launch a new product or a new range of products, or one may only wish to give a boost to a product that is already well known. One may be working on a revised version and only wish present sales to keep ticking over and maintain goodwill. Such different 'jobs to be done' will call for very different promotion budgets. Whatever the job to be done, the budget is only just enough to do it, so that strict control of expenditures will be necessary whatever the figure agreed upon, and if there is a danger of exceeding the budget in one direction we shall have to cut back somewhere else. Advertising staff are prone to think 'big', and budgetary control is essential.

Types of advertising

Advertising is a feature of modern life which is essential to the type of prosperity and wealth creation which seems desirable to most people, yet it meets considerable opposition from all sorts of people on the grounds that it is anti-social and leads to many types of exploitation. If we analyse advertising we find that it divides into two main sectors, informative advertising and persuasive advertising.

Informative advertising

This tells us about the product or service being advertised: what it does, why it is helpful, the technical details, various do's and don'ts when using the product, and so on. There can be no serious objection to informative advertising. How else, in a busy world, shall we find out about products or become aware of their attributes, advantages and disadvantages? Every product or service meets a 'want' felt by some section of the community. If it is to find those who 'want' it, the information that it is available must be advertised. A popular misconception, especially among politically motivated people of a certain type, is that goods and services are created to make profits. They are not; they are created to satisfy wants somewhere in the community, and those that meet a widely felt need make profits in the process. Many that prove to be less popular than expected make losses, as the bankruptcy and liquidation notices in any local or national newspaper will confirm.

Persuasive advertising

This type of advertising is less praiseworthy, though those that engage in it may argue that it is still essential if enterprise is to be encouraged. The fact is that the capital costs of some forms of production are so enormous that failure to find a market means the collapse of the company concerned. The new product cannot be allowed to fail, for failure means bankruptcy. If a market is not available it must be created by persuading the public that they do need the product. This is far less meritorious than informative advertising, and the mindless jingles and endless repetitions on television of such advertisements can be tedious. It may also verge on the unsavoury, as where young children are persuaded at Christmas time that they need expensive toys far beyond the pockets of many parents.

The Advertising Standards Authority has a duty to investigate public complaints about advertising and has a key phrase which helps it to assess the quality of any particular advertisement. The phrase is: an acceptable advertisement is one that is 'legal, decent, honest and truthful'. While the Authority is necessarily conservative in its approach to complaints – many people dash off a letter of complaint without seriously weighing up the pros and cons of the advertisement concerned – it has done a considerable amount to set good standards in advertising. Many advertisements have been discontinued by agreement with the advertiser concerned, who may not have appreciated that the wording used or the illustrations used could be offensive in some way to sectors of the public.

Advertising agencies

An advertising agency is a business which operates as a middleman between the advertiser and the media. The agency devises advertisements and plans campaigns on behalf of the advertiser, but places them with the media selected. Its rewards are earned partly from the advertiser if the planning and designing work is extensive, but also partly from the media source as a commission on the revenue earned by the medium concerned. The agency has expertise in designing and writing material which will have a good impact on the market. The copy should be clear and related to the needs of the market concerned. It should give all the facts, speak with authority and invite a response which is simply made and easily dealt with by the advertiser's sales department which is triggered off into its usual routine by the customer's enquiry.

Types of advertising media

The business press
Table 7.1 (page 106) gives a list of advertising media, from which it can be seen that the business press takes a major share of the advertising budget of British advertisers. This would also be true of many other countries around the world. The business press consists of some 350 leading journals which cater for the major sectors of British business. Journals such as *The Grocer, The Chemist and Druggist, Business Equipment Digest*, and so on, go, either on subscription or on a 'free circulation' basis, to all the important firms in their particular fields. Such journals not only cover the whole range of products in their particular field but include feature articles on particular trends and developments which bring the subject area under constant review. A busy administrator who needs to be kept up-to-date finds such magazines the most useful guide to what is going on in the industry generally, and may often participate in the information-gathering process by giving his/her own point of view, or feeding press releases to the editor of the journal concerned. The trade association argues that since most businesses sell much of their product to other businesses, who are very considerable 'consumers' of products of every kind, the publicity departments of all firms would do well to reconsider the British business press. They provide a couple of checklists in their brochure *Better media planning for business to business advertising* which are extremely detailed and helpful. The first of these, for example, deals with advertising objectives and reads as shown in Table 7.2.

Table 7.2 Checklist for evaluating an advertising proposal

Source: Better Media Planning for Business to Business Advertising (courtesy of British Business Press)

Advertising objectives: key headings and some options

Heading	Option
1 What is the overall marketing strategy?	Increase sales of current product/service by £ x 000 – by expanding the market Increase market share by taking sales from competitors Launch new product Widen customer base Create quality sales leads Change attitude to company Increase awareness of company
2 What am I advertising?	An existing product/service A product range A new product A new aspect of the company/product A competitive, relevant image for the company An offer of information, demonstration, etc
3 To whom am I advertising?	Which types of business employ them? What size of company? What title? What job function? Where are they located? How many are there? How often must I reach them to be effective? Quote sources for these judgements – market research, sales records, analysis of response, exhibition records, etc
4 What do I want to achieve?	New product launch Provide detailed information Reach specific target audience Create effective sales leads Increase product awareness among target firms Have the right business environment Provide effective sales support Increase company reputation Broaden customer base Provide cost-effective advertising Communicate detailed information Product demonstration
5 What customer benefit do I offer?	Is it competitive? Is it relevant? Will it change attitudes or awareness positively? Will it be news? Can I prove it? Can I deliver it? Can it be used to enhance the company, as well as product sales? Justify against competitive analysis, customer feedback. Ensure that the product benefit is valuable and relevant to customers and expressed in their language.
6 What action do I want?	Telephone call/letter Request for more information Identified visit to my exhibition stand Visit to my website New awareness of my product/service

Positive change of opinion
Increase in my company's reputation, etc
Internal discussion in prospect company
Review of existing buying practice
Opportunity to quote
Clipping and filing for future reference
New sale and repeat order

7   How can I check whether the advertising works?   a   *Response*
Have I planned to record the following information?
date received
source of enquiry*
action taken
customer reaction
follow up
sales result
*e.g. for a press advertisement, record magazine title, date, specific advertisement, colour, page cost, etc, for future planning purposes.

b   *Communication*
Have I pre-tested the advertising concepts for communication of the key points in the advertising brief?

c   *Opinions*
Have I researched current attitudes and opinions of the company product/service and is a check on changes planned for next year? This data will be used to plan future promotions.

Brochures

Brochures are an important form of advertising and probably better value for money than many other types. They can be fairly expensive to produce, especially as they are usually in full colour, but their great advantage is that they deal specifically with your product or products in fuller detail than is usually possible in an ordinary advertisement. The brochure lends itself to a response-producing invitation, for example by including an order form, or a request for a visit by a demonstrator, or by giving a telephone contact for the nearest stockist, and so on. It enables you to set out any customer benefits you can offer in detail, and to include your standard terms and conditions of supply if these are important in your trade.

Direct mail

The difficulty with brochures is to get them into the hands of the people most likely to need them, and the range of approaches is wide. You may try direct mail-shots, but the problem is to get the addresses. There are many mailing houses which supply lists but the costs are usually fairly high. Some lists are about £25 per 1000 addresses but many specialised lists are £75 or £100 per 1000 addresses. The bigger the list the cheaper the price, but if you pay even £25 per 1000 for a list that includes 350 000 addresses, you are budgeting for a very large expenditure. You have to supply 350 000 brochures and envelopes, and pay postage besides paying for the list. Of course you may be able to participate in a shared mailing, but this reduces the impact.

A huge mailing often results in promotion staff being overwhelmed with enquiries. A more controlled response can be obtained by selecting sections of the *Yellow Pages* telephone directories and making up one's own lists. Any city centre library has all copies of *Yellow Pages* for the whole country and the relevant pages can be photocopied for a few pence. For small businesses with a limited advertising budget this is often the better way, and staff can produce labels for 50 envelopes in half an hour every day to build up a reasonable mail-shot.

It is possible to run a mail-shot campaign using the fax machine, but it is not always popular with recipients. It pushes costs on to the recipient which he/she would often prefer not to bear; it uses up the fax roll or other paper source which may fail later when some more vital message is arriving and the labour required to cut out the advertment from other more vital materials is often a nuisance.

E-commerce

Electronic commerce is trade in goods or services carried out electronically across the extended trading community and with the general public via the World Wide Web. The three main areas are 'business to business', 'business to final consumer' and 'government to nation' (which includes both citizens and the business community). E-commerce is believed to be on the point of rapid expansion, but as late as October 1998 one major detergent advertiser with a $3 billion advertising budget was only spending $3 million on the World Wide Web (that is, only 0.1 per cent of the budget). The complex arrangements which have led to E-commerce on a worldwide scale are described more fully in Chapter 8 (see page 151). To advertise on the World-Wide-Web involves the design of a website, or websites, and brings problems associated with the type of product, the terms of payment and the security of the data used when paying by credit cards.

Exhibitions

Participation in exhibitions is a relatively inexpensive way of contacting customers. With specialised exhibitions, such as those organised by trade organisations, the charges are usually reasonable, but the better positions are naturally more expensive than others. Sometimes sites are drawn by lottery and it depends on the luck of the draw whether you get a good one or not. Since these exhibitions are annual affairs, those who get a very poor site one year may be given a biased opportunity for a better site in a subsequent year. However, although the sites are reasonably priced, the expenses of producing clean up-to-date display material which has been fire-proofed to reduce the risks of fire are a further expense, and so are hotel charges for staff staying near the exhibition centre for its duration.

Merchandising assistance at the point of sale

Many retailers have limited facilities for preparing advertising material and point-of-sale marketing aids are essential to them if they are to display and promote products in a satisfactory way. All sorts of posters, stickers, brochures, leaflets, price lists, and so on, may be devised and even display cabinets, racks, and so on, are often necessary. Making these particular to your own product is essential – for instance, the provision of book -racks which are filled with other publishers' books is no advantage to you. **Packaging** of the product may be in itself a promotion device, and the point-of-sale advantages of attractive packaging should always be borne in mind.

Other media

The list in Table 7.1 shows most of the other popular media for advertising purposes. Each has its particular features, and the advantages and disadvantages must be weighed. The chief considerations in each case are:

1 How relevant is the media type under consideration to our present promotion activity?
2 Which type will best meet the advertising objectives set at this particular time for this particular promotion?
3 Is the question of frequency important? Will the outlet proposed be a one-off activity or does it lend itself to repeated approaches?
4 What is the likely cost relative to the budget agreed (or under consideration)?
5 How can we check the response to the medium chosen? For example, posters are widely seen and sometimes become collectors' items, but it is very difficult to know whether any increase in sales is attributable to them, or to other factors.

7.5 Pricing policy

In Fig. 4.4 we saw that the price to the customer in theory has to be large enough to cover not only the costs of production (material, labour and direct overhead) but also the selling expenses and the indirect overhead (the overhead not related directly to the product concerned). The difference between the total costs and the selling price is the profit we have made.

Pricing policy is a major consideration for the marketing director, and the following considerations enter into the picture:

1 The production of any unit of our product requires a certain amount of raw materials, labour and overhead expenses (such as supervision and quality control expenses). These costs are called the variable costs, because they vary with output. If we make 1000 items the amount of variable costs will be ten times more than if we make 100 items and if we make 10 000 items the variable costs will be ten times as great again.
2 Other costs, such as the purchase of buildings, plant and machinery, and so on, are called fixed overheads because they do not vary with output. For example, the managing director's salary is a fixed overhead. Whether we make 100, 1000 or 10 000 items, the managing director will still draw his/her salary.
3 The selling price we decide upon has to recover these costs, the variable costs and fixed costs. If the product is new and unique, and we can draw it to the public's attention so it becomes desirable, we shall be able to price it in the way suggested in Fig. 4.4. We shall be able to recover both the variable costs and the fixed costs and we shall be able to make a good profit on it, because no-one else has the product. Economists call this type of profit 'monopoly profit' because the lucky producer has a monopoly and can charge a higher price. However, we cannot demand too high a price because even a monopolist is subject to the authority of the consumer to some extent. If the price is so high that it renders the product too expensive relative to all other things a family needs, the consumer will refuse to buy it – having other items higher on his/her scale of preferences. Assuming, then, that we have very little competition we shall be able to make our sales

at the price we are asking, and as sales rise we shall reach the point where we 'break even' and move into profit. This is usually shown on a break-even chart such as the one in Fig. 7.2. This diagram is based upon the following figures:

Fixed costs £20 000   Variable costs £15 per unit   Production (up to 2500 units) Selling price £35 per unit. Now study Fig. 7.2 and the notes below it.

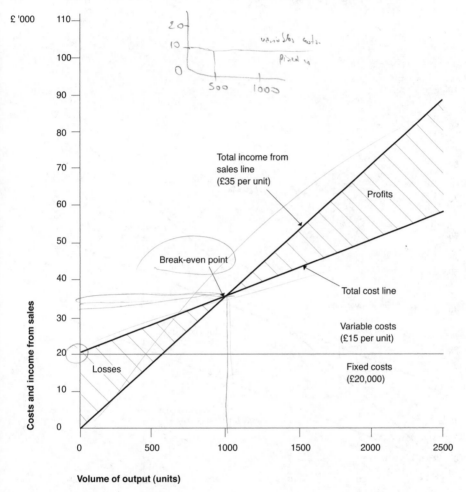

Fig. 7.2   A break-even chart

Notes:
i   The fixed costs of £20 000 are incurred before any production can begin at all.
ii As we start to produce we incur extra costs which vary with output of £15 per unit. This gives us a total cost line as shown.
iii Sales increase to the point where we are selling our entire output at £35 per unit.
iv At the break-even point (1000 units) the profit on each unit (£20) is enough to cover the £20 000 fixed costs as well as the variable costs of £15 000. From now on we are making profits of £20 on each item over 1000 units.

We can see the effect of price on profits if we look at the same diagram in slightly rearranged form to bring out the contribution made by each unit sold to profitability. In Fig. 7.3 we see the break-even chart redrawn with the variable costs drawn at the bottom and the fixed costs above. The result enables us to see that at every level of output the units produced recover their own variable costs and then make a contribution towards fixed costs as well. Now study Fig. 7.3 and the notes below it.

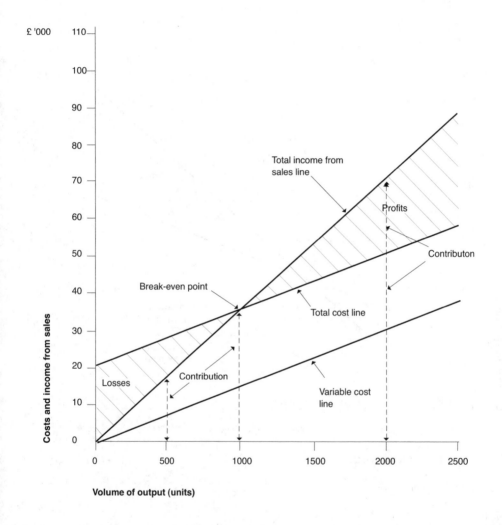

Fig. 7.3   Contributions to fixed costs and profits at varying outputs

Notes:
i   At an output of 500 items the sales income of £17 500 achieved covers all the variable costs, £7500, and makes a contribution of £10 000 towards the fixed costs. However, as the fixed costs were £20 000 we have not yet broken even. *(Continues opposite)*

ii At an output of 1000 items the income received covers the variable costs of £15 000 and makes a contribution of £20 000 to fixed costs. This is therefore the break-even point.

iii At an output of 2000 items the sales income contributes enough to recover all the variable costs, and all the fixed costs, and still leaves profits of £20 000.

iv What contribution would be made by sales of 2500 units?

4 The idea of contribution is important because it leads straight on to a system called **marginal costing**. Marginal costing is the ascertainment of costs by differentiating between fixed costs and variable costs to bring out clearly the effect on profit of volumes of output. For example, suppose we are selling 2000 items in Fig. 7.3 and could produce 2500 items with our present capacity. We are approached by someone to supply 500 items at a privileged price of only £27 per unit. Since the extra output will have variable costs of £15 per unit and bring no extra fixed costs we might as well take the order and add to our profits by 500 x £12 = £6000. This is not as satisfactory as 500 x £20 but it is better than nothing at all. So long as the new order covers the marginal cost and does not require any extra fixed costs we might as well take it.

5 Other pricing considerations are:

a In monopoly conditions or monopolistic competition (where we are selling goods under a brand name which others cannot use and, consequently, to some extent we have an element of monopoly even in a competitive industry) it is usually possible to command a better price than in other conditions of pure competition.

b We cannot price our goods without any prediction at all of what competition will do. Thus to cut price in order to increase market share may be counterproductive, since our competitors may follow us down into a spiral of falling profit margins which may produce bankruptcy. 'There is always one fool who cuts' says an old proverb.

c Price lining is a frequent practice. Traders stock goods at three prices – a good standard item, a cheaper line and an up-market line. Consumers in various brackets know what line they usually buy but may move up a line for special occasions and down a line (or cease buying) when times are hard.

d Where markets can be separated, we can often sell at different prices, discriminating in favour of one group because the other group cannot buy in the cheaper market. For example, publishers sell cheap editions to book clubs because the ordinary public cannot buy unless they join the club – which many of them are unwilling to do.

e The method of distribution influences pricing. For example, if we are selling direct to the customer we only have to add on one profit margin – our own. If we sell to the retailer, who sells to the customer, we have to price the article in such a way that two profits are available, the profit we require and a further mark-up to give the retailer a profit. If we sell to a wholesaler who sells to a retailer who sells to the end-user (the actual customer) three profits have to be achieved. In a competitive market, where there are many sellers of the same product, it is very difficult to add on three profit margins, and the marketing manager may be forced to share the profit with one of the other parties. Where a product is a branded article, selling under a trade mark of some sort, the system is said to be one of monopolistic competition (in other words, there is an element of monopoly in trading even though it is fairly competitive). Bloggs football gear is a 'different' product from anyone else's football gear and consequently people who know of the product will 'prefer' it, and be prepared to pay a little extra for it. In such situations it is possible to ask the extra price which enables all parties to obtain a reasonable profit.

f A sound marketing strategy can often enable a company to review its pricing policy to its own advantage. Instead of a crude cost-plus policy, a more sophisticated system can be used which includes a consideration of costs, order size, spare capacity for production, market desirability and the appropriateness of a particular order for the company's future marketing strategy. For example, a company which wished to move up-market into a better class of work might take a particular order because in fulfilling it the staff would be able to exercise new skills and move in a desirable direction. This could lead to more specialised products, the fuller development of which in the future would mean the company could command premium prices for new products.

7.6   Credit control

Credit control is a vital element in sales policy and should never be overlooked. Some important aspects may be listed as follows:

1 New customers are always welcome; but will they pay? It is usual to demand cash with order, or cash on delivery for an initial period while the customer is as yet unknown to us.

2 When regular orders have been placed, the customer may ask to be treated as an ordinary account customer – in other words, payment will be made at the end of the period usual in the trade. This is as short as three days in some trades in perishables, but more commonly is for one month. Large firms are notoriously bad payers and some will not deal with a trader unless 90 days' credit is allowed. This is grossly unfair. An application for ordinary credit terms should normally only be granted if banker's references or references from a trade association or firms in other industries are available. If these are not available the application may still be granted. For all accounts the possible loss should be limited by setting a credit limit. Goods will not be sent out once this limit has been reached unless the outstanding account is settled. The limit should be clearly stated in writing to the customer, and it should be made clear in the same letter that the acceptance of all orders, including telephone orders, is subject to the credit limit and will be invalid if that is exceeded. It is a common practice of dishonest people to place several small orders and pay in accordance with the terms of the agreement, but then to place a massive order for which it is not intended to pay.

3 If an order is received for a further supply which leads to the credit limit being exceeded, a good response is to telephone the customer and tell them that they have exceeded their credit limit and therefore can only be supplied on pro-forma terms. Pro-forma means 'in the form of', and what happens is that we send them a document called a pro-forma invoice which is exactly like an invoice, but it is not for goods supplied –it

is only for goods we are prepared to supply if they pay the pro-forma invoice. When we get the money, we will dispatch the goods. Firms hate to be put on pro-forma terms. If they pay and we send the goods, when the next order comes in , we repeat the process. They really hate that. When they protest it is possible to make it quite clear to them that we do not deal with people on credit unless we know they will abide by the agreed terms.

The reader may feel that in the present competitive climate such actions may drive the customer elsewhere. If the customer is intent on obtaining goods for which he/she does not intend to pay, we may well prefer that he/she goes elsewhere. If the customer genuinely wants our product, and none other, let him/her state a convincing case for the restoration of the credit limit formerly enjoyed.

4 Failure to pay any monthly statement within the time limit should mean a written request for payment at once. If this is ignored, a solicitor's letter requiring the customer to pay the amount due within a limited time period should follow, and if this does not result in payment a writ should be served. Since many bad debtors only pay the people who actually sue them there is no point at all in being shy about taking legal action. The costs are negligible and nearly always produce payment, since their business will almost certainly fail if court orders are made against them.

7.7   Sales administration

The marketing director (who may also be the sales manager) has a major interest in the work of the sales department. Selling situations vary. For example where a head office has its own chain of retail outlets the selling problems are rather different from where a team of salesmen is selling to middlemen in bulk, or trying to achieve one-off orders for machinery and similar capital items. The aim in all cases is to use the sales team as efficiently as possible in its particular situation, whatever that may be.

Functions of the sales manager

The sales manager must do the following:

1 Set up and control a sales office which not only brings the company's products before the public in an attractive way but can supervise all aspects of work that follow from the sale of goods – for example, packing, dispatch, delivery, servicing, handling of complaints, credit control, observance of warranties, standard conditions of sale and carriage, and so on.

2 Appoint, induct, motivate and supervise whatever sales team is required, including the whole question of their remuneration.

3 Set up in co-operation with other departments a system of documentation which will ensure efficient conduct of the sales office, keep selling expenses as low as possible and keep management fully informed.

4 In association with the advertising department and promotions department, arrange for such a range of publicity and sales literature as will meet all the needs of sales staff in answering enquiries about the company's products and seeking new business, repeat orders, and so on.

The sales team

A sales team can only be effective if the sales staff have been selected for their interest in and knowledge about the general area of merchandise to be handled. They must if necessary be taught the basic principles of salesmanship: how to approach clients, how to deal with enquiries in a courteous and helpful way, how to resist temptations to vary the terms of trade by cutting prices or yielding to unfair delivery demands, or promising extended credit periods, and how to close an interview in such a way as to leave lines of communication open with goodwill intact. They must be trained in all aspects of product knowledge, anything less than complete familiarity with the product's characteristics, construction, uses, price, and so on, being regarded as unsatisfactory. They must then be trained in the company's procedures, its sales policy, its documentation, report system, conditions of employment, and so on. This formidable list of introductory training must usually take place before any selling can begin, since a raw recruit released into the marketplace without a basic grasp of all these matters could lose the company both orders and goodwill.

Remuneration of the sales team

Remuneration presents a problem in any sales organisation. A flat salary irrespective of the sales achieved provides no incentive to the sales staff, whereas payment by results may be unsatisfactory too, especially where sales are seasonal or there are 'dead' patches in the year when no-one is buying. A beginner nearly always needs a basic salary for survival purposes while he/she establishes a clientele. Some sales are one-off sales, unlikely to be repeated, while other trades may offer the chance of repeat orders without further work. Thus a seller of plain paper copiers has to work hard to achieve a sale with little chance of a repeat for at least three years, while the person supplying the paper for use in the copier may get a new order every three months for several years.

Commission is a method of rewarding sales staff according to the orders received. It gives the salesman an incentive to sell, but may lead to aggressive methods which invite public criticism. The degree to which staff are free to make a sale in any territory is often a cause for disputes since a salesman designated to a particular area would expect that sales made in that area would bring some commission. Sometimes an outsider making a sale in the area may be forced to share the commission with the designated member of staff for that area. Some crossing of territorial boundaries is inevitable if sales are not to be missed, because a customer of A may have a friend in B's territory. If the customer puts a bit of business A's way it would be a pity for it to be refused because the new customer was in B's territory.

Some sales managers organise *special drives and events* which offer either a *financial bonus* or a *prize* – such as a weekend in Paris or the Bahamas. While anything that motivates sales staff is *prima facie* helpful, it does lead to trouble on occasions. Such events are easily taken advantage of by unscrupulous sales staff who may soft-pedal in the weeks before the event (when there is no penalty for soft-pedalling) and then bring in a host of orders in the event week to scoop the prize.

Organisation of the sales office

A sales office may be situated in various positions: at the factory, at head office, at a specialist showroom or in some logical geographical centre for keeping control of the selling staff. The sales manager must be efficient and have a good grasp of the system in use so that maximum support can be given to sales staff, not only with a problem, but as a matter of general routine. Note that the sales manager is not necessarily a good salesman who has been promoted. Many salesmen do not make good managers, because they are not fond of sitting behind a desk offering back-up support to others. They want to be out in the field selling themselves. The sales manager must be calm, unflappable and respected for his/her general integrity and fair-mindedness. The marketing director should lay down the duties of the sales force, so that the sales manager knows the volumes of sales that are being looked for and the budget within which the department must operate. Basic elements in the sales organisation are as follows.

Territory allocation

Sales staff should be allocated territories which represent a reasonable area to cover with an adequate number of potential customers to ensure a good living. Where the area is already established they will have to service existing customers and also extend the clientele with new calls. They should preferably live in their own territory, where they can keep the local calls as far as possible for 'bad weather' calls and times when the car or van is out of commission, but at other times make circuits through the surrounding territory at regular intervals. Where the goods are such that regular orders can be expected, the customer appreciates regular visits which ensure that the representative looks after his/her interests as a routine matter. Where the goods are not the subject of regular re-orders but are one-off sales of a capital item such as a machine and a new call comes up in a particular area, a circuit from home incorporating the new call might take in a number of other past customers at the same time. Cold-calling has its disadvantages in that staff may find the customer unavailable or too busy to see them, but where a circuit has to be covered anyway on a particular day it is better than phoning in advance – which often means the customer will try to arrange a different time. With such customers, who only require supplies intermittently, it is an opportunity to leave an order form, or a new brochure, or just a business card with a telephone number and an invitation to phone whenever the representative can be of assistance.

An experienced sales manager can assist considerably with helping sales staff to plan their visits, and get as much system as possible into the arrangements. For example, a degree of priority must be given to good customers, and less attention to those who order more rarely or in small quantities.

Sales stationery

The sales manager can offer support to sales staff by providing a full range of sales stationery. This can save staff time and ensure a standard for quality responses to enquiries. Typical items include business cards, compliments slips, standard reply letters to acknowledge the receipt of enquiries, brochures, price lists, draft estimates, requests for references (new customers), advices about sanctioned credit limits, order forms (arranged in warehouse order for easy order picking), and so on. A special briefcase which has compartments for such items is convenient. The stationery should include an appropriate form for easy completion for each call made, notifying the sales manager of the outcome. The representative should complete this form, preferably a two-part NCR (no carbon required) set, after each call while all the facts are clearly remembered. A suitable form for completion is shown in Fig. 7.4.

The top copy of each form completed should be posted in at the end of the day, to be examined on arrival by the sales manager. If it refers to an attached order, this should be acknowledged and started off on its journey through the order procedure, credit control, invoicing, order assembly, packing and dispatch.

It is helpful to have an extra copy, called the representative's copy, added to the set of invoices issued when an order is fulfilled. This copy is sent to the representative who can produce it should the customer complain on the next visit that the order has not arrived. This confirms dispatch, and may lead to a claim on the carrier for non-delivery. Where a customer is busy and wants to get rid of the representative, it is commonly the case that he/she will say 'Oh, well, repeat that order for us then – we're almost out of stock.' Such 'forms' can now be completed electronically from the rep's car, and the order received can be invoiced and dispatched with breath-taking speed.

Information for representatives

The representative must be fed with all the latest information about the products, the servicing arrangements (if applicable), the promotions coming up and the advertising to be undertaken in the near future. It is easy to feel neglected on the road, and out of touch with the area office and head office. Sound arrangements must be made to establish contact at regular intervals and times, and the sales manager should make a point of establishing this contact personally whenever possible rather than through a secretary or other subordinate. New selling features, changes in trading methods or methods of approach, new advertising and the media to be used, supplies of give-away advertising materials such as pencils, ball-point pens, memo pads and so on, should be provided. The sales department should not be seen as a supervisor seeking to gain control of the representative with endless checking-up procedures, but as a source of help and encouragement, and appreciative back-up.

Sales conferences

Although these can rarely be more than annual events, they are the best opportunity to generate new enthusiasm among the sales force and to set new targets for the year ahead. Usually lasting two or three days and held in pleasant surroundings (even the Costa Brava is not too far these days), they give a unique opportunity to correct past errors, introduce new methods of work, generate interest in new products and reward meritorious service.

Salesman's Report

Name of Salesperson .... Report No. ....

Territory .... Date ....

Call made upon: Name .... Time of Arrival ......

Address ....

.... Time of ....

.... Postcode .... Departure ....

Person Interviewed ....

Result of call: ....

....

....

....

....

Is an order submitted with this report?   Yes ....   No ....

Had the customer any complaints? ....

....

....

....

Did the business appear in good heart? ....

....

Is the present level of credit   (a) adequate? ....

                                   (b) excessive? ....

                                   (c) too small? ....

Did the customer express any views on the climate of business? ....

....

....

....

Any signs of competition? ....

Any need for promotional material, point of sale material, etc ....

....

Fig. 7.4 A report form for calls made

The presence of wives (or husbands) is much to be recommended, with special programmes arranged for them and recreational opportunities provided. Much of the day-to-day back-up provided to selling staff comes from the marriage partner, who may help with circularising customers, answering the telephone, advising about problems, and so on. This sort of service should be recognised occasionally.

The sales conference should have a theme, or several themes. A product theme is a common one, or a publicity theme, but such matters as sales performance, meeting the competition, general finance themes (including credit control, bad debts, VAT and so on) may become important from time to time.

Evaluation of sales effort

The sales office must on a regular basis and usually not less frequently than once a quarter assess the efforts of each member of the sales team and issue an assessment report – a copy of which must go to the sales person concerned. A typical form is shown in Fig. 7.5.

Sales-staff Assessment Report

Name of Sales Person .... Territory ....

Period of assessment   from ....   to ....

Target for period   £.......................................

Actual sales achieved   £.......................................

Excess   ....   Shortfall ....

Number of calls notified ....

Of which .... existing customers; .... new customers

Total orders obtained .... Average value £ ....

Percentage of orders to calls ....%

Total number of live accounts ....

New accounts opened in period ....

Assessment Rating: ....

(A = Very good; B = Satisfactory; C = Poor)

Sales Manager's Comments ....

....

....

....

....

Response by staff member: ....

....

....

....

Note: You need not comment above but if you do please photo copy the complete form and return it to Sales Department for information, and to complete your record file. Thank you!

Fig. 7.5   A sales staff assessment report

7.8   Transport and distribution (logistics)

Two more subsystems under the general control of the marketing director are distribution and transport. These are often called by the general term **logistics** today. While these two areas are closely related, and the general term **physical distribution management** is commonly used to cover the whole area, it is convenient to consider the aspects separately.

Distribution is concerned with the movement of goods from the point of production to the point of consumption. Since production and consumption may be separated both geographically and in time, we have two 'gaps' to bridge, the **geographical gap** and the **time gap**. The geographical gap is bridged by transport, and the time gap is bridged by merchandising skills – which vary from product to product. Thus the merchandising skills for dealing with strawberries or bananas are quite different from those required for books, or newspapers, or bedroom furniture or ironmongery.

The distribution process

The first problem with distribution is to clear the production lines, which otherwise become cluttered with finished goods. We may clear the product into temporary storage pending dispatch to wholesalers or distribution depots around the country, but all handling is expensive, and double handling is doubly expensive. Therefore, frequently, much of current output is loaded straight onto vehicles for onward delivery, reducing the need for factory storage space. An important concept here is the **unit load concept**, which means that small items are consolidated into a single unit which can be picked up by some sort of mechanical handling device. Thus if eight boxes of envelopes can be placed in a single layer on a pallet, and the boxes are strong enough to stack four high, we can lift 32 boxes on the pallet in one unit load. If a container divided into an upper and lower deck can hold four pallets wide and 20 pallets deep in each floor, we have 5120 boxes of envelopes in one container. The container must be stuffed using a fork-lift truck and the whole container must be lifted by a heavy-duty fork-lift truck or a container crane, but this type of unit load is a very efficient method of distribution.

Unit loads are commonly made up by stacking cardboard cartons, drums, work boxes of various sorts and sacks of product on simple devices such as stillages (a low platform) or pallets (wooden or metal frameworks which can be picked up by a fork-lift truck). Pallets can be two-way entry, four-way entry and even eight-way entry platforms. In the latter case the fork-lift truck can pick them up from the front, from the back, from either side or from any corner – making 'pick-up' and 'put-down' very easy, however cramped the working space. Some pallets have cages, so that goods cannot easily fall off the pallet or be pilfered. Some of these caged pallets can be folded compactly when not in use (on return journeys) so that they can be carried economically when not loaded. **Containerisation** began in the early 1960s and now completely dominates the distribution scene. This revolution in transport has cost a fortune, the biggest investment in transport facilities since the railways were laid down in the nineteenth century.

Channels of distribution

Channels of distribution vary greatly. The biggest influence on the choice of channel is the nature of the goods concerned. These include:
1 *Perishables* These must have as direct and simple a distribution network as possible. Thus fish are sold direct from the quayside in many areas to housewives and hoteliers who come to buy personally. More distant markets are reached by a wholesaling sys-

tem, which delivers from the port daily to inland retailers. The wholesaler's 'premises' are his lorry, and he starts his journey empty, goes to the market for supplies, and finishes empty, having picked up the fresh fish and delivered it over a circuit of retailer-calls.

2 *Foods and household items* Such items are so numerous and the variety is so great that it is essential to market them through wholesalers, though many multiple shops, chain stores and department stores act as their own wholesalers and distribute goods to branches as if they were wholesalers selling to retailers. The essence of the wholesaling system is that the wholesaler acts as an intermediary performing useful functions to both manufacturers on one side and retailers on the other. Suppose every retailer had to deal with every manufacturer. To sell 1000 lines it would be necessary to open accounts with every supplier, to place orders separately for each line, to take delivery of hundreds of small consignments, and so on. If one wholesaler takes bulk deliveries from 1000 suppliers, he/she can supply everything the retailer needs.

The advantages to the manufacturer are:

a the wholesaler takes goods in large quantities as they are produced, clearing the production lines

b transport, warehousing and depot location problems are reduced, the wholesalers assuming responsibility for these matters

c wholesalers pay promptly, thus reducing working capital requirements, bad debt problems and so on

d the wholesaler bridges both the geographical gap and the time gap, using whatever expertise is required

e the wholesaler may develop an own-brand image for marketing purposes.

The advantages to the retailer are:

a the wholesaler delivers everything required in a single delivery

b the retailer may be given credit, thus helping with cash-flow problems

c the wholesaler often grades, packs and prices goods, and may supply point-of-sale advertising material

d the wholesaler runs a showroom for easy inspection of the full range of goods available, including new lines, fashion items as they appear in season, and so on.

3 *Durable consumer goods* Here there is often an element of servicing and repairs to be done. Consequently, we need a system of agencies, where the retailers who actually make the sale to the customer either have trained staff to operate a servicing workshop or at least have an agreed link with an area workshop to which repairs can be sent. The agents will take supplies in reasonable bulk, national or local advertising feeds customers through to the agency in their own home area, and the costs may be shared by the manufacturer and the retailer in some agreed way. These shorter communication lines which eliminate the wholesaler can result in increased profitability, more direct feedback when problems arise, increased customer satisfaction and consequent goodwill.

Transport

Transport is a study in its own right. In the United Kingdom the alternatives are road and rail transport, with a heavy bias towards road transport except for two main areas. With long-distance loads the advantages still lie with rail haulage, and with bulk transport of basic materials (stone, sand, gravel, iron ore, coal and petroleum products, for example) the train is still the economical way to move. Even car transporters illustrate the superiority of rail haulage as those who have travelled to Dover by road and then to the South of France by this method can testify.

Leaving rail transport aside, there are three chief methods of moving goods by road, own-account operations, contract hire fleets and public hauliers. We may summarise these as shown in Table 7.3 (see page 126–7).

The sequence of dispatch activities

Obviously the whole field of transport and distribution is a complex area, with a great variety of movement – every load varies. However, we can consider a number of headings which are important.

1 *Packaging* Packaging serves several functions. Its main aim is to protect the goods in transit, though this protection is often reinforced by packing, which is a separate process. Where packaging, in effect, is the packing as well it is usually the result of specialist design to ensure that the goods move safely and easily. This may be achieved by the use of foam or polystyrene shapes, filling material, and so on. The outside of the packaging may serve as an advertisement, but not if the goods are pilferable or worth stealing because they have a ready market. Such goods are best sent as inconspicuously as possible. Packaging may form part of the marketing effort, in that the package itself constitutes point-of-sale material – merely to display the box is to present it in an attractive way. Polythene wrapping may strengthen and preserve more flimsy but colourful packaging, without detracting from the marketing impact.

2 *Packing* Packing is designed to protect the goods in transit, and in many situations may need to be of a quality which is above criticism. While this is particularly true in export trade, even home trade containerised cargo needs to be properly packed. An insurance clause may read 'warranted professionally packed'. Sea cargoes are particularly vulnerable because ships roll and pitch, so that the contents of a container may move if it has not been properly stuffed. Even road and rail movements are subject to fore and aft forces, and centrifugal forces at bends in the road or track.

3 *Documentation* The invoice usually signals the start of dispatch activities. The top copy is taken off first and sent to the customer by post, while the second copy goes to the accounts department for the book-keeping records. The third and fourth copies come to the dispatch department and lead to the picking of the order from the stores. Of course it may be just a single item, but in large warehouses with racks arranged in lines with narrow paths between, an order-picking lift-truck may be used to assemble the order required. The goods are then packed, and the advice note (the fourth copy of the invoice) is packed with the goods or attached to them in an adhesive envelope. The

third copy (the delivery note) is used by the carrier to bring back a clean signature. A clean signature is one given by the addressee reading 'Received in apparent good order or condition'. A dirty signature would be claused to read 'Appears damaged' or some such wording.

4 *Marks and identification* Most sets of invoices are accompanied by labels (often computer-generated adhesive labels these days). For small orders these may be adequate but where an order consists of a large crate or several large crates, deliveries are simplified if clear marks are stencilled on the crates. For example, four crates addressed to Kitchen Fittings (Camelot) Ltd might be marked KFC 1 of 4, KFC 2 of 4, KFC 3 of 4, KFC 4 of 4. This would ease identification and ensure that a partial delivery was not made.

5 *The transport programme* This is a list of journeys to be made to meet customer needs. It is a schedule of regular deliveries to known customers with the nature and size of the load, address for delivery, and so on. Additional space each day must be allocated for one-off deliveries and new customers. The loads will then be allocated to appropriate vehicles according to vehicle availability, since many vehicles will be away on deliveries on any given day and some will be out of use because of servicing, and so on. Much effort is required in journey planning, costing, recording vehicle allocation and problems arising from returned loads, damage in transit, theft of vehicles, and so on.

Table 7.3   Road haulage transport: advantages and disadvantages

Own-account operations

Advantages

1   You own the fleet and use it entirely at will.

2   You have complete control over the drivers, loading, timing of departures, etc.

3   The vehicles are available for other uses, personal use, personnel welfare, trade association functions, etc.

4   They are a moving advertisement in your company's distinctive livery.

Disadvantages

1   Return loads are difficult to find, which means a certain amount of 'light running'.

2   You have to service the vehicle and garage it.

3   The fleet may be too small at peak times, and too large in slack periods.

4   There is a temptation to think of the costs in terms of running costs only (petrol and wages) and forget the heavy capital costs incurred with an own-account fleet.

5   Other departments may use the fleet as a way of reducing their own costs.

6   There are 'hidden' costs: insurance, breakdown time, etc.

Contract hire

Advantages

1   You hire the fleet but do not own it, maintain it, or garage it. These costs are borne by the haulier.

2   Complete control over drivers and the operation of the vehicle.

3   The costs are known and agreed in advance.

4   The hire charge is a fully deductible revenue expense for income tax purposes.

Disadvantages

1   Return loads are difficult to find, which means a certain amount of 'light running'.

2   The hirer will expect the vehicles to be fully employed during the period of the hire and if not may make a charge for 'dead freight', i.e. under-use.

3   It is more expensive than own-account operations (but there are no hidden costs: these are borne by the fleet owner).

Public hauliers

Advantages

1   The haulage industry is competitive and you can shop around for a cheap price for the job.

2   There is a variety of vehicles available. You choose your haulier according to the job in hand.

3   There is no worry about return loads.

4   There is no idle time for vehicles in slack time. You just pay for the actual jobs done.

5   The haulier is an expert and knows his job.

6   The charges are a deductible business expense for tax purposes.

Disadvantages

1   A haulier owes you no loyalty (especially if you shop around for low prices) and at busy times your goods may not move.

2   There is no control over the vehicle or its driver. Once in the system you are unable to influence what is happening. If a strike occurs, for example, your goods stop.

3   There is no advertising advantage on the vehicle.

7.9   Export marketing

If a nation was endowed by nature with such varied resources that it never ran short of minerals, fuel and other resources, and if it also had an equable climate, abundant water supplies, a bountiful soil and a skilful population, it would be in that happy state which the Greeks called **autarchy** or self-sufficiency. A few large nations, like the former USSR and the USA, are almost self-sufficient and could, if circumstances required it, manage on the resources available to them for a considerable time. Such a nation would not need to engage in export marketing. Overseas trade is not essential, except to those whom nature has not endowed with the necessary resources, or whose stock of a particular resource has already been consumed. For example, the United Kingdom's copper, lead and other metals have been almost completely consumed by two centuries of industrial activity.

The problems of export marketing

These may be listed briefly as follows:

1   We are dealing with a foreign country, subject to foreign laws which in many cases may be difficult for us to enforce against a customer who is more familiar with the laws than

we are, and able to employ competent lawyers at close range. This sort of problem is generally described as a 'conflict of laws'. Fortunately many such problems have been reduced over the years by the adoption of internationally agreed conventions in particular areas of dispute. The idea of a convention is that all the parties get together at an international conference and draw up agreed procedures called the 'convention'. The individual parties go back with this agreed set of procedures and enact them into their own national laws, a process known as 'ratifying the convention'. When the required number (usually 20) of nations have ratified the convention it comes into force between the member states, replacing former national law by the new one now enacted. This ends the conflict of laws. New nations join in as their own national legislations introduce the necessary enactments.

Where no such convention exists, conflicts of law may still arise, but multinational companies with a sufficiently firm foothold in a foreign country can usually operate quite satisfactorily using local law.

2 There may be difficulties affecting the product, including such problems as climatic differences, standard voltages in electricity, technical specifications, packing and packaging regulations. Even colours can be a problem, as the manufacturer who sent fertiliser in green sacks to the Middle East found when his cargo was regarded as an insult to the religion, green having a special religious significance in Muslim countries. A handbook from Croner's, the *Reference Book for Exporters*, gives useful guidance on many such problems in the pages which refer to particular countries.

3 There are difficulties of language – labelling, instruction booklets, guarantees, pricing, and so on.

4 Documentation is an important aspect of overseas trade. Not only must the ordinary invoices be made out as in home trade, but frequently special 'consular invoices' must be obtained at quite considerable expense. These are certified copies of invoices showing that the foreign customer has been authorised to purchase the items concerned because they are in the national interest. Many countries restrict the types and quantities of imports in this way. They may also require certificates of origin and of value, the first to show that the goods are not coming from a country which is in disfavour with the importing country and the second to show that the price is a fair one for the goods in question. Such certificates have to be validated by an agreed authority, usually a Chamber of Commerce. Other documentation includes insurance cover, methods of ensuring payment is received, instructions to bankers in foreign parts, and so on.

5 Products which require servicing after sale may make exporting difficult for some companies. The cost of appointing agents, training staff in servicing, and so on, can be enormous, but for those who can set up the necessary basic organisation the rewards can be very great – in fact we move into the concept of global marketing where the entire world is our marketplace.

Methods of exporting

The chief methods of exporting are as follows:

1 *Through an export merchant* This is a firm or company already operating in overseas markets which is prepared to add your products to the range of goods at present being sold. The term 'merchant' implies that the company buys to sell again, and is actually the owner of the goods sold. You are therefore virtually selling to a home customer – the merchant – who is invoiced in the usual way and pays in the home currency. In fact the goods will be sold abroad, but the merchant handles all the export difficulties, using the expertise already acquired.

2 *Through a confirming house* A confirming house is one which obtains goods required by foreign customers, placing orders for them with suppliers. The house confirms that the order is a genuine one, for which it will be personally responsible – so that once again the exporter is not really engaged in export trade but is dealing with a home customer, who will take delivery of, and pay for, the goods before they go abroad. The confirming house consolidates all the goods it is buying from a host of suppliers into a number of container loads, sees to all the documentation, freight bookings and so on, and thus relieves the exporters of all the problems.

   A confirming house is triggered into activity by an indent, a request for stores from a foreign importer. This may be an open indent: 'Please obtain ten million 5-cm sterilised bandages at the best price possible.' This leaves the confirming house free to place the order with any supplier. On the other hand it may be a closed indent: 'Please obtain ten million Florence Nightingale 5-cm sterilised bandages.' This requires the confirming house to obtain the particular brand requested, and no other.

3 *By direct selling to an overseas customer* It is possible in certain trades to sell direct to overseas customers – for example, textbooks are often sold to foreign students in this way and so are many other mail order items. It is usual to insist on *cash with order* terms, including a clear margin for postage and insurance. We may also sell to foreign visitors in our own country – for example, visitors to the United Kingdom can be sold items free of VAT. Naturally a charge for packing, carriage and insurance has to be made and the necessary export documentation should be checked out before engaging in this kind of exporting activity. Payment will be made on ordering by the foreign visitor, in the home currency, so that foreign exchange problems do not arise. We can also deal direct with foreign nationals in their own countries by post, telephone, fax and the Internet, but we do have to overcome the language barriers, the problems of getting payment, and so on. This is very much like real exporting and requires the full expertise of export trade.

4 *By using an overseas agent* Where an overseas agent is used, the agent acts on your behalf in finding customers for your products, and in securing payment. Whether you find the agent, or the agent seeks you out and offers to act on your behalf, there is a problem of establishing a sound business relationship. References should certainly be taken up and credit reference agencies such as Dun & Bradstreet may be able to provide a report on an agent, and on any individual customer. The position of an agent is that he/she acts as an intermediary in bringing parties (suppliers and customers) into contractual relationships with one another, for a fee called commission. This means that in the event of

any dispute about quantity, quality or payment the agent drops out of the picture, and you are left dealing with the foreign customer, at long distance, in a foreign language, and perhaps under foreign law. As far as payment is concerned, it is possible for the risk to be reduced if the agent is prepared to take a *del credere* commission extra (usually about 2.5 per cent) in return for running the risk of any bad debts. The words *del credere* mean 'in the belief that' the buyer is solvent. The agent enters into the bargain in the belief that the buyer is solvent, and backs his judgement of the debtor's financial status by being prepared to carry the risk of any bad debt, in return for the extra commission. If all is well and the debtor honours the debt the agent forwards the payment less the agreed commission. If all is not well, he/she pays the debt, less the commission, on the due date and pursues the debtor through the local courts, which is not a difficult procedure at close range, with a local lawyer.

5 *By setting up an overseas branch office* When a company sets up overseas branch offices it moves into the global marketing field with a fully sophisticated export marketing system which treats an overseas market as just one more market to be treated in the normal way as if it was a home market no different from the true home market. Such overseas branch offices are often welcomed by the host country because they mean employment for their own nationals, not only in the selling organisation but possibly in manufacturing or at least assembly offshoots of the foreign company. There are problems – the repatriation of profits, for example, may be a matter for some discussion – but usually some reasonable basis can be arrived at with reasonable repatriation of profits in return for a continuing and developing manufacturing base in the host country.

Getting paid for exports

There are five main ways of getting paid for exports. The problem is twofold. The exporter naturally does not wish to proceed with manufacturing an export item or obtaining it from a supplier, and with the expensive and time-consuming export procedures, unless payment is forthcoming. Similarly, the importer does not wish to put up funds immediately for something which will not arrive immediately and when it does may prove defective in quality or unfit for the purpose intended. Fortunately there are clever ways of overcoming the problems, and plenty of trustworthy intermediaries well used to all the problems who can help the nervous exporter or importer. The five methods are:

1 cash with order
2 letter of credit
3 documents against payment
4 documents against acceptance
5 open account terms.

1 *Cash with order* Already referred to earlier, this method is used for small orders where the foreign importer is prepared to pay cash straight away and rely on the business integrity of the exporter to honour the bargain for which he/she has already been paid. Having the payment in hand, the exporter proceeds to make or purchase the item, arranges the full documentation required and sends the goods on their way.

2 *Letter of credit* There are several types of letters of credit and a full explanation cannot be given here, but the confirmed, irrevocable letter of credit is the best. Under this system the foreign importer either deposits funds at the bank to the value of the order being placed or, more likely, simply arranges a credit for the amount required with a local bank (a loan). This enables the importer's bank to send a request to a correspondent bank in the exporting country asking them to notify Anne Exporter that an irrevocable credit is available for the purchase of certain items of a given description, quality and price as previously discussed between importer and exporter. Irrevocable means that the importer cannot withdraw from the bargain without Anne Exporter's permission. If the importer's bank asks the correspondent bank to confirm the credit it means that the correspondent bank will itself honour the credit as soon as the exporter presents it with a stated set of documents, as listed in the letter of credit. These usually mean a 'shipped on board bill of lading' (or an air waybill if carriage is to be by air), an invoice, a certificate of insurance, and so on, according to the legal requirements for that class of cargo.

The exporter can now go ahead, knowing payment will be forthcoming provided he/she does everything that should be done. When the goods are loaded on board ship, according to the terms of the contract (see Incoterms below) the master of the vessel signs the bill of lading and the exporter presents this with all the other documents to the correspondent bank. As this is a confirmed credit the correspondent bank, after checking the documents, releases payment and sends the documents out to the foreign bank in the importer's country. The foreign bank reimburses the correspondent bank, calls in the importer and releases the documents. The importer's deposit is now used (or the loan arranged is brought into effect) so that the importer has paid for the goods which are on the high seas. If they arrive safely the bill of lading presented to the master of the vessel secures the release of the cargo. If they fail to arrive the insurance policy entitles the importer to claim for the loss.

The system gives both parties complete security as far as the business transaction is concerned. It cannot give complete security in other respects – for example, government action in the importer's country – but these risks can be covered by an export credit guarantee. Your local BusinessLink will tell you how to arrange such a guarantee.

3 *Documents against payment* With this system payment is secured by a sight bill of exchange drawn on the foreign importer. The importer places an order with an exporter who manufactures or obtains the goods, ships them on board a vessel and obtains a bill of lading signed by the master. This bill of lading represents ownership of the goods while they are on the high seas. The invoice for the goods, the bill of lading, a certificate of insurance, a sight bill of exchange and any other necessary documents are presented by the exporter to his/her local bank. The local bank sends them out to a foreign correspondent banker, who calls the importer in and presents him/her with the bill of exchange, which is payable on sight. If the importer pays the bill, the correspondent bank releases the documents which can be presented to the master of the vessel when it arrives, to claim the goods. If the vessel is lost the importer claims on the insurance policy. Meanwhile the money received from the importer, less charges, is relayed back to the exporter, who has thus been paid for the goods.

4   *Documents against acceptance*   A bill of exchange may be payable on sight, as explained above, or it may be payable at some future time. Suppose this time is 90 days after sight of the bill by the importer. When the documents arrive in the foreign country the correspondent bank to whom they are sent calls in the importer and asks him/her to 'accept' the bill. This means 'to accept the order to pay' written on the bill, which reads something like this: *90 days after sight pay Anne Exporter the sum of one thousand five hundred euro, for value received.* The importer writes 'accepted' on the bill and signs it, thus becoming the primary person liable to pay the bill. The documents are released to the importer, who uses them to claim the goods on arrival, and at the expiry of the credit period the bill is honoured. This is called the 'due date'. However, because of the adaptable nature of a bill of exchange, the exporter has probably discounted the bill with a bank, taking its face value less interest for 90 days at an agreed rate of interest. When the importer finally honours the bill it is not the exporter who is paid, but the person who presents it for payment – the 'holder in due course' – who is thus reimbursed with interest for the loan made to the exporter. This useful system really means that the exporter can give the importer a period of credit before payment becomes due (time to sell the goods at a profit, it is hoped) while at the same time getting paid straight away for the goods by discounting the bill with a bank prepared to take it and hold it until the due date.

5   *'Open account' terms*   If we know the foreign importer sufficiently well to be confident of good faith in all dealings between us we can trade on 'open account' terms. The foreign customer is treated exactly like a home customer, and given the same credit period, paying on a statement issued monthly or, perhaps, quarterly. This is a sign of a fully developed export market, with a sound business arrangement between the parties. There is a more secure arrangement involving the use of a bill of exchange. Each time the importer places an order the goods are sent together with a bill of exchange offering the usual period of credit that would be given to an 'open account' customer in the home trade. The importer signs this (accepts it) and returns it. Now, not only has the importer given a valid promise to honour the debt on a definite due date, but we have a bill of exchange which we can either keep to maturity or – if we need the money – we can discount it at the bank for the loss of a few euro interest.

Incoterms

Overseas trade takes place across national boundaries and is liable to be affected by 'conflicts of law'. To resolve many of the difficulties in making contracts across national boundaries an international agreement on the meaning of contractual terms has been reached and is revised from time to time. The current version is Incoterms 1990 which is a list of 13 terms, each with an internationally agreed three-letter code which is convenient for computer use. The 13 Incoterms are:

EXW = Ex works – named place
FCA = Free carrier – named place
FAS = Free alongside ship – named port of shipment
FOB = Free on board – named port of shipment

CFR = Cost and freight – named port of destination
CIF = Cost, insurance and freight – named port of destination
CPT = Carriage paid to – named place of destination
CIP = Carriage and insurance paid to – named place of destination
DAF = Delivered at frontier – named place
DES = Delivered ex ship – named port of destination
DEQ = Delivered ex quay (duty paid) – named port of destination
DDU = Delivered duty unpaid – named place of destination
DDP = Delivered duty paid – named place of destination

There is not room at this point to explain all these terms but the marketing manager with special responsibility for exports must be absolutely familiar with the legal implications behind these terms. The best guide is *Guide to Incoterms* published by the International Chamber of Commerce, 14 Belgrave Square, London sw1 8ps, telephone 0207 823 2811, www.ICCUK.net. The ICC has offices (or agents) in every country. Each term states quite clearly what the responsibilities are of the buyer and the seller in each case, and the *Guide* explains where the risk passes – an important point for insurance purposes.

Export documentation

Again, this is not the place for a full discussion of export documentation, but it is important to know that internationally agreed arrangements require export documentation to be based on an agreed A4 layout which permits **aligned documentation**. This means that every document, invoice, bill of lading, insurance certificate, certificate of origin and value, air waybill, transit document, and so on, has the same information in the same place. Thus the exporter's name and address always appears on the same spot whichever document you are looking at, and so does the customs reference number, or the description of the goods, or the carrier's signature. This means that anyone, anywhere in the world, whatever language he/she speaks, knows where to find the box with the information which is of interest to him/her. The United Kingdom body for liaising with other bodies world-wide on these matters is SITPRO, the Simpler Trade Procedures Board. It publishes most export documents in a booklet called *Topform*. The address is Sitpro Ltd, 8th Floor, 76 Oxford Street, London, w1d 1bs, www.sitpro.org.uk. Ask for customer services and they will give you the current price, including postage and packing. Copies should be ordered cash with order. The whole range of SITPRO materials, checklists and so on, is absolutely invaluable and SITPRO is a constant reference point for all export managers. Similar bodies exist in all countries.

The information for aligned documentation is collected together on a master document, a copy of which is reproduced as Fig. 7.6, by courtesy of the SITPRO Board. It can then be used with a series of overlays or masks, to reproduce all the different documents required, the overlay obscuring any information not required on a particular document. Thus the same master document can reproduce a great variety of documents in a very cost-effective way, without any chance of a typing error such as might have occurred if they had been prepared individually.

MASTER DOCUMENT

Exporter VAT no.

Invoice no.

Customs reference/status

Invoice date

Carrier's bkg. no.

Exporter's reference

Buyer's reference

Forwarder's reference

UNIC

Consignee VAT no.

Buyer VAT no.

Freight forwarder VAT no.

Country of despatch

Carrier

Country of destination code

Country of origin

Country of final destination

Other UK transport details

Terms of delivery and payment

Vessel/flight no. and date

Port/airport of loading

Port/airport of discharge

Place of delivery

Insured value

EUR 1 or C. of O. remarks

* DANGEROUS GOODS : Refer to IMDG, ADR, IATA, CIM and UK regulations as appropriate and specify: proper shipping name; hazard class; UN no.; flashpoint °C.

Shipping marks; container number

Number and kind of packages; description of goods *

Item no.

Commodity code

Quantity 2

Gross weight (kg)

Cube (m³)

Procedure

Net weight (kg)

Value (£)

Summary declaration/previous document

LIMIT OF SAD BOX 31 ▶

Commodity code

Quantity 2

Gross weight (kg)

Cube (m³)

Procedure

Net weight (kg)

Value (£)

Summary declaration/previous document

Commodity code

Quantity 2

Gross weight (kg)

Cube (m³)

Procedure

Net weight (kg)

Value (£)

Summary declaration/previous document

SPECIMEN

Identification of warehouse

FREE DISPOSAL

Invoice total (state currency)

Total gross wt (kg)

Total cube (m³)

Freight payable at

Signatory's company and telephone number

Number of bills of lading Original Copy

Name of signatory

Place and date

Signature

Fig. 7.6 The SITPRO master document (courtesy of the SITPRO Board)

Sophisticated information technology systems are also available which enable all export transactions to be correctly documented and available 'on line' for immediate access by any interested party. An export document can rarely be completed at any one moment: it has to be built up over the course of a few days. By having the documentation on line anyone anywhere who has information to input can access the master document and key in the point concerned (for example, the weight of the consignment). This is called DTI (direct trader input). Keying it in on the master document automatically feeds the information to all other related documents.

Intermodal transport

In export marketing we are nearly always concerned with intermodal (or multi-modal) transport. This is the movement of goods which can be transferred from one mode of transport to another as a unit load, with no need to handle the individual units and unpack or repack them. The unit of transport is the container, a metal box with a strong steel frame which permits stacking (often as high as seven containers). They are of internationally agreed size, 8 feet square at the end and 10 feet, 20 feet or 40 feet in length. The container ship has holds which are of the correct size to take 40-foot containers and are called cellular ships because the empty holds are cellular in appearance. At the corners of containers are clamping devices which can be used to clamp the container to the road vehicle, rail wagon or deck, and also to the containers above it or alongside it to give a stable and solid structure. The side, end and roof panels may be of a variety of materials, such as stainless steel, aluminium, plastic or plywood.

Handling containers requires heavy-duty cranes, straddle carriers or heavy-duty fork-lift trucks, while other cargoes (such as packaged timber) may be lifted by special side-loading fork-lift trucks. The maximum weight is 32 tonnes (metric tons). The advantages of containerisation are:

1 They make a unit load of otherwise small cargo which would need much more handling. Once properly stuffed (packed so that goods cannot rattle around) the load can be moved easily and cheaply.
2 Much less packing is required – cartons and crates can be of such a size that they fit the container exactly (for example, four 2-foot cartons make an exact fit in an 8-foot container).
3 Pilfering is reduced; the container is sealed and no-one knows what is in it – not even the driver of the vehicle in many cases.
4 A container moves under a single document. Groupage firms will group odd packages together under house bills of lading and the whole container moves as a single package.
5 Customs clearance can be arranged at both ends at the premises of the freight forwarder, to avoid delaying the ship. Turn-round time is usually about one day, compared with several weeks for a general cargo ship loading and unloading individual packages, subject to immediate customs inspection.
6 Insurance costs are reduced, provided containers are warranted professionally packed by competent stevedores.

With intermodal transport we can have road–sea–road, road–sea–rail, rail–sea–road and similar movements, operated by **combined transport operators (CTOs)**. A combined transport operator takes full responsibility for the load throughout the entire journey. If anything goes wrong the dissatisfied consignee claims from the CTO for loss, damage or delay, leaving the CTO to find out who actually caused the problem and to recoup the compensation paid from the ship, airline, railway or road haulier at fault. An internationally agreed set of rules called the Uniform Rules for a Combined Transport Document is available from the International Chamber of Commerce (ICC Publication 298).

8 The information technology (IT) function

8.1 What is information technology?

Information technology is a general term to describe a range of technologies concerned with the availability of information, and its transmission around the business and scientific communities to establish a knowledge-based society. It is of the utmost importance to governments, although they were fairly slow to appreciate its potential. It began as a number of computers, provided with bespoke software, and aiming to carry out basic activities such as accounting, record keeping, statistical analysis, and so on. As computers proliferated and became more powerful the applications increased to embrace almost every aspect of business, scientific and academic life, while millions of families had their PCs (personal computers) for domestic and for entertainment purposes.

Some explanation of the characteristics of computers is given below, but there is little point in detailing the history of computerisation except to emphasise how short its history is and how all-embracing its influence is today. What began with large teams of systems analysts writing software for huge computers, known as mainframe computers, which needed special dust-free environments, became a world-wide industry with a whole computer on a chip of silicon the size of a thumbnail. The process of miniaturisation was very rapid. The mainframe computers costing millions of pounds became mini-computers costing about £50 000 and these in turn became micro-computers costing as little as £250. Instead of a team of programmers writing dedicated software for in-house use software became available in the form of 'packages' which anyone could use. Thus a payroll package could be purchased off the shelf for a few pounds.

How did computer technology become information technology? Taking the simple payroll package as an example, the computer was told by the program what sort of data to expect. Data about the names and addresses of employees, their hours of work and rates of pay, their tax situations (some had large families and paid no tax, while others had few responsibilities and could be taxed fairly heavily). The program also told the computer how to manipulate this data. Multiply the hours worked by the rate of pay and deduct... and so on. The information fed in – the data input – became a new set of information – the data output. The data could be put out in various ways, as printout, as a screen display, as records in a data bank for use next pay day, and so on. The person who was interested in this new information was now more knowledgeable than he/she would have been before computer technology.

Information technology has an infinite number of applications, and it all happens at enormous speeds. A single process can take place in a nanosecond, one billionth of a second. Someone called the last decade of the twentieth century the 'nanosecond nineties'. No matter how much it has to do the computer can manage in seconds what had previously taken hours or days.

The ultimate effect of these high speeds is that we can experiment with many things. If we feed in all the data about an economy (quite a lot of work to do it) we can then try 'What if…?' experiments. What if we lower taxes? What if we make all education a direct cost to parents? We become more knowledgeable as we try out such ideas. The knowledge based society has arrived.

The last requirement is that this new knowledge has to be communicated to everyone who needs (or wants) to know it. To do that required another development, digitisation. A simple explanation is provided by the ordinary telephone.

8.2   The telephone system

Before the microprocessor revolution an operator seated at a PMBX (private manual branch exchange) connected executives with one another or with outside exchange lines through a system of plugs which when inserted into sockets gave a continuous line between them. Today the new internal exchanges are known as 'phone systems', the heart of which is a microprocessor which can be programmed to make connections. Large installations still have an operator, but the vast majority of the work involved is done automatically, and the operator only interrupts the system when it requests assistance by a winking light or an audible signal for help. The cumbersome switchboard has been replaced by a compact console, and the electrical circuits inside it have been replaced by 'solid-state' electronic components. Some idea of the facilities programmed into the microprocessor may be gained from the following list:

1 *Call queuing* Incoming calls are queued automatically in the order of arrival and are answered in sequence. Until the operator answers, no charge is made, so the caller is not wasting any money. On some systems where there is no operator the extensions are all alerted when an unanswered call is coming in and anyone can answer the telephone. Every extension is able to call every other extension, so if Mr A answers a call and it proves to be for Miss B, he simply keys her number and the telephone rings on her desk. The call is switched automatically to the extension required.
2 *Call storing* Numbers which are dialled regularly are keyed into a memory and can be called at the touch of a button. Many numbers now, with their STD codes, are 10 or 11 numbers long, while overseas calls may number as many as 15 digits. A single touch on the button will dial the number in seconds with no fear of miskeying. Most fax machines can hold both the telephone number and the fax number. If you raise the handset a touch of the button gives you the telephone number. If you put a fax message in the machine ready for transmission the machine detects this and dials the fax number required instead.

3 *Last number redial* The telephone will remember the last number dialled. A simple code will tell the telephone to redial the number to try again for a connection.

4 *Conference calls* Sometimes it is helpful for users in several different parts of the country to confer together over the telephone. Even international calls can be shared in this way. For example, a top-level Australian executive applying for a job in the United Kingdom could be interviewed by a panel on a conference call much more cheaply than by flying him/her over and paying air fares, hotel bills, and so on. If videophones are used the parties conferring can see one another as well. This is known as video conferencing, and can be more economical than flying overseas staff in for discussions, saving the inevitable disruption of their normal routines.

5 *Call barring* Call barring can be used to restrict an extension from making outside calls, or from making trunk or international calls.

6 *Executive intrusion* Top executives on selected telephones and the operator can break into an established call with a warning note that a top priority call is trying to get through. The extension user closes down the non-urgent call and the priority call gets immediate access to the extension.

7 *Call diversion* An extension user can programme the extension to relay any incoming call to another extension for as long as required – either to prevent interruptions or to visit a colleague without fear of missing important calls.

8 *Mobile telephones* Mobile telephones give immediate access to staff outside the building, on sites, or in vehicles. They have obvious advantages for sole traders working away from the office. Over 1 billion mobile phones are in use today (2003).

9 *Voice mail* A voice mail system is one where a caller who wishes to speak to a particular executive who is not available can be diverted to a voice processing system (more sophisticated than an answer-phone). The system usually says something like 'You have reached Mary Lewis's voice mail box.' It then may give information about Mary's whereabouts, or may invite the caller to leave a message. If someone else will do just as well the voice mail may offer a visit to the main switchboard so that the call may be answered by some suitable executive who *is* available.

These examples of telecommunication services are only a small part of a huge range of services, but we are trying to see how 'Information Technology' could transmit information all over the country, and all over the world. The answer is by 'going digital', but what exactly does that mean? Fig. 8.1 explains. *(See overleaf)*

Notes:

i A traditional telephone works by turning the pattern of sounds made when a person speaks into a wave of electricity caused by the pressure of the voice on carbon granules. The variations on this wave are transmitted to the receiving end and are turned back into audible speech when a magnet in the earpiece attracts a thin metal disc in exactly the way the wave varies. It thus repeats the message at destination. The trouble is that at long distances the wave distorts and background noises increase.

ii The solution was found to be the measuring of the wave at its starting point. How do you measure a wave that is constantly varying? The answer is that you have to be quick. If you can measure the wave every 125 millionths of a second (which is 8000 times in a second) you can say 'Well at this moment the wave is 2 cm high and 1 cm from the start-

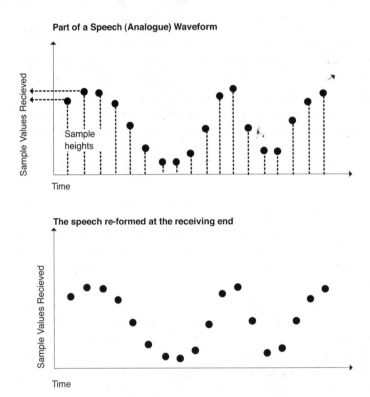

Fig. 8.1 Changing analogue (wave form) messages into digital messages (courtesy of British Telecom PLC)

ing point.' You have turned the wave into a couple of numbers, the dimensions of the wave in digital form.

iii These measurements are then turned into binary machine codes called bits, and are sent off as a 'bitstream' to the destination.

iv At destination the digital information is turned back into a wave form and becomes audible on the telephone.

v The device which turns the analogue wave into a digitised bitstream is called a **modem** (a modulator/demodulator). The system is called 'pulsed-code modulation' and at destination another modem converts each pulse back into speech. By clever devices it is possible to send 2000 separate conversations over a single cable without getting them muddled – which requires 140 million bits of information to be sent every second.

The use of a bitstream to send information is not confined to the human voice. Every letter and every number in a piece of text can be digitised and sent as a stream of electronic information to any destination. Similarly any map can be digitised and transmitted. The effects of such miraculous developments are far reaching. For example, the law is slow to recognise anything but documentary evidence, although in recent years there has been some change in the direction of recognising electronic information as evidence in the courts. For example, the Carriage by Air and Road Act 1979 says that, if the consignor agrees, an air waybill – which recognises the acceptance of goods by an air carrier for carriage – may be replaced by a record in any other form (for example, on the memory banks of some computer). If the consignor does agree he/she may ask the carrier for access to the computer record. This has made possible the concept of DTI (direct trader input) of information to the computers of HM Customs and of various airlines and shipping companies.

A fax machine turns a document into a bitstream of information. It uses a transceiver (a device that can both transmit and receive bitstreams of information). The document is scanned by electronic eyes which 'read' the document as a collection of black and white spots, which are relayed in electronic form over the telephone lines. The receiving instrument at the other end turns the information back into an exact copy of the document. The process only takes 20 seconds to transmit an A4 document, which means documents can reach foreign customers, banks and customs houses long before even the fastest plane can deliver the goods. Fax is an abbreviation of facsimile (exact copy).

Now that we can see how information can be supplied to all the people who need to know it, it is time to look at the various services that can be offered to clients. By this term, clients, we mean anyone who needs the knowledge, perhaps an 'in-house' client like a marketing department or an accounts department, or an outside client prepared to pay for the use of our stored data (for example, our list of addresses).

First we must just recapitulate what we know about computers.

8.3   The characteristics of computers

Today computers are everywhere. In commerce, manufacturing, design, banking, investment, telecommunications, schools, colleges, the kitchen – even the nursery – we use computers every day of our lives.

The power of a computer lies in its ability to perform certain simple functions (basically, addition and subtraction) immeasurably faster and more accurately than a human being can. Because of this enormous speed of operation a computer can be programmed to do millions of calculations every second, and certain activities like book-keeping and accounting are made very simple as a result.

Computers began as huge machines powered by thermionic valves and needing large inputs of power. Later, transistors replaced valves as a means of controlling electron flow, and later still the silicon chip was developed as the basis for an integrated circuit, the equivalent of a computer on a single chip of silicon.

There are three main types of computer, mainframes, mini and micro-computers. Mainframes were the original computers, large machines with a very large memory capacity and backing store. They are still widely used, but mainly for very large organisations which serve a very wide area with 'client server' facilities. The main argument in favour of mainframes serving large numbers of clients is that the software updating is in the hands of the finest programmers in the world and the need to update the software being used by millions of PC users is avoided. Mainframe computers provide centralised updating and data back-up. Their wide area networks (WANs) are the basis of the Internet (international network).

Mainframes were followed by mini-computers. They cost about £50 000 and could do all the things that mainframe computers could do. Where we need a very large computer these days a mini will usually do all we require.

Today the vast majority of computers are personal computers (PCs). These are micro-computers, which use VLSI circuits. VLSI stands for very large-scale integration with complex patterns of circuits on silicon chips. There are many qualities of PC but even the smallest of them will carry out most of the work required by a small business. The larger PCs will do most of the work required by a large firm, especially if a local area network is set up. This is explained later.

Hardware and software

A business that is thinking of buying a computer system has to consider both the machine required (often called the hardware) and the instructions or programs (software) that are needed to run them, and which tell the computer exactly what it has to do. Whatever the size of the computer the underlying principles of the equipment remain the same. We have to feed information (under the general term, data) into the machine by some sort of input device. This data then has to be processed (data processing) by means of a program of instructions. Finally, the results have to be put out of the machine in readable form by some sort of output device. The essential components are shown in diagrammatic form in Fig. 8.2.

Input devices

As the diagram shows, these are of many types, and include the following.

Punched cards and paper tape
The earliest types of input devices were punched cards and paper tape inputs and these may still be met, especially in companies using large mainframe computers. They are relatively slow methods of input. It is possible to process about 1500 cards per minute, with 80 characters per card, or 1000 characters per second on paper tape. They are read by bands of photo-electric cells which pick up light through the holes and pass the data in a machine-readable form to the computer.

Terminals
Today the terminal is the chief way to communicate with a computer. A terminal consists of a keyboard which acts as an input device and a visual display unit which acts as an output device. Thus in accounting, a question asking the computer to search and find a particular account will lead to its display on the screen of the VDU. This may enable the terminal operator merely to note the state of the account, or it may be necessary to update the computer's records by adding a further charge or recording settlement of the account. Any such alteration to the account will usually be the subject of safeguarding actions before the change is made. For example, keying in an instruction 'Delete £50 (cheque received)' may be met by a statement on the screen:

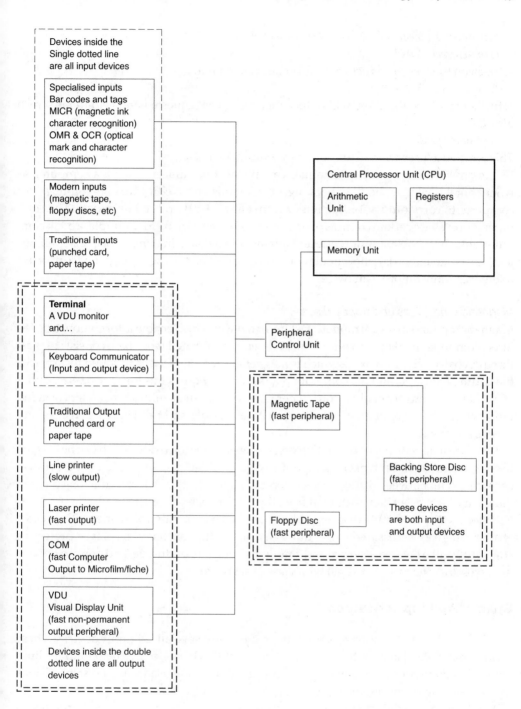

Fig. 8.2   A typical (generalised) computer configuration

You are asking me to reduce Smith & Co's debt by £50.
Is this correct   Y/N?

A touch on the Y key produces a double-check statement:

Are you sure   Y/N?

A further touch on the Y key will reduce the account as requested and lead to the screen display:

Next entry please

This is called a 'user-friendly' program in computer circles.

It is possible to have many terminals capable of communicating with a computer, as where hotel bookings, holiday bookings, bank cards and credit cards are 'on-line' to a computer to carry out various activities from conveniently placed terminals. The computer will exercise certain controls over the activities concerned - for example, a bank computer will check the amount requested against the balance in hand. It will also remove 'hot' cards (stolen cards) from circulation, and cards whose 'owner' has given an incorrect reference number more than twice.

Magnetic tape, discs and floppy discs

Magnetic tape and discs are modern fast input devices which enable information to be fed into a computer quicker than with punched cards or punched tape. Tape consists of plastic tape, coated with iron oxide which is magnetic. Each character is in coded form across the width of the tape, and the computer reads them in sequence as the tape passes. About 1600 characters are normally recorded per inch with about 45 million characters on a full tape, which can be read at about 180 000 characters per second. Higher densities and speeds are possible.

Discs are magnetic packs of rotating discs, coated with iron oxide which can be magnetised to record data. Each pack has about 12 double-sided discs with about 800 tracks to each disc, with between 8 and 20 blocks on each track. Each block can store one piece of data, which can be written to or read from the block by a read – write head.

A floppy disc is a single disc of flexible material coated with iron oxide, with a read – write head given access to the disc through a slot in the cardboard or plastic protective cover. They give between 640 000 and 2 million characters of storage, and one can have as many discs as one wishes, to deal with various sets of records.

Specialised input devices

Besides the devices mentioned above, there are many specialised input devices. These include **bar codes** (such as the one on the cover of this book), a unique pattern of lines which the computer can read through a light pencil. They are used to record sales of stock for stock-taking purposes, the issue of library books, and so on.

MICR (magnetic ink character recognition) is achieved by printing number codes on items like cheques, paying-in slips, and so on, which can then be read by the computer. When a cheque is made out it already has all the account details printed on it, and the only part not printed in magnetic ink is the amount of the cheque written in by the drawer. This is encoded in the branch by the keyboard operators, before the cheque details are read, so that the message read from the cheque by the magnetic ink character reader includes the account details and the amount to be paid. The cheque can now be cleared electronically through BACS (the bankers' automated clearing service).

OMR and **OCR** inputs refer to **optical mark recognition** and **optical character recognition**. These are methods of reading examination papers and other documents electronically. For example, in multiple-choice examination papers the student ticks a particular box which is believed to be the correct answer. This tick reduces the light being reflected from the paper and the box ticked can thus be detected. If it is a correct answer the computer gives the student a mark for it.

The processing of data

The computer itself is called the **central processor unit** or **CPU**. It consists of a control unit, an arithmetic and logic unit and a main memory or main storage. The stages of processing are as follows:

1 The appropriate program is 'loaded' into the main memory from storage, either in the backing store discs or magnetic tapes associated with the computer or from a floppy disc through a disc-drive unit.
2 The current data situation for the program concerned is then also loaded. Thus with a payroll it would be the situation on the last payday; all the personnel files of employees, pay to date, PAYE (pay as you earn) codes, and so on. This would either be in the backing store or on a separate floppy disc called the 'data disc'.
3 The new data to be processed would then be input. It might be keyed in individually from a keyboard or, if this had been done earlier in batches and stored, this stored material either on tape or disc, would be fed in.
4 The control unit would now carry out the program, at speeds of between 5 and 12 'mips'. The word mips stands for 'million instructions per second'. At this enormous speed the computer reads the instructions one at a time, designates some part of the arithmetic or logic unit to carry out the instruction and stores the various results ready to be put out.

The detailed procedures by which an instruction is read, data values are loaded into the arithmetic unit, the calculation is performed and the results are unloaded and stored at an appropriate 'address' in the main memory is too complicated for an introductory chapter of this sort, but at several million instructions per second an individual item is completed instantaneously.

Output devices

Once data has been processed and the results achieved, the 'output data' (unless it is required immediately for display on a VDU) will be held in main storage until a sufficient volume is available to present it to an output device. The output device may be a storage device which will preserve the data in electronic form (as where the revised payroll records are put out to a data disc for storage until required on the next payday).

Alternatively, it may be put out to a printer or other device which will convert the binary code into characters (letters and numbers) in readable form.

VDU outputs

These are instantaneous, non-permanent screen displays which can also provide hard copies if a printer is attached. The speed of response makes them ideal for certain activities like hotel bookings, home-banking services (which enable the customer to see his/her bank account on a domestic television set), airline reservations, and so on.

Printers

There are many different types of printer but their common feature is that they all produce the computer's results on paper, in legible form. The printout may be in the form of correspondence, tabulated statistics, invoices, statements of account, salary slips and many other documents. The types include line printers (which print a line at a time, usually of 132 characters and at speeds of up to 4000 lines per minute). Another type, the matrix printer, builds up the characters by printing a series of dots. They are slower than line printers, and print about 200 characters per second. A third type is the daisywheel printer, which has characters embossed on petals like a daisy. The daisywheel rotates until the correct character is in position. It is then struck through a ribbon on to the paper. Speeds are slow, about 90 characters per second (cps).

A more specialised printer is the thermal printer, which makes characters by bringing heated wires into contact with special heat-sensitive paper. There is no impact, so the printer is quiet, but the speeds are low, about 100 cps. Another type is the ink-jet printer, which sprays droplets of ink to make the characters and can be used to print several different colours. A laser printer is another non-impact printer capable of printing a whole page at a time. It is very fast, printing 200 pages per minute on the fastest machines.

Graph plotters

These are devices which are able to reduce the data to diagrammatic form, giving graphs, bar diagrams, pie diagrams, maps and drawings. Used mainly in the scientific and engineering industries, they also have business applications. Basically they consist of pens whose movement is controlled by computer programs.

COM

Computer output to microfilm (or microfiche) is a method of storing images on rolls or sheets of film. The reduction that can be achieved is such that up to 270 A4 pages can be held on a 6 x 4 inch microfiche sheet of film. Some of the main uses of COM are long-term records, for example library records, the records at Companies House, banking records of customers' account details and insurance records. The reduced images can be read in special viewers, which magnify the image to full size again. The viewers also permit copies to be taken from the full-size image concerned, so that, for example, customers at banks can be given a copy of statements when required.

8.4 The computer as a local area network (LAN)

While a computer has numerous uses in a small or medium-sized business as a stand-alone facility for payroll, purchasing, sales and similar aspects of business, its uses are enormously enhanced if it is available as a host computer in a network of terminals serving every part of a business. It is not stretching credibility too far to say that networks are altering the whole way businesses work and democratising the whole working environment. More of this later.

Fig. 8.3 gives a diagrammatic layout of a corporate network where a high quality computer acts as host to an extended pattern of terminals and input and output devices, most of which are on-line to the computer with immediate access to its memory. Others may not be on-line but results are queued to be output later, usually after normal working hours.

The diagram is largely self-explanatory, and can be extended to give everyone in the business access to a terminal so that everyone can interrogate the computer on routine matters, whereas more confidential matters can be made available by the use of passwords or codes. Such a network is called a LAN (local area network). They are often called corporate LANs, because they only apply to the company or corporation that set them up. They are a private network to keep in touch with branches, depots, etc.

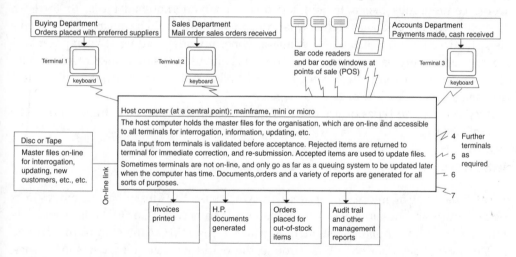

Fig. 8.3 A network of terminals around a host computer

When this LAN is extended to enable access to the corporate computer by customers, suppliers and logistical firms and companies, we have a much more extensive network. What was just a corporate facility becomes an 'electronic community' facility, where orders can be placed, the status of a job can be established by electronic enquiry, transport space can be reserved on ships and aircraft and clearance through Customs can be effected, all by computer-to-computer links. These sophisticated EDI (electronic data interchange) and DTI (direct trader input) systems have established the United Kingdom's leading firms in the forefront of European electronic practice. Such 'community networks' (the word does *not* refer to the European Community but to the 'electronic community') have become known as VANs (value added networks).

The trouble with VANs is that they take quite a lot of work to set up. If we are going to have other people sending messages to our computer we must be sure that our computer knows what the other computer is sending, which bits to receive first, and so on. We need to train staff in many new areas and once we have agreed on standards (for example a standard way of sending messages) everyone must stick by the standard adopted. The whole thing tends to benefit big companies rather than SMEs (small and medium enterprises) because (for example) we shall hesitate to change from a supplier who knows EDI to one who does not know his/her EDI even if the new supplier is cheaper. The safe thing is to use a supplier who is in the electronic community.

8.5   The Internet, intranet and extranet

LANs and VANs are all very well but in the modern world the globalisation of business calls for world-wide solutions rather than local ones, and even the wider electronic community that results from EDI, the VAN, is not a world-wide system. In the 1980s the electronic communities began to join together on an international basis, to form an international network. The Internet was born, but before it could be much use it needed a new standard format which would enable anyone, anywhere, sitting at a computer keyboard to access any part of the information data bank using a single link (interface) with the Internet. This eventually became the World Wide Web, with electronic pages of text and images rather like the pages of a magazine.

This led to three types of use of the Internet, as an intranet, an extranet and as the Internet itself.

Intranets

We are imagining an international company which has a LAN for its basic activities in its own country, and possibly also a VAN (value added network) for EDI (electronic data interchange) with suppliers, customers, logistical firms, HM Customs, and so on, around it. However it does not have links around the world with more remote subsidiaries, branches, suppliers and customers. It approaches an internet service provider (ISP) and asks for limited access to the Internet to operate an intranet. This is an internal corporate-controlled network using internet communications protocols and web-browser technology. The company (corporation) has full control over who uses its intranet, which is a private link between branches, subsidiary companies and head office. Head office can deny access to certain types of information by using passwords and codes, and the whole system is denied to all ordinary net-surfers. However it would be usual to have an external connection to the open Internet, through a secure link. This would give branches and subsidiaries an opportunity to browse the Internet for ordinary purposes.

The chief uses of an intranet are to make company information available to all branches, and subsidiaries around the world. Such information as policy changes, training programmes to meet skill shortages, product information, sales support, and so on.

Extranets

Now imagine a whole community of companies dealing with one another around the world and wanting to streamline their links by means of internet technology. They all know one another; they have proven creditworthiness stretching back over a number of years; they wish to exchange information about matters of mutual interest; to make binding contracts and make payments in a secure environment. An ISP will again make access to the Internet available to all agreed members of this community, using the agreed standard technology, which is TCP/IP. TCP stands for transmission control protocol and IP stands for Internet protocol. These protocols are international agreements reached between nations, and signed by the representatives of those nations, to make clear the best methods of sending electronic messages internationally.

The extranet is a more sophisticated organisation than the intranet, which can only reach down into the company itself for information, sales support, and so on. The extranet links a whole community of companies, who can buy and sell, pay for goods and services, reach into any company in the community to confirm the state of a contract, or the stage of manufacture of a bespoke product, and make secure payments without fear of interference from ordinary Internet users. The extranet is therefore like a VAN on a world-wide scale.

The Internet

Ignoring for the moment the use of the Internet to a company, it is a fact that millions of people world-wide are applying for access to the Internet with a view to sampling the information and entertainment that is available on the various web sites. Another chief reason for joining the Internet is to make use of the e-mail facility, which is free of charge apart from the cost of your local telephone call. A description of e-mail is given on page 209, so there is little point in repeating it here, but it was the original use of the Internet, as a forum for academics and technologists interested in keeping in touch with one another, relatively inexpensively. Since such messages travel at electronic speeds it is possible to hold virtual conversations with anyone around the world, though e-mail messages tend to be succinct, practical and down to earth. While e-mail will always be a major use of the Internet, the move to web sites giving company information, details of general-interest societies and non-profit-making organisations' activities has extended the network enormously.

Many companies and even family businesses find that it is essential to have a web site which can tell enthusiasts surfing the net about the products or services they offer. Even a presence on the web is worthwhile, but if this can be developed into an e-commerce centre trading on-line with customers around the world, it can be very lucrative. One family business selling smoked bacon had a turnover of £90 000 in 1997. After spending £1600 to set up a web site, its 1998 turnover was £750 000. Orders came in from as far afield as Peru, Japan and South Africa. Clearly a web site is a powerful marketing tool.

An essential part of orders achieved in this way is the need to ensure payment in advance by credit card. Overcoming the reluctance of customers to give their credit card details over the Internet is being achieved by SET credit cards (secure electronic transactions) and the 'secure merchant servers' system set up by some of the internet service providers. Secure merchant servers take over the procurement activities on their own private website; obtaining the card details over their secure links, not available to casual Internet surfers.

A new Code of Practice for secure elecronic commerce has been published by the British Standards Institution (BSI). BS 7799 'Information security management systems' is available in paper and electonric formats from DISC, part of BSI. BSI-DISC also manages a DTI-backed BS 7799 certification scheme known as 'c:cure' which offers independent certification of an organisation's BS 7799 system. The c:cure scheme uses independent auditors appropriately qualified in IT matters to approve the information security management arrangements of companies, relative to a risk assessment of the company's trading situation.

For more information visit http:\\www.c-cure.org or call BSI-DISC on 0208 995 7799 for a free information pack.

8.6   The effect of LANs and other networks on companies

In Chapter 2 we referred to the problems of the multidivisional company as it faced fierce competition from the emerging NICs (newly industrialised countries). Not only were the NICs able to take advantage of their low-cost labour forces and the keenness they displayed for a place in the industrial world, but they were also highly innovative and adaptable. They used the new technology with enthusiasm and devised new applications of it. By contrast, traditional industries in the industrial nations were unwilling to change over to computerisation from the smoke-stack industries which had served so well. Slowly the more alert industries began to dismantle their old plants, and to get rid of their middle-management layers of staff, but it took 20 years before the trickle of more entrepreneurial corporations became a flood. It was at this point that LANs began to be used, and their effect was to democratise the industrial process and do away with the hierarchical structure of the multidivisional companies.

If anyone can access the computer to discover the current situation on orders, goods in transit, and so on, anyone can handle the queries of outsiders that come in every day. Anyone can update a document which is waiting for a final statistic before it is sent across the world. We do not need people at higher levels to make routine decisions – there is no higher level than the computer, for it tells us the state of play.

When LANs became VANs, because the state of the computerised art enabled other firms and companies to access our computer to update documents and raise queries, and place orders and make deliveries, the whole organisation became more democratic. Every person was of equal importance, and grass-roots experience was just as valuable as top-level decision-making.

Finally, the move to global operations was solved by the use of Internet technology, to set up intranets and extranets. This carried the democratisation of industry into the international field. Every employee could be fully informed about the affairs of the company over the intranet, and every employee anywhere could act within the larger community of secure relationships provided by the extranet. Add to this the ability to surf the Internet itself (through a secure 'firewall') and to devise web sites for the World Wide Web and we can see that any employee is in a position to find new suppliers, customers and products.

The jury is still out on the success of information technology. There are, we are told, three views on the degree of success achieved. Some thought that the actual Internet technology would produce the great leap forward that had been so confidently predicted for humankind. They felt that business efficiency must improve if high-speed decisions, manufacturing output and improved logistical arrangements were made possible by the new technology. The second view is that technology is not everything and that even the most perfect systems will not help if the company is weak and insensitive in its approach to suppliers, customers, the financial sector and associates of every sort. We have to be clear what the data is telling us, and quick to respond to it. We need to avoid wasteful repetition of analytical work – there is no need to re-invent the wheel by endlessly pushing buttons to get almost identical results. The data has to be supported by good practices, turning information into action which is persevered with long enough to produce the results envisaged.

The third group recognise that both good systems and good practices in applying the knowledge provided by them are only likely to be successful if the people in the company have really understood and whole-heartedly support the change to a full IT technology. People can still keep their own counsel about the true situation, still safeguard their own positions, still genuflect in the direction of the new technology but innovate very little and care about innovation still less. 'Tell me what to do and I'll do it' is an attitude that can all too often be held, and falls far short of a 'new enterprise' culture.

The many take-overs and mergers, soon to be followed by de-mergers and management buy-outs, illustrate the problems. There is little point in taking over a company if you do not know what to do with it when you have got it, and eventually sell it back to the people who used to run it, and do know its ethos. The real wealth creators in the future will be the people who understand the technology, the good practices that follow if the technology is to be of real benefit, and can lead a company charismatically to make and distribute better products and services world-wide.

Security aspects of IT

Information technology presents many security problems and both specialist IT staff and the Chief Administrative Officer of a company have an interest in ensuring that routine precautions are taken. The value of computers alone (especially the latest items which are often in short supply) makes them vulnerable to theft. Even more the loss of a computer which has stored in its memory many aspects vital to normal business activities can be a real burden. It is essential to take back-up copies of this data at frequent intervals so that any losses will mean only the last day or so's entries need to be repeated. The back-up copy will restore the rest.

With a network which gives access to the computer from a number of terminals there is the risk that someone may do serious damage to our records. The most likely person is a disgruntled employee, and it is usual when personnel leave a department for any reason, such as dismissal, redundancy, etc to refuse them access (even to collect their personal belongings). Clearly the wider the network the more chance there is of some malpractice occurring. Thus with a VAN, or an intranet or an extranet there are outsiders who can reach into our computer for legitimate purposes such as direct trader input (DTI) or electronic data interchange (EDI). A disgruntled employee or a disappointed trader seeking revenge on someone for some perceived grievance may do us serious damage incidentally.

When a company has a permanent connection to the Internet, with a leased line and the internet service provider giving access 24 hours a day, the risks are much greater. The usual aim of an interloper would be to obtain credit card details, but there are many cranks who may wish to gain access to other details. Some individuals, known as hackers, break into private circuits to get secret information, for example industrial espionage is quite common. An even more unsavoury practice is sheer mischief making – electronic vandalism, for example by injecting viruses to destroy data or cause disruption. The mere threat of such a virus has been used to blackmail major enterprises such as banks; the hacker demanding ransom money. A number of anti-virus programs are available.

A major source of problems in the modern electronic office is the misuse of the internet and e-mail systems by staff. There should be a clear policy on e-mail and internet use, and it should be formally set out and distributed to all existing staff. It should also be a distinct element in any induction programme and new staff should be required to sign a declaration that they have read the policy and accept compliance with it as part of their conditions of employment.

Some of the chief abuses are:

a Searching for pornographic or sexually explicit material, and saving 'screen saver' images of any sort of offensive material.

b Downloading of software for other than business purposes. Where software is downloaded, all licensing requirements must be complied with and payment made.

c Careless wording of e-mails and of attachments to e-mails can give rise to legal action for libel, or for harassment or abuse infringing laws on race relations or other discriminatory practices. Such offences could be used in complaints to tribunals of various sorts, since they show a climate of discrimination in the company concerned. Care in wording e-mails is essential.

d Most states have enacted legislation on computer misuse, and often they require employers to institute a monitoring system to discover inappropriate or fraudulent use of terminals.

e Finally, use of terminals for non-business purposes wastes time, adds to the general costs of internet systems and overloads systems. Administration officers should do their best to discourage such activities.

9 Personnel department

9.1 The need for staff

Every business needs staff. Even sole traders cannot do everything for themselves and need to employ staff, even if only on a part-time basis, supplemented by freelance services from outsiders who are not, technically speaking, employees but independent contractors. As firms and companies grow, it is the number of staff employed which is the usual measure of size. The Bolton Report in the 1970s, which reported on the small firm, was empowered to investigate and hear evidence from firms employing 200 or less employees. This does not seem very small in today's climate, when about 1000 firms are being established each week by sole traders under various 'Business link' schemes, most of them with no employees at all. Larger firms employ very large numbers of people – the largest employer in the United Kingdom, set up in 1947, was the British Transport Commission with 900 000 employees. It proved to be hopelessly unwieldy and by 1953 was in the process of being broken up, a process which is still continuing even today with the privatisation of further sectors of transport.

In large firms the department charged with securing staff for the organisation is the personnel department. Its function is to secure for the firm or company such staff, with such skills and abilities, as are required from time to time. There is a popular misconception that the personnel department is a sort of welfare department, whose function is to take care of employees and be solicitous of their general welfare. This is not really the case, except that it is hoped a personnel department will always do what it can for an employee with a problem. The true function of the personnel department is to serve the organisation and achieve its general objectives. Thus at times the personnel department might be more concerned with shedding labour than recruiting it, and in many other ways it may act against an employee who for some reason is not in tune with company objectives. The disciplining and, if necessary, dismissal of staff is a major function of the personnel department. Equally the recruitment and induction of staff, the training and retraining of staff are major activities, and play a vital part in its work of ensuring that the organisation is never starved of labour of the right types and qualities. Promotion within the firm is usually a desirable feature of personnel policy and the personnel department must regularly review the development and progress of staff, so that future executives are being developed to take over responsible posts which become vacant through natural wastage, retirement, death or transfers out to other businesses.

9.2   The functions of the personnel department

We may list the functions of the personnel department as follows:

1   To secure for the organisation staff with such skills and experience as are required from time to time, to ensure that the organisation is never starved of the human resources it needs to carry on its varied activities. This involves a recruitment and selection procedure which ensures that staff of the quality required are made available at wages and salaries which are economic, and reflect an employee's value to the organisation. As part of this main function the personnel officer would draw up with senior management a general personnel policy aimed at securing harmonious and cooperative pursuit by all ranks of the general objectives of the organisation. This idea is developed later in this chapter.

2   To induct new staff by a proper induction procedure so that they are aware of their duties and responsibilities, and particularly of any health and safety aspects arising from their employment.

3   To keep records upon and monitor progress made by staff, giving help and encouragement where required to develop each employee's skills and understanding of the organisation's work. This includes some element of training, both in-house and by part-time education and training elsewhere, as part of a 'grow your own' management development programme.

4   To ensure compliance with the law in respect of all legislation bearing upon employment, including health and safety at work, conditions of employment, payment of wages legislation, and so on.

5   Participation in all matters relating to wage negotiations, joint consultative committees and similar bodies where these exist, and the furtherance of arrangements designed to secure harmonious labour relations.

6   Dealing with difficulties which arise within the labour force, such as improper or irresponsible behaviour, the cautioning of staff, disciplinary procedures and, where necessary, dismissal of staff.

7   Acting on behalf of management in devising schemes of redundancy, early retirement, and so on, where these become necessary. If redundancy can be avoided by retraining, the personnel department will devise schemes to assist orderly transfer of staff to new types of employment. A general supervision of pension arrangements may be part of this area of responsibility.

8   Various types of welfare activities may be carried out, particularly where bereavements or major illnesses requiring termination of employment call for assistance to the families affected. There will usually be clubs for social or recreational purposes to be supervised, and canteen facilities may also come within the personnel officer's span of control.

We must now study each of these general activities in greater detail.

9.3 A personnel policy

At times of full employment the personnel officer puts a telescope to his/her eye and scans the far horizon for staff with the required skills and abilities. At times of mass unemployment it is the employee who puts the telescope to his/her eye and scans the horizon for employment opportunities. In developed countries with an established social security system, even at times of high unemployment the employee may not search the horizon quite so diligently, for securing employment has ceased to be a matter of life or death, however unpleasant unemployment may be. Even the long-term unemployed will not take up work unless the pay is an adequate recompense for the efforts made and the personnel policy of the employer is favourable, or even generous. It follows that even in times of high unemployment devising a personnel policy which offers attractive rewards to staff is still essential if a firm is not to be starved of willing, able and cooperative employees. What are the characteristics of such a personnel policy? They include the following.

Remuneration

The employer requires employees with a variety of skills and abilities, and at as economical a price as possible. However, the costs of acquiring staff are great (many advertisements in local and daily newspapers cost hundreds of pounds) and a policy of paying the lowest rates possible will mean a heavy turnover with consequent disruption and expense. A sound personnel policy will therefore envisage paying at least the rate for the job, and possibly a little more, with regular reviews and merit rises designed to ensure that reliable staff stay with the organisation. We do not live in a crudely capitalist world, but in a world where developed capitalism has widened the scope of ownership of businesses and has meant that the ruthless entrepreneur (Charles Dickens' Iron Gentleman ruthlessly pursuing profit) has been replaced by a corporation which pursues 'management-satisfying' policies. Few boards of companies wish to be known as ruthless exploiters of their employees, but prefer a quiet life offering a reasonable standard of living to all who genuinely pull their weight in the organisational boat. Such policies, which avoid industrial unrest and lead to steady output and endeavour by all ranks, may well be cheapest in the long run.

Security of employment

The average employee is family orientated, and family life requires a certain degree of stability. Security of employment is therefore of great importance to most people. Economists have called labour the 'immobile factor' for it is difficult to uproot labour and move it to a new site because of the family commitments and other roots it has put down into the local community. A sound personnel policy aims to offer secure employment to all staff who work well and do their utmost to advance the organisation's activities. In particular, unfair dismissal or arbitrary behaviour by management or supervisory staff may lead to perverse 'bloody-minded' behaviour by employees in return.

Advancement and self-realisation

We have already seen (see section 2.4) that approval by the workforce of management policies is most likely to occur where the individual is able to achieve self-esteem, the esteem
of others and a large measure of self-realisation in the working situation. This requires the
individual to have the chance of self-advancement within the firm, where a general policy
of promotion from within should be pursued except in circumstances of an unusual
nature. For example, occasions may arise when there is no logical successor to a particular individual, perhaps because the logical successor has been 'head-hunted' away by a
rival firm. Another example would be where the existing staff had become too inbred after
years of internal promotions, and it is felt that an infusion of new blood from outside is
desirable.

'Promotion' in this context does not necessarily mean elevation to a higher rank, since
this is not possible in many jobs of a fairly routine nature. Where an employee of poor ability is doing a very routine job, which is repetitive and would perhaps be boring to another
employee showing greater initiative, it is still necessary to recognise that person's contribution to the firm. Such a person can be just as difficult to replace as a managing director.
There are people who take pride in being a small cog in a big machine, and if they are
absent the machinery still stops. For such a person all the 'promotion' needed may be an
annual review of the job, a word of appreciation and a merit rise or bonus payment. The
important point for many employees is that their work is appreciated and that their view
of any aspect of it is important to management and will be taken into account.

For other people, promotion must depend upon increasing skill and experience, coupled with professional advancement through sound educational and training policies. It
cannot be too strongly emphasised that a management today that fails to encourage
younger members of staff to pursue full professional qualifications is doing both itself and
the nation a disservice. There is not enough real drive for professional qualifications in
industry and commerce today. Of course some of the professional staff thus generated will
inevitably go elsewhere for their promotion, but this is not necessarily a total loss to the
business. Wide contacts in other firms, especially with staff who remember the original
firm as their source of skill and experience, may bring worthwhile spin-offs at some future
date, and lead to new lines of work not envisaged earlier. Encouragement to take up professional training, much of which is carried out in the employee's own time, does not cost
much. It may mean little more than help with correspondence course fees or evening class
enrolment fees. Compared with the cost of wages for even one ordinary employee, the
sums involved are negligible, and since training takes some years the labour force tends
to be more stable until full professional qualification is achieved (let alone full experience
in the practical affairs of the business).

Freedom from discrimination

In the last 25 years the United Kingdom Parliament has enacted a number of major anti-
discrimination acts of which the three most important are:
1 the Sex Discrimination Act 1975

2 the Race Relations Act 1976, and
3 the Disability Discrimination Act 1995.

Discrimination because of marital status is a fourth type of discrimination referred to in the above acts. Similar legislation exists in many countries.

Today the avoidance of discrimination of any type is an important aspect of personnel policy. For example, in racial discrimination and sex discrimination, a firm or company which does not employ a proper proportion of ethnic minorities on its staff or offer female employees equal job opportunities in the higher fields is automatically suspect. The locality in which the firm operates may influence the proportion that ought to be employed, but ideally the question of race or sex should not enter into the employment picture at all, and suitability for the post itself, qualifications, experience and potential should be the only criteria for selection. Equality of opportunity, both in the selection procedure and after recruitment, should be constantly of concern to the personnel officer and the board, so that justice is not only done, but is seen to be part of personnel policy at all levels. Proper appeals procedures should exist and be widely publicised and incorporated into written conditions of service.

While the Disability Discrimination Act is clearly an act which will apply to many employment situations, it goes wider than that. For example, access to premises by disabled people is a matter of concern to all disabled people, whether they are employed on the premises or not. Those who supply goods, or services, or facilities of any sort must make arrangements to meet the needs of disabled people unless they can show that refusal to do so is justified. The wide range of such services includes access to many different places, means of communication, means of transport, accommodation, banking, insurance, loans, credit or finance, entertainment and the services of any profession, trade, local authority or public authority.

The many rules and regulations about such matters are a study in their own right and a good source of information is Croner's *Reference Book for Employers*, which is available in most libraries, or by subscription.

Fair treatment

Today in the UK a considerable legal apparatus exists to ensure that employees are protected against arbitrary dismissal by employers. Alleged unfair dismissals can be brought before an industrial tribunal. Representation at such tribunals and the preparation of a defence can be quite expensive to an employer, and it is better to avoid such hearings if at all possible. Certainly evidence of the existence of fair arrangements about dismissal procedures is the best rebuttal of claims about unfair dismissal. The basic requirement is that the laws of natural justice should have been followed. The two main rules of natural justice are:

1 the rule against bias: no-one should be a judge in his/her own case, and
2 the right to a hearing.

The rules will generally have been met provided there is some right of appeal to senior management against the allegedly unfair dismissal, and the employee has had a full opportunity to explain the case from his/her own point of view, or has been allowed to be represented by a friend or colleague, trade union representative, and so on. There will be less question of unfairness if an employee has been warned on previous occasions that similar behaviour was not approved of and might lead to dismissal. In general, summary dismissals should not be made except for the most serious offences, theft of money or stock, serious assaults on other workers, and so on. In all other cases the employee should be given a chance to state a defence and should be warned about the consequences of any repetition. Formal notice of intention to dismiss should be given if persistent misbehaviour, unpunctuality, absenteeism, and so on, occurs. Policy on these matters should be published and drawn to the attention of all staff.

The right to a hearing embodies several points: a right to know the nature of the complaint; a right to prepare a defence in advance of any hearing; a right to be heard; a right to be represented if necessary; and a right to know not only the decision made, but the reasons for the decision. Generally speaking a breach of natural justice makes the decision taken by management ineffective; the employee is entitled to reinstatement and if this is refused considerable compensation will be payable.

Codes of practice on industrial relations

The industrial relations scene has changed considerably in recent years, due to government legislation introduced to curb the abuse of powers by trades unions themselves. Initially designed to reduce the exploitation of working people by unscrupulous entrepreneurs, the trade union movement in some areas became an arbitrary power in its own right, to such an extent that managements have in some situations been quite unable to manage, and whole industries have collapsed because of their inability to react and adjust to new situations in a competitive world. The position now is that firms and trades unions act within a tight framework of employment law. Where an established trade union does act reasonably and management can, through some sort of joint consultation procedure, draw up a code of practice acceptable to both parties, this is much the best procedure. Under the Employment Act 1988 the Secretary of State may take steps leading to the issue of codes of practice in certain areas of industrial relations, for example about the conduct of union elections and ballots, or about disciplinary action against members acting in good faith in alleging union misconduct.

9.4   Human resource planning

Having a clear policy on personnel matters is important, but it then has to be turned into a practical exercise in human resource planning. From an initial small labour force in a firm which is struggling to establish itself, the organisation grows to fulfil the many functions and activities which expansion requires. The expansion is difficult to predict, and growth may not be uniform and rounded. Certain areas may grow faster than others. Human resource planning seeks to anticipate growth and ensure that the right numbers and types or staff are developed or recruited; that back-up personnel are trained to ensure continuity should a particular key member of staff leave, or die, or be promoted to a new post.

Failure to meet the plan may reveal that there are certain areas where high labour turnover presents problems and the causes may need to be investigated. Such a personnel plan serves as a reference point against which recruitment, training programmes, promotion and succession programmes can be examined.

The elements of human resource planning are:

1 *Review the existing situation* Does it meet present needs, and can we pinpoint any weaknesses? Are the various jobs in each sector of the business clearly delineated and graded, and are staff regularly reappraised for performance?
2 *Assess the future situation* Does it lead us to believe that the present system will be able to meet the future objectives? If not, where are the likely shortcomings to be revealed? Can we train people to meet the future requirements while we still have time?
3 *Draw up a plan of the future organisation* Whatever the changes envisaged, determine the detailed staffing requirements and ponder who will be occupying the key posts, and who will be filling the subordinate posts if staff changes do not occur.
4 *Make detailed plans for training staff* This can be an element in raising morale, because it sounds out people for possible future promotion. It gives them a chance to think about their future, starts them off in seeking self-improvement, develops company loyalty and equates future staff requirements with skills, abilities and experience. Where there is no existing employee capable of being trained into the required category, the shortage should be noted and, at the most suitable moment as the need becomes urgent, the post should be advertised.

Human resource management

Human resource management, formerly referred to as the human relations movement, seeks to achieve the harmonious growth (or contraction) of the labour force so that both the staff and the company suffer the minimum of disturbance while at the same time achieving as close a fit as possible to perfection between staff required and staff available. Human relations enter into almost all the changes made in an organisation, but they are often not considered early enough, especially in such situations as acquisitions and mergers. If the personnel officer has established as routine the retraining of staff whose situations may be expected to change due to business fluctuations, the climate of employment within the firm will be one that is favourable to change. Change should be seen as inevitable, but rarely critical in its effect on staff. When a situation such as an acquisition or merger takes place, the envisaged situation must be fully appraised from the human resource management viewpoint.

A detailed list of areas for concern should be drawn up for both the parties concerned. To what extent will the workforce change and what kinds of staff will need to be retained? How shall we prevent vital staff leaving just because they are uncertain of the situation? What level of redundancies can be expected and what will be the cost of such settlements? Will voluntary redundancies solve the situation, or will some measure of compulsory redundancies be inevitable? Open communication will reduce rumours and may have helpful side effects (such as the early departure of those who realise their situation is insecure, the willingness of others to retrain for jobs that will be needed, the avoidance of discrimination procedures, and so on).

Acquisitions and mergers do not always succeed, and failure to appreciate the human resource problems is often a chief cause. Legal actions alleging an absence of 'due diligence' are common. Such an action alleges that one party did not do its utmost to reveal the true situation to the other party, who was consequently misled into making an acquisition which would not have been made if the full facts had been known.

9.5   Employee records

Every personnel department needs a comprehensive set of records on each employee. The best thing to do is to use one of the sets of employee records available commercially at reasonably economic prices. The examples used in this section are taken from the set of employment forms produced by Chancellor Formecon Ltd, Gateway, Crewe CW1 6YN, whose permission to reproduce them is gratefully acknowledged. Some idea of the comprehensive nature of the forms available is given by the following list, which covers all the problem areas usually to be met in personnel management. Although the forms referred to necessarily reflect United Kingdom practices, readers elsewhere will find them interesting. Chancellor Formecon Ltd would be interested in licensing their use in translation, or adaptation, to suit the needs of other nations.

Recruitment
The aim of recruitment is to select the 'right person for the job' but we must not discriminate against applicants on the ground of sex, marriage, race or religion. It is also an offence to employ anyone who does not have permission to work in the UK. A detailed set of records is essential for recruitment.
FS30   Pre-recruitment job description and person specification
FS31   Document wallet for job application
FS33   Application for employment – concise version
FS34   Application for employment – extended version
FS35   Occupational health – medical assessment
There are eight further forms in this recruitment range.

Employment
The Employment Rights Act 1996 and other acts require employers to observe many rules about the rights of employees. Careful records using the forms listed below will ensure compliance with these Acts of Parliament.
FS52   Employee's induction checklist
FS55   Employee training history record
FS63.1 Contract of employment – principal statement
FS63.2 Contract of employment – supplementary statement
FS64   Changes to particulars of employment
FS65   Standing statement and authority to deduct from wages
There are fifteen further forms in this employment range.

Absence and attendance
Absence may be authorised, in which case the employer can take steps to cover the work of the absentee. Unauthorised absence causes resource and administrative problems, disruption of the work of others and a general loss of efficiency. Good records are essential and a system of self-certification is required under the Statutory Sick Pay regulations(SSP).

FS80   Record of hours worked
FS83   Attendance record card
FS84   Timekeeping monitor
FS85   Employee holiday record
FS121   Self-certification of sickness and absence
There are six further forms in this range.

Discipline and grievances
We show discipline when we observe rules and procedures. Employers must acquaint staff with the rules they have laid down and the procedures to be followed for conduct, safety, attendance, and so on. When grievances arise they can be met by reasonable discussion, and possible relaxation of the rules. The following forms assist in record-keeping about any such matters.

FS 700   Record of grievance or disciplinary matter
FS701   Grievance procedure notice
FS703   Employer's disciplinary procedure
FS704   Employer's disciplinary investigation
There are seven further forms in this range.

Statutory maternity pay (SMP)
Forms to acquaint women staff with the rules about SMP, and to document the procedures as the months pass, are:

FS151   Employee SMP data card
FS152   SMP – notice to female employees
FS153   Notification from employee of maternity absence
FS154   Details of entitlement (to employee)
FS155   Maternity absence and returning to work
There are eight further forms in this range.

Statutory sick pay (SSP)
In former times employees who were sick were not paid wages, but instead received a cheque from National Insurance for 'sick pay'. Then it occurred to some bright civil servant that as employers were deducting tax under the PAYE system from the employees' wage packets and holding it for the government, some of this money could be used by the employer to pay the 'sick pay' on behalf of the government. Statutory sick pay was born. The following forms keep track of SSP.

FS111   Employee SSP data folder
FS112   SSP Notice to all employees
FS113   SSP Entitlement check – flowchart
Note: two new forms of statutory pay, Statutory Paternity Pay (SPP) and Statutory Adoption Pay (SAP) were introduced in the United Kingdom on 6 April 2003.

Redundancy

Redundancy leads to many problems. Often in the past the person made redundant could claim discrimination on many grounds: age, sex, racial origin, handicap, and so on. Compliance with new laws calls for careful record-keeping, as the forms below indicate.

FS720   Redundancy procedure – guide for employers
FS721   Redundancy appraisal – data folder
FS722   Proposed redundancy – employee assessment
FS723   Proposed redundancy – notification to appropriate representatives

There are four further forms in this range.

Termination of employment

FS77   Employment termination – summary for employer
FS78   Employment termination – summary for employee
FS79   Leaving employment folder

These forms leave a tidy conclusion of employment on file, and eventually archived. Employees often write in, years later, for confirmation that they worked for the company, and as a matter of courtesy it is convenient if we can easily turn up their records.

Data protection

FS 410 A2 Data protection 'What you should know'
FS 411   Employee consent to process personal data
FS 412   Record and verification of personal data

Public Interest Disclosure Act.

An act to protect workers drawing attention to malpractices or wrongdoing at work.

FS 480   Employer's Guide to the Public Interest Disclosure Act
FS 481   Employer's policy and procedure
FS 482   Interview summary
FS 483   Protected disclosure data folder
FS 484   Initial response to discloser
FS 485   Investigation/inquiry summary
FS 486   Feedback to discloser

Working time regulations

FS 122   Night worker average hours calculation sheet
FS 123   Average working time (calculation sheet and monitor)
FS 124   Employee request to take paid annual leave
FS 125   Average 48 hour weekly limit, opt-out agreement
FS 126   Provision of health assessment for night worker
FS 127   Work force agreement
FS 128   Hours worked in other employment
FS 129 A3 The Working Time regulations

Clearly this is not a specialist book on personnel matters and it is not possible to illustrate all these forms here, but specimen copies or starter packs are obtainable from the publishers at the address given above.

The best form to illustrate at this point is the Employee Data Folder, which is shown in Fig. 9.1. It is larger than A4 size, so that it can contain all the records relating to an employee, which are usually printed on A4 paper. The front cover is illustrated in Fig. 9.1; the back of the folder includes a remuneration record (as increases in pay are awarded over the years), a bonus record, a disciplinary record, a maternity record, and a leaving interview record. The inside of the folder is a wallet, which holds all the forms on other aspects of the employee's records, the whole making a complete coverage from recruitment to leaving.

It cannot be too strongly emphasised that personnel records are confidential and must be kept safely, preferably in locked drawers which are not opened except for temporary removal for updating or return. Files should not be available to other staff, or be risked in any way (for example, by taking them home for work to be done out of office hours).

They do need updating from time to time, for such matters as changes of address, changing family circumstances, attachment of earnings by court orders, and so on. Such matters may be highly personal and it is important that personnel department staff observe strict confidentiality.

9.6   Recruitment

The personnel requisition

Just as the purchasing department is triggered into ordering goods by the receipt of a requisition from the department needing them, the personnel officer needs to know the details of staff required. A 'personnel requisition' requests the personnel officer to recruit staff. It includes details of the type of post to be offered, permanent or temporary, full-time or part-time, whether the post is additional to present staffing or a replacement for someone leaving or taking temporary leave of absence. The form includes a job description summary, which may be briefly expressed when it is one of the known existing categories of labour, or may be a detailed account of a new post to be offered. Since a detailed job description has to be sent out to applicants and may be needed to devise a suitable advertisement, it is often preferable for the requisitioning department to attach a full job description to the requisition form. The rest of the requisition form can be quite detailed, giving full particulars of the days and hours of work required, the possible overtime, the place of attendance, the experience looked for in the applicant, the professional or other qualifications looked for, whether the applicant should be able to drive and any special inducements offered, for example company car, pension scheme membership, and so on. All firms are required by law to employ a certain percentage of disabled people and if the post is considered suitable for such a person this should be stated, as it is preferable to fill the company's quota of such staff (or even overfill it) when an opportunity arises to offer suitable employment.

EMPLOYEE
DATA FOLDER

Ref./Works No.		FORENAME(S)
Date of birth		
/ /		

Place of birth
Town
Country

Ethnic

Nation

EMERGENCY CONTACTS

Name
Relationship to employee
Address

Home telephone
Work telephone
Name
Relationship to employee
Address

Home telephone
Work telephone

Personal Doctor
Name
Address

Tel. No.

Marita
Single
Marrie
Separa
Divorc
Widow

EMPLOYMENT DETAILS

Employment commenced on	/ /

Employment is
e.g. Indefinite, Fixed term, Temporary, Seasonal, Casual, Annualised hours, Job share

Childr
/
/
Other

Full-time (✔)	Part-time (✔)
Probationary period	

Period of Employment	From	/ /
	To (if fixed term)	/ /

Trade

Contract amendments	/ /	/ /
	/ /	/ /
	/ /	/ /
	/ /	/ /

Attach
From
To

DISABILITIES (tick any applicable to this employee)

☐ Blindness/has a visual impairment
☐ Continence problems
☐ Deafness/hearing impairment
☐ Dyslexia/learning difficulties
☐ Failure to perceive risk of physical danger
☐ Manual dexterity difficulties
☐ Mental health difficulties
☐ Mobility difficulties/wheelchair user
☐ Speech impairment
☐ Physical co-ordination difficulties
☐ Unseen disability, e.g. diabetes, epilepsy, asthma, MS, arthritis, heart condition
☐ Needs personal care support
☐ Has a disability not listed above
....

Date(s)	Job Title - Position	Section or Department	Reason
/ /			

CONFIDENTIAL – KEEP SAFE

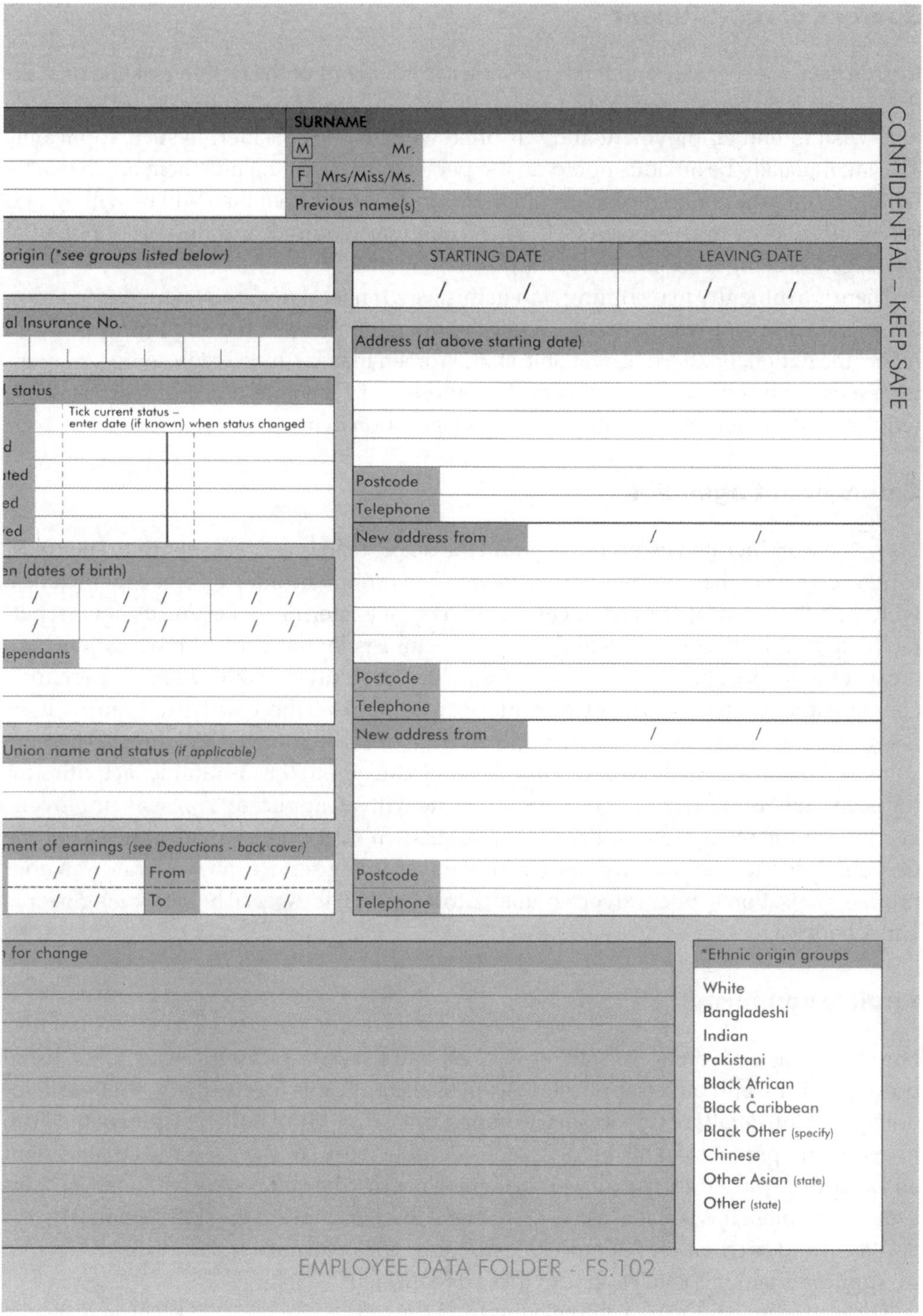

SURNAME

M Mr.

F Mrs/Miss/Ms.

Previous name(s)

CONFIDENTIAL – KEEP SAFE

origin (*see groups listed below*)

al Insurance No.

status

Tick current status –
enter date (if known) when status changed

d

ated

ed

ed

en (dates of birth)

/ / / / /

/ / / / /

lependants

Union name and status (*if applicable*)

ment of earnings (*see Deductions - back cover*)

/ / From / /

/ / To / /

for change

	STARTING DATE	LEAVING DATE
	/ /	/ /

Address (at above starting date)

Postcode

Telephone

New address from / /

Postcode

Telephone

New address from / /

Postcode

Telephone

*Ethnic origin groups

White
Bangladeshi
Indian
Pakistani
Black African
Black Caribbean
Black Other (specify)
Chinese
Other Asian (state)
Other (state)

EMPLOYEE DATA FOLDER - FS.102

Fig. 9.1 The Employee Data Folder (Courtesy of Formecon Services Ltd)

Sources of recruitment

Recruitment is expensive and if it is possible to find labour of the right type at no or at little cost this is obviously desirable. Frequently, existing staff may have relatives or friends who wish to find employment and it is often worthwhile considering such applicants. They will usually be anxious not to do the person who recommends them any harm by failing to fulfil the confidence placed in them, and to that extent they will be willing and cooperative. They must, of course, have the qualities required, and the sort of potential envisaged as being associated with the position offered.

There is a difficulty in recruiting staff in this way. If new staff are always recruited from the friends and relatives of existing staff the overall pattern of the employees may not reflect the national pattern of available staff. Women may be under-represented, or over-represented, and ethnic variety may not be represented. Personnel officers must bear these requirements under the equal opportunities legislation in mind.

Employment agencies

These have proliferated in recent years and the whole field is very competitive. They exist to relieve a firm of the laborious work involved in recruitment and are perhaps at their best when handling specialist recruitment. Thus an agency catering for fashion designers, pattern cutters, quality controllers and sample machinists for the fashion trades would take most of the work out of finding staff in this field. The result would be that only perhaps a couple of applicants would need to be interviewed, since all those with irrelevant skills or the wrong sort of interests or experience would have been eliminated and directed to more suitable positions. A higher-level type of agency carries out 'head-hunting' activities for top-level staff, undertaking not to communicate with an applicant's present employers, nor inform the head-hunting firm if one of its own staff applies. At another level the Careers Guidance Services, formerly a local government service, now operate as a non-profit organisation to offer careers guidance to all ages, with special help to young people and school leavers.

Application forms

For firms which advertise for staff, or just respond to applicants who write in, the usual procedure is to send out an application form to all applicants together with a job description giving full details of the job, salary offered, and so on, and a potted history of the firm, its work and prospects. This involves considerable work for the personnel department and also for the applicant since a well-designed form can be quite extensive – four A4 sides is quite common. It is usual to ask for references, both to confirm the skills claimed by the applicant and as character references. Testimonials from former employers are often sent by applicants and it is usual to return these if requested.

The responses have to be acknowledged and considered, and a list of applicants results who are then called for an interview. References need to be taken up and if these are called for by telephone a form is available in the Formecon series for conducting the enquiry.

Thus it is necessary to confirm that the applicant did work for the referee, that the circumstances of leaving were as stated in the application, that punctuality, health and so on were reasonable, and honesty above reproach. The final paragraph on this form notes the previous employer's general attitude towards the candidate, with choices which read 'enthusiastic, praiseworthy, noncommittal, discouraging, critical', and so on. Clearly a record of such a telephone enquiry is desirable and this 'Pre-employment reference enquiry by telephone' form is a useful aid.

Interviews for selection

Selection interviews are serious matters, for the selection of a totally unsuitable person is a great burden to any firm. It is extremely difficult to get rid of unsuitable people, and even an unsuccessful candidate can cause problems if sexual or racial discrimination is alleged. It is therefore important to prepare for an interview carefully beforehand and to have a panel of interviewers rather than a single individual. The candidates will equally be preparing from their point of view. Interviews are a two-way process. The employer wishes to confirm the claims made in his/her favour by the applicant on the application form, and to extend the investigation to assess the attitude, compatibility and potential of the recruit. The applicant wishes to discover fuller details about the terms of employment, the nature of the work, the scope of the employment in the future and, in short, whether the job is the right one for him/her.

A proper interview record should be kept, preferably by each member of the panel, and time should be allowed at the end of each interview for members to complete the record and write a short summary – especially if the recommendation is unfavourable – since these may be helpful in the event of any complaint. It is unwise for the chairman of the panel to seek to influence the other members into writing uniform reports since this would tend to indicate that the interview was loaded against the applicant. A set of frank, personal reports would indicate a more open-handed, fair treatment of the applicant.

During the interview, 'open' questions are best at giving the applicant a chance to speak up and make an impression on the panel. For example, the question 'Did you pass in mathematics?' is a closed question, the answer to which is yes or no. The question 'Do you think a knowledge of mathematics would be helpful in this clerical post?' gives the candidate a chance to be enthusiastic (or otherwise) about mathematical aspects of the job.

The purpose of selection interviews is to compare the candidates who have applied, not only with one another but with the job specification as given in the personnel requisition. If we have a bad bunch and we pick the best of them it does not mean that the requisitioning department will be happy; the new employee does not solve their problem. It is for the personnel officer to find the right kind of labour, not recruit inferior substitutes just because they present themselves. Re-advertising with an improved offer to attract better applicants may be necessary at times.

Appointment

Appointment is a formal process, and should always be put in writing even if it is offered orally and accepted at the end of an interview. The applicant may not get to the point of refusing the appointment until it is actually offered, being perhaps unable to make up his/her mind that this is not the job that he/she wants. The offer of employment finally convinces the applicant that the moment for a decision cannot be postponed any longer. A copy of the letter of appointment becomes part of the employee's records and the formal letter of acceptance makes a contract of employment between the parties (though in strict law the actual contract may have been made orally at the end of the interview).

9.7   Induction

Induction today is a slightly more formal procedure than in earlier times because the Health and Safety at Work Act 1974 has imposed a duty upon all employers to provide a safe system of work and to bring it to the attention of employees. The most vulnerable employee is the new arrival who has not had any chance to appreciate the layout of the plant or the potential hazards. It is essential that these hazards are mentioned at the induction session, which should take place either on the first day of employment or in an initial induction period before employment commences. The atmosphere should be formal, with the personnel officer dealing with the initial phases of the induction, welcoming the new employee(s), and dealing with major aspects of employment in the firm, the rules laid down by the employer, and so on. Later, he/she may yield the floor to more specialised personnel if the nature of the employment calls for instruction in safety regulations of a technical nature, hazardous materials, and so on. All the items dealt with should be listed on an induction check-list, preferably a two-part set, perhaps an NCR (no carbon required) form which the employee is required to sign at the end of the induction period as a recognition that all the points listed have been covered. One copy is retained by the personnel department and is filed in the employee's data folder; the other is given to the employee. Such a check-list is illustrated in Fig. 9.2.

The induction period should be concluded by a tour of the premises, and introduction of individuals to the members of staff who will be supervising them or acting as their closest colleagues. The location of all emergency exits, fire alarms, fire equipment, first-aid services, and so on, should be pointed out and any special features of the plant referred to earlier in the induction period should be referred to again at the appropriate points so that warnings or advice can be repeated *in situ* where they will be most meaningful.

L.AW

PERSONNEL MANAGEMENT

Employee
INDUCTION
Check List

Employer *(name of organisation)*	
EMPLOYEE SURNAME	
Forename(s)	
Dept./Section	
Employee Ref. No.	Employment start date

The object of induction is to help a new employee settle down into the job as soon as possible. It is important that information is given in a planned and systematic way to maximise the benefits to both the employee and the organisation.

Induction should commence on the first day of employment and be completed as soon as is practicable. The items shown in **bold print** are those which should be dealt with on the first day. Complete the form by entering the inductor's initials and the date alongside each item as the information or documents are given to the employee. If the induction is carried out by one inductor only and all on the same day, enter a tick in the 'initials' column alongside each item after it has been explained to the employee and complete the box 'Date induction completed' at the foot of the form.

	Initials	Date			Initials	Date
GENERAL — Explanation of induction procedure			**EMPLOYER'S Health and Safety Policy Statement**			
Introduction to manager/supervisor/colleagues			**Fire precautions, procedures and drills**			
Location of department/work area			**First-aid and accident reporting procedures**			
PERSONNEL — Employee details for personnel file			**Workplace security arrangements**			
Contract/Statement of Employment Particulars			**Risks to health and safety and protective/preventive measures**			
Staff handbook or other necessary written information			**Use and availability of personal protective equipment**			
PAY and BENEFITS — **Basic pay, additions, e.g. overtime, shift allowance pay etc. and deductions, e.g. PAYE, NI**			**Emergency procedures and escape routes**			
When and how paid and payslip format			**Smoking and Alcohol - rules/restrictions**			
Obtain P45, NI number, bank details			Reporting of health hazards			
Bonuses, commissions			Good housekeeping and tidiness			
Pension scheme, health insurance, savings schemes, company discounts			Safety officer/representatives			
Other benefits, e.g. social and recreational facilities			Health and safety training			
HOURS of WORK — Normal hours, lunch and other breaks			**JOB and ORGANISATION** — Job description and departmental information			
Overtime/flexible working arrangements			Security arrangements - cash, valuables, computers			
Timekeeping and recording procedures			Canteen/refreshment facilities			
TIME OFF — Arrangements/qualification			**Transport and parking arrangements**			
Application for time off/holidays and pay entitlement			**Use of company communications systems**			
Current commitments of employee			Company structure, quality management system(s), history, products and services			
SICKNESS — Sickness absence notification procedure			Performance appraisal, education, training and prospect of promotion			
Company sick pay arrangements			Trade union membership/recognition			
SSP entitlement and qualifying days			**TOUR of PREMISES** — Draw employees attention to the location of washroom facilities, cloakrooms, lockers, exits and			
RULES and DISCIPLINE — **Equal Opportunities Policy - employee responsibilities**			entrances, emergency and fire exits, fire alarm points and extinguishers,			
Employer's rules and procedures			first-aid points, canteen, prohibited areas, hazards, notice boards and any			
Disciplinary, grievance and appeal procedures			areas to which the employee will need to go in the course of his/her job.			
Periods of notice			Introduce staff in other departments with whom the employee will have personal or telephone contact.			

WHO TO CONTACT		OTHER IMPORTANT INFORMATION
Job Supervisor/Manager		
Personnel and Welfare		
First-Aid		

Signature for Employer	Employee signature	Date induction completed
Induction approved by	I have received the above induction training	/ /

Once signatures have been appended, pass the bottom copy of this formset to the employee and retain the original in the employees personnel file

Fig. 9.2   An induction check-list (Courtesy of Formecon Services Ltd)

9.8   Training

It has been said that every recruit to the British army has a potential field marshal's baton in his knapsack and, similarly, every new employee has the key to the managing director's desk available if he/she just works long enough and hard enough and acquires the wide range of knowledge and skills necessary. Training is very much part of personnel activities, and the personnel officer must be alert not only to the needs of the firm for labour of various types, but also to the abilities of the potential staff for future development. Not only must training and education be encouraged (and even insisted upon) but the types of opportunity to staff must be appropriate to their abilities and inclinations. The aim should be to develop each employee so far as possible, even if that means running some risk that they will move elsewhere.

Job training

This is the first requirement once an employee has been inducted. It starts at once, and need not at first be formal in any way. The process called 'sitting next to Nellie', where the employee is shown how to do particular tasks and then given some time to become skilled in the procedure, being checked and helped when in difficulty by an experienced supervisor, is still one of the best ways of learning simple skills. Rotation around the various jobs in a department or cost centre soon makes the employee a useful addition to the staff, and the wasted work and spoiled units of production are minimal if the supervisor is firm and encouraging. Some jobs require more formal training in an in-house training department. For example, one firm of international reputation in the colour film development industry has to train staff to work in total darkness. This requires special training which cannot really be picked up adequately by sitting next to an invisible work-mate.

Apprentice training

With apprentices who are learning a trade there is usually some combination of theory and practice. Formal instruction, and formal education, will usually be a part of this type of training, with skill tests and examinations to be completed from time to time. Recruits may be at several levels, graduate apprentices, student apprentices with good elementary educational qualifications joining to acquire professional status by part-time study, and craft apprentices learning a trade and taking day-release education at a local technical college as part of their apprenticeship.

Official policies on training

It is debatable to what extent training should be sponsored and the last quarter of a century has seen the abandonment of rigid training structures in many industries in the UK. The idea that an industrial training board financed by a levy on all the firms in an industry must ensure an improvement in training in any company that adopted the scheme has to some extent proved abortive. The levies raised costs in many industries already meeting severe foreign competition, and the courses provided were often irrelevant to many firms, who resented paying for training which yielded little result for them. Training for small businesses has in many cases been found to be most helpful when related to sound business advice from organisations such as the BusinessLink service. For example, if the business advice recommends changes to new technology and arrangements are then made for staff training to convert to computerised equipment, the results give an immediate impact upon the firm's prosperity and are seen to be worthwhile. Similarly, an area which has been insufficiently developed (usually marketing) may be pinpointed and managerial training and staff training to improve the neglected aspect can be introduced.

Management training

Eventually all skilled workers and qualified staff take on elements of managerial activity, usually beginning with minor supervisory duties leading to full supervisor status, and often with some responsibility for budgeting, cost control, documentation, and so on. Generally speaking, the drive for full professional status in any field eventually includes management training, for it is simply not possible to reach full professional status without moving up the hierarchy in any firm and taking on responsibilities of a management nature.

Generally, management training modifies the behaviour and drive of the trainee concerned, revealing his/her strengths and weaknesses as a manager. It points the trainee in new directions which it is hoped both satisfy personal ambitions and strengthen the company's ability to operate. This is achieved by providing for its planned management resources an individual of known ability whose work has been appraised during the training period and regularly thereafter – usually at six-monthly intervals – unrelated to merit awards or salary reviews.

9.9   Performance appraisal

In the section on job applications (see 9.6 above), reference was made to the use of **job descriptions**, now widely adopted as a helpful aid in personnel matters. The great benefit of a clear and detailed job description is that it requires the departmental head needing staff to set down a clear account of the work to be done by the member of staff concerned and to specify the standard of education, training or skill required. This is very helpful in deciding what rate of pay should be paid or what scale of salary the new recruit should receive. It is also helpful in enabling staff to see what jobs are comparable with other jobs, and thus clarify any situation where unfair discrimination is alleged. It also provides a standard against which appraisal can be made of the employee's ability as it develops, and this appraisal can be the basis for merit awards or ordinary increases of pay. However, experience tends to show that it is better to hold appraisal meetings at a different time from the annual 'pay increase' time, since the true purpose of the appraisal is wider than just a pay award decision.

Once again, it is helpful to use one of the published **performance appraisal forms**, and an **employee job performance self-appraisal form** is also available. The latter form is drawn up by the person being appraised (the appraisee) before the appraisal interview is held.

The purposes of a performance appraisal are:

1 To compare the job-holder's performance with the ideal performance described in the job description and assess his/her degree of success in meeting the requirements.
2 To the extent that the performance falls short of perfection, to identify the causes of the shortfall. Is it the job description that is inadequate or does the job-holder not have the necessary intelligence, skill or knowledge? What remedial action is called for?
3 To assess the employee's range of performance, for example productivity, reliability, compatibility with supervisors and colleagues, drive, determination, and so on. Where the appraiser records an unsatisfactory level of performance on any point there should be a space on the form for the appraisee to rebut the criticism or offer some justification for the shortfall in performance. This may bring to light an injustice not previously known to management, or a difficulty (either of a personal nature or due to some item of poor equipment, and so on) which was not appreciated.

The result of the appraisal is a summary, or set of conclusions, preferably followed by a clear account of future objectives. These should be signed by both appraiser and appraisee and should be photocopied for the appraisee. These future objectives would then be the starting point for the next appraisal in six months' time. The objectives outlined naturally bear upon the career development of the member of staff concerned, and could be instrumental in helping staff to see their future training and educational requirements in clearer perspective. There is one difficulty here – that appraisal is usually carried out by supervisory staff, not personnel staff. The supervisor or head of department may not have an overall view of staffing and may draw up objectives which would distort the pattern of employment in the firm. It is for the personnel officer, when these appraisal forms are returned for filing in employee data folders, to review the objectives set and, if these appear to be unsatisfactory in any way (for example, some heads of department may see all their geese as swans), to draw attention to a need for balance.

9.10 Promotion and transfer

Promotion is part of the general personnel policy discussed earlier. It must not only be fair, but be seen to be fair, so that generally speaking the main basis for promotion should be merit and ability. A difficulty immediately arises in certain industries where the tendency is for those people who have no skill to get promotion. Thus in hairdressing the persons who can cut hair with flair and artistry are in such demand that they are endlessly engaged in using their particular talents. It is the person who cannot cut hair who has the time to make the appointments, take the money, keep the books, and so on, and eventually become the manager. Such cases apart, promotion for any other reason than merit and ability is bound to cause discontent. Even where a promotion is fair, the filling of the vacancy to which several had aspired may cause the unsuccessful ones to leave now that their promotion prospects cannot be fulfilled. Some reassurance of those not selected or even of all staff before the interviews are held may reduce this tendency by making it clear that all staff's efforts are appreciated and valued. It is usually necessary to take seniority (length of service) into account, provided other factors do not override it. For example, in fairly routine situations length of service and experience may be given more consideration than in a situation where flair, or a particular type of skill, or experience in a new area of work, overrides the humdrum experience of longer-serving staff.

Opportunities should be given to all staff to reach the highest grade within their level of competence, which means that posts should be advertised widely in-house. Those not short-listed should be called in to the personnel department to be given an explanation, which will give them some hint for their future path to advancement, though the present occasion is deemed to be inappropriate.

Transfers (moves between departments) may be made for a number of reasons. First, the general review of personnel may indicate surpluses developing in one area and shortages in another. To meet the situation the most appropriate people should be asked to retrain, or move sideways if the work is within their present competence. A different situation arises where an employee requests a transfer, either because a particular area of work is found to be interesting or because of incompatibility with colleagues. Similarly, where a supervisor requests that an employee is transferred away there is a further series of considerations, and tact, diplomacy and a fair hearing of the employee's viewpoint are essential.

9.11 Termination and dismissal

Employment may be terminated by summary dismissal, by dismissal, by giving notice and by redundancy. The Employment Rights Act 1996 lays down all the rules about the individual rights of employees, and a code of conduct produced subsequently gives practical guidance on how these rights may be preserved. The code calls for all employers to have written rules and disciplinary procedures, copies of which should be available to all staff. The rules should state clearly the objectives of the disciplinary procedures, the types of conduct which are deemed unsatisfactory, and those types of conduct which are deemed serious misconduct and gross misconduct. The Formecon rules referred to earlier regard as 'gross misconduct', which merits instant dismissal, without any second chance, if proved, the following:

1 Clocking on or off for someone else.
2 Malicious attack on a fellow employee, or other person on the employer's premises.
3 Acceptance of bribes to the detriment of the employer or employees.
4 Falsifying time sheets or giving false information about your own or another employee's time records.

5 Unauthorised removal or possession of the employer's or fellow employees' property (theft).
6 Indecent or immoral behaviour.
7 Wilful destruction of the employer's property or sabotage of products.
8 Extreme cases of insulting behaviour on the employer's premises.
9 Wilfully endangering the life of any person.
10 Unauthorised disclosure of sensitive information (for example, contravention of the provisions contained in the Company Securities (Insider Dealing) Act 1985 or in the Data Protection Act 1998).

However, the disciplinary procedure provides that senior management will have discretionary powers over all disciplinary proceedings dependent upon special circumstances and the gravity of the offence, so that even summary dismissal for gross misconduct might be reduced to a final written warning, with summary dismissal for a subsequent offence.

The procedure is shown as follows:

	First occasion	Second occasion	Third occasion	Fourth occasion
Unsatisfactory conduct	Verbal warning	Written warning	Final written warning	Dismissal
Serious misconduct	Final written warning	Dismissal		
Gross misconduct	Dismissal			

In view of the likelihood of claims for unfair dismissal if the code of conduct is not adhered to, it is vital for administrators to proceed formally with all investigations and enquiries. These should take place without delay, but should be preceded by a calm collection of the facts on the day of the incident, or at the latest the next day. All statements should be made before several witnesses, including a friend or representative of the person whose behaviour is under investigation, and written statements should be drawn up which are agreed to be the facts as given. These will be used at the subsequent investigation, which will issue the appropriate warning or dismiss the employee. The employee has a right to appeal and to be represented at the appeal, which will be held before an adjudicator from senior management not previously involved. If this is not possible a panel of three persons will be appointed by the most senior manager present to act as adjudicators.

Redundancy

Under the Employment Rights Act 1996 redundancy is defined as a dismissal due to the fact that an employer has ceased to carry on the business for the purposes of which the employee was employed, or where the work available has diminished, or where the firm or company has relocated. An employer who proposes to make employees redundant is required to consult with any recognised trade union as soon as possible. If the numbers exceed 99 persons, the employer must start negotiations at least 90 days before the first dismissals take effect, giving the reasons for the redundancies, the numbers involved, the method of selection, and so on. A trade union which believes that persons to be made redundant are not covered by the method of selection may bring a complaint before an industrial tribunal. An employer must also notify the Secretary of State of a redundancy situation affecting 10 or more people at least 30 days before redundancies take effect, and 90 days beforehand if 100 or more are involved.

An employee who is made redundant or who is dismissed with or without notice in circumstances which appear to be related to redundancy is entitled to a redundancy payment. The amount is based upon length of service, and amounts to half a week's pay for each year of service from age 18 to 21, one week's pay for each year of employment from 22 to 40 years of age and 1.5 weeks' pay for each year from age 41 to 64. The rules about all these matters change from time to time. The only way to keep really up-to-date on such matters is to subscribe to a handbook such as Croner's *Reference Book for Employers*, which has monthly updates on all the changes affecting employment. It is sold by Croner Publications Ltd, Croner House, 173 Kingston Road, New Malden, Surrey KT3 3SS.

9.12 Industrial relations practice

Until the end of the 1970s the field of industrial relations practice was an expanding one. The power of trades unions had been enhanced to such an extent that it was almost universally agreed that co-partnership in industry between management and trade unionism was the only way forward for British industry. Legislation about trade union rights was advanced almost annually. Unfortunately it advanced at about the same pace as British industry declined and led to some serious soul-searching about whether there was a link between the two. This is not a specialist book about industrial relations and cannot attempt either to review the evidence about the increased influence of trade unionism in recent years or to draw any conclusions about the decline of British industry in the 1970s or its partial recovery in the 1980s. What is clear is that there is much to be said for the advances which trade unionism has achieved in the standard of living of British workers in the course of the last 150 years. It is equally clear that abuses of trade union power do occur, and that recent legislation to ensure that fundamental freedoms to dissent from trade union policies are preserved, and to limit trade union exemption from civil actions where outsiders are harmed, are probably justified. The personnel officer is often involved at the sharp end in industrial relations negotiations and he/she must be aware of the three aspects which enter into the discussions. These are:

1 the legislation about industrial relations and collective bargaining, including any code of practice issued officially or drawn up in-house
2 the union regulations of any recognised trade union or trades unions
3 company policy on industrial relations as established over the years, and the views of any employers' organisation to which the company belongs.

Once again, this field is a very important one where the legal situation is hotly contested and to some extent highly politicised. It is essential to keep up-to-date on the position by referring to a handbook such as the *Reference Book for Employers* (see above).

The Employment Act 1988 (as amended) is a major piece of legislation on what is now a complex field of industrial relations law. This is based not only on Acts of Parliament such as the Trade Union Act 1984, the Trade Union and Labour Relations Act 1974, and so on, but also on codes of practice issued by the Advisory, Conciliation and Arbitration Service (ACAS).

Essentially the personnel officer has a difficult balancing act to perform. He/she has first of all to see that the needs of the firm for particular classes of labour, at prices it can afford, are met at all times. In doing so it is necessary not to deny to the employee any rights to which he/she is entitled in law, including the right to be a member of, and represented by, a trade union of his/her choice. Equally it is necessary not to deny to the employee other rights, such as the right to choose not to join a union if he/she prefers, and the right to remain at work, even during a strike, if peaceful persuasion fails to persuade him/her that the strike is a correct action in the circumstances. Obviously, if all parties are equally convinced of the need to be reasonable and to act only within the legal framework existing at the time, the vast majority of difficulties can be solved by negotiation. Political activity to change the law is outside the field of industrial relations itself, and is best left to those who feel a dedication to one viewpoint or the other.

The Race Relations Act 1976

This makes it unlawful to discriminate against a person, directly or indirectly, in the field of employment. Direct discrimination means treating a person, on racial grounds, less favourably than other people. Indirect discrimination is not clearly defined but might, for example, include less favourable treatment because the employee had a poor command of English when this was not required for the job concerned. What was fair treatment on language grounds for a person with poor English seeking a post as a telephone operator might be discrimination against a seamstress whose command of English was weak.

The Code of Practice for the Elimination of Racial Discrimination and the Promotion of Equality of Opportunity in Employment recommends that all employers should adopt, implement and monitor an equal opportunity policy which should be communicated to all employees, through the usual channels (notice boards, contracts of employment, written notifications, and so on).

Particular care has to be applied when advertising vacancies, or when using the services of employment agencies, and it is unlawful to give instructions to discriminate or to bring pressure on such agencies to exclude certain groups. Similarly recruitment from the friends of existing staff where this is likely to produce a disproportionate number of people from a particular racial group may amount to discrimination.

Victimisation is discrimination against a person on the grounds that he/she has brought action on the grounds of racial discrimination, or is to give evidence or has made allegations of racial discrimination.

The Sex Discrimination Act 1975 as amended by the Sex Discrimination Act 1986

These acts make it unlawful to discriminate against women by treating them less favourably than men. It also applies to men if they are treated less favourably than women and to married persons of either sex if they are treated less favourably than a single per-

son. Exceptions apply in a number of situations where sex is a genuine occupational qualification. A related matter, sexual harassment, can constitute sexual discrimination where
it can be proved that the claimant has been treated in a way which would not have applied
to someone of the opposite sex, or where it led to constructive dismissal (where the
employee resigns rather than endure the harassment). As with the Race Relations Act, discriminatory advertisements, instructions and pressure to discriminate are unlawful.

9.13 The remuneration of staff

The remuneration of staff is a vital aspect of personnel work and a close liaison between
the personnel department and the wages department is essential at all times. The personnel department must keep the wages department informed about appointments, promotions and demotions, retirements and dismissals, since all these matters require action by
the wages department. Other matters affecting pay are changes in rates agreed at board
level or at joint consultation meetings on the industrial relations front, rises which start on
birthdays, attachments of pay by court orders for the support of separated wives and families, and so on. By contrast, wages department may alert personnel department to such
matters as absenteeism, notices of sickness, compensation claims being pursued by
injured employees, and so on.

There are many ways of remunerating staff, particularly production staff, and some
of the schemes are very elaborate. They produce numerous queries to the wages department, some of which may find their way to the personnel department, because they produce anomalies as between grades of staff. One popular method of paying wages is the
Kalamazoo system.

9.14 Labour turnover

Where there is a high rate of labour turnover it almost always means extra costs. The chief
of these are recruitment costs, retraining costs, spoilt work, damage to machinery and
equipment, and industrial injuries leading to claims for compensation. It is usual to calculate rate of turnover of labour as a percentage, using the formula:

$$\text{Percentage rate of labour turnover} = \frac{\text{Number of leavers in the year} \times 100}{\text{Average number of employees in the year}}$$

Thus if 74 staff move in the year out of 356 employed on average, the figure is:

$$\% \text{ Rate of turnover} = \frac{74}{356} \times 100$$
$$= 20.8\%$$

About one-fifth of the entire labour force is having to be replaced each year. This is a high rate of turnover and we should investigate the causes. What is it: the unattractive nature of the work, the low rate of pay, a martinet disguised as a supervisor? Common faults pinpointed by high labour turnover are poor selection procedures and insufficient attention to career structures. Thus a person placed in the wrong job may feel that it is better to move on than to get trapped in a job which really has no interest and no prospects for him/her. The same person might have held the job cheerfully for a year or two in the knowledge that it was appreciated by the company that this was a stop-gap only and another opportunity was being lined up for a better, permanent post in due course.

9.15 The Data Protection Act 1998

In most countries there is now an awareness of the need to keep records about personnel confidential, and available to the employee (the data subject) so that he/she may be aware of the records being correct and may correct any untrue statements. In the United Kingdom the regulatory Act is the Data Protection Act 1998. Starting as a concern about computerised records, the Act now covers paper-based records as well.

The principles behind data protection are as follows:

a Information about an employee must have been obtained fairly and lawfully.

b It must be on file for a legitimate purpose.

c It must be accurate and be kept up to date.

d It must not be excessive, or kept for longer than is necessary.

e It must be protected against accidental loss, or damage, by the use of suitable barriers to unauthorised access.

f It must be treated as confidential.

g The employee must have a right of access, obtainable by a simple and well known procedure.

Some data, so-called sensitive personal data, may only be kept on record with the consent of the data subject, or if there is a legal obligation to keep a record of it. 'Sensitive' data includes racial or ethnic origins, religious beliefs, political opinions, physical or mental health, sexual orientation, criminal records, trade union membership (or non-membership) and details of any disability.

An employee may request to know the nature of records kept about him/her, why any particular record is necessary and who routinely sees such information. On receipt of such a request the employer must comply with it within 40 days but need not respond to it if only a short time has elapsed since a previous request was complied with.

10 The accounting function

10.1 The nature of accounting

Accountancy is a fundamental function in all businesses. It is all-pervasive, ranging from the most trivial expenditures of petty cash to the very topmost level of financial management, take-overs, mergers, amalgamations, reconstructions and winding-up procedures. Every student of business administration should ideally be pursuing at the same time the study of accountancy, unless a sound background has already been achieved earlier. For the benefit of those who have no background in accountancy, this chapter begins with a brief account of double-entry book-keeping based upon the author's best-selling publication *Book-keeping Made Simple*. It cannot be more than a brief introduction to show how routine book-keeping records are used to find the profits of a business. Every type of business uses these records, in either manual or computerised form, but the preparation of the final accounts section varies with partnerships, limited companies, public authorities and non-profit-making societies such as clubs and associations, for example the Automobile Association. We cannot linger, however, to go into these matters, which are part of the study of elementary accounting. We must press on to consider higher-level matters. First, then, a brief recapitulation of basic accounting as we consider Fig. 10.1.

10.2 Basic accounting: a recapitulation

In the explanation which follows, the numbered sections refer to the numbers on the illustrations in Fig. 10.1.

1 *Every transaction has an original document* Documents trigger off all accounting activities, except in a few very advanced systems where the computer accepts information in machine-readable form and will (if requested) print out a document later. The chief documents are:

   a The top copy of other people's invoices, which become our purchases record.

   b The second copy of our invoices, which become our sales record (the top copy has gone to our customer as his/her record of the purchase).

   c The top copy of other people's credit notes, which become our record of purchases returned for some reason to the supplier.

   d The second copy of our credit notes, which become our record of sales returned (the top copy having gone to the customer to prove he/she has returned goods to us).

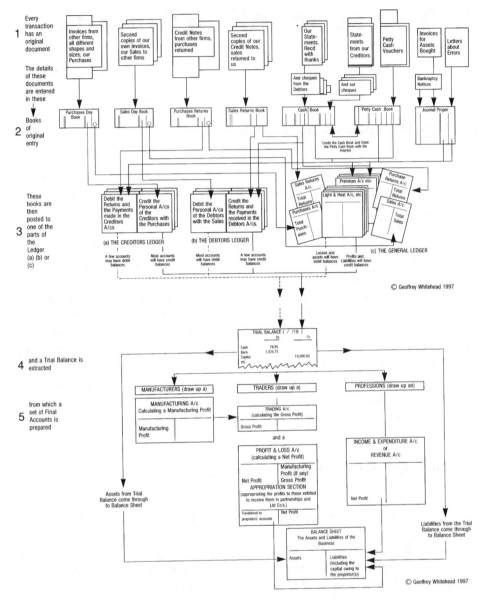

Fig. 10.1   How the double-entry system works

e All sorts of other more formal documents, deeds, bankruptcy notices, and so on, which are fairly rare events notifying us of various business transactions.

f Our cheques paid out and other people's cheques received. Today we may move money electronically, as 'direct debits' and 'direct credits'.

g Petty cash vouchers for minor disbursements.

What sort of entries do all these documents generate?

2 *The documents are entered in books of original entry* This gives us a permanent record of documents, in date order, in books of original entry such as those listed in the diagram, the purchases day book, the sales day book, and so on. In fact these days we have many ways of avoiding all this rather unnecessary work. Some systems are called simultaneous entry systems, where several records are made at once using carbon paper or NCR paper (no carbon required). A famous name in this field is Kalamazoo, who specialise in these systems. Another way is to put the material on to a computer and let it print out a day book once a month. Another way is to bind the documents in loose-leaf binders.

3 *The original entries are now posted to the ledger* Whatever system we use for original entries in (2) above, every single transaction must be posted from the book of original entry to the ledger. A ledger is simply a book full of pages, called accounts. Every single page is entirely separate from every other page. It has a name at the top. This could read:

Geoffrey Whitehead A/c	(a personal account)
Mrs Amy Jones A/c	(another personal account)
Furniture and fittings A/c	(a real account, because the thing it is keeping account of is a real thing)
Wages A/c	(a nominal account. Nominal means 'in name only'; there is nothing real there, the real money has been paid to the workers, but we need to keep a record of how much has been paid in wages)

Every account is either personal, real or nominal.

The other thing to know about these accounts is that every time one is debited (receiving goods, or services, or money) another account has to be credited (giving goods, or services, or money). For example, if I pay out postage £2.40 on a parcel, Cash Account gives £2.40 (credit the giver) and Postage Account receives £2.40 (debit the receiver). Of course, Postage Account does not really receive £2.40 – it is stuck on the parcel as stamps – but then Postage Account is a nominal account; the money is there in name only.

It is these double entries that give the system its name, double-entry book-keeping. A good accountant spends his/her life thinking in double entries, and very interesting it is too. For those not yet able to think in double entries, the rules are as follows:

Debit the account *(that is, make the entry on the left-hand side of the page)* **if it is receiving goods, or services, or money. Credit the account** *(that is, make the entry on the right-hand side of the page)* **if it is giving goods, or services, or money.** This may be abbreviated to: debit the receiver; credit the giver.

A few examples may help. What is the double entry in each of these cases?

a R. Brown sends us goods worth £1800, which we are purchasing. Answer: Debit Purchases Account which receives the goods. Credit R. Brown who gives them to us. He is now our creditor and we owe him £1800.

b Margaret Jones asks us to supply £500 of goods. We do so. Answer: Debit M. Jones who receives the goods. She is now our debtor and owes us £500. Credit Sales Account, as we have sold the goods and are the givers.

c Helpful Bank PLC lends us £15 000 which it puts into our current account at the Bank. Answer: Debit Bank Account, it has received £15 000. Credit Bank Loan Account – we now have a new creditor, Helpful Bank PLC, to whom we must repay this money under the terms of the loan agreement.

There are millions of such transactions in a year, and they all require double entries, because one account receives and another gives.

4 *A trial balance is extracted* A trial balance is simply a process of extracting from the ledger a list of all the accounts which have balances on them. Some of these will be debit balances and some will be credit balances. If we have done a correct double entry, the total of the debits should balance the total of the credits. That is why we call it a trial balance – we try to see if the ledger balances. If it does we can assume that the book-keeping is correct.

5 *A set of final accounts is prepared* A set of final accounts consists of a Trading Account, a Profit and Loss Account, and a Balance Sheet. In the Trading Account we work out the **gross profit**, which is the difference between the cost of goods sold and the selling price. This gross profit is then taken to the Profit and Loss Account, where the various overhead expenses are deducted from it. This leaves the **net profit**, which means the clean profit. This profit belongs to the proprietor, but if there are several partners or a large number of shareholders the net profit is taken to an **Appropriation Section** of the Profit and Loss Account, where it is shared out in the appropriate manner, according to the terms of the partnership agreement or the recommendation of the directors of the company approved at the annual general meeting.

Finally the assets and liabilities are listed in the closing Balance Sheet, which becomes the starting point for a new financial year.

Conclusion about double entry

Obviously the study of double-entry book-keeping is a study in its own right, and cannot be undertaken in a few hours. It is a very worthwhile subject for all business administrators. We must now consider the accounting function in all its major aspects.

10.3 A definition of accounting

Accounting is the art of controlling a business by keeping accurate book-keeping records, and instituting budgetary controls and other control procedures so that the profitability of the business can be ascertained and reported to management, which can also be alerted to changes or undesirable trends in the business.

10.4 The functions of financial managers

The functions of financial managers may be listed as shown below. For convenience, reference has been made to a company, but the same functions apply to sole trader enterprises, partnerships, non-profit-making organisations and public authorities of all types. The functions are:

1 The raising of money to provide the original capital of the enterprise.

2 Financial decisions on resource allocation. The accountant has to oversee the expenditure of the money raised, whether it is spent for the purchase of assets (land, buildings, plant and machinery, and so on) or on consumable items, such as stationery, postage, wages and salaries, and so on. Money spent on assets is often called **fixed capital** (because it has been turned into fixed assets) while other money is referred to as **working capital** because it has been spent on things which keep the fixed assets at work. Plant and machinery can only be worked if we have staff to work them, raw materials and components to work on, documentation to ensure payment is received, and so on. The accountant has to keep a nice balance between fixed capital and working capital. Shortage of working capital is called **overtrading** and is a common cause of failure. Even if it does not lead to failure it means we have to borrow from banks at high rates of interest and this creams off a lot of the profits into the banks' pockets and leaves our business less profitable. Excessive working capital is called **undertrading** and means the business could increase its activities by buying more fixed assets and taking on more staff. While this is true, expansion of the business is not always possible at a given moment in time and a company which is cash-rich (plenty of working capital) can always put it on deposit temporarily to earn some return from it. The director who always wants to expand to the last penny of working capital is not likely to please the accountant, for prudence is one of the basic principles of accounting. **Cash flow** (ensuring that there is always enough cash flowing in to cover future activities) is a major preoccupation of accountants.

3 All the activities mentioned in 2 above require a great deal of routine accounting, kept on the double-entry system, though possibly in computerised form.

4 Another important function is budgetary control. The resources needed to carry out the planned activities are limited, and any department which is in danger of overspending has to be reined in and controlled well before the danger point arrives. People have to live within their budgets.

5 All departments which handle cash, or stock, or capital assets of any sort, are subject to internal audit procedures, which seek to detect weak control in departments and malpractices of every kind. Besides these internal audit procedures which are part of the accountant's control of all other staff, companies and public authorities are subject to external audit under a variety of statutes, notably in the United Kingdom the Companies Act 1985–9 for companies and various acts for local authorities, public authorities, and so on. All countries have their own laws on the audit of accounts.

6 Costing activities are the accounting activities associated with production, pricing and profitability. To a certain extent they are a separate division from the ordinary financial accounting, and a specialist profession, management accountants, deal with this aspect.

7 A main preoccupation of accountants is with the final results of the year's activities and the preparation of the final accounts of the business. This requires the drawing up of a Manufacturing Account (for manufacturing organisations), a Trading Account, a Profit and Loss Account, and a Balance Sheet. Some firms do not trade but provide services,

and some professional people do not talk about profit (doctors and dentists, for example) but refer to 'surplus of income over expenditure'. For many organisations the accounts have to be published. The most important examples are the public limited companies (PLCs), quangos (quasi-autonomous non-governmental organisations), and local and central government bodies.

8   Finally, a continuing preoccupation of accountants is with giving advice to management about every aspect of the business's activities. No-one is better placed to notice adverse aspects of the business that need to be drawn to management's attention – for example, that sales of certain products are falling off, that orders are drying up, that cash is getting tighter, that credit periods are being extended, that a customer is under pressure from lawsuits, trades unions, take-over bidders, and so on. Equally, no-one is better placed to notice surpluses of cash becoming available, special opportunities to buy stock as rivals get into difficulties, special bargains in property or plant and machinery, the likely availability of specialist staff as rivals close down or reduce their activities, and so on.

10.5 Control and the accountant

Although routine book-keeping matters are a large part of the work of the accountant, this book is not the place for them. Here we are interested in the administration of businesses and their control by senior management. The accountant has much to do in helping to secure this type of control and some of the measures must be studied here, although they can only be introductory and more specialist studies follow at higher levels.

The general principles of control apply. These are:

1   The accountant must know and, if necessary, set standards of financial performance.
2   Actual performance must be measured and compared with standards.
3   The results must be fed back into the system and used to correct deviations from standard.
4   The corrections must be monitored to see if they were effective.

In setting up financial controls such as budgets, standard costs, break-even charts and accounting ratios, we must be careful to ensure the following:

1   The controls instituted must be appropriate to the job and the type of organisation concerned. The larger the organisation the greater the need for controls, since management is more remote from the actual operations.
2   The collection of information and its feedback to management should be as immediate as possible and, if necessary, regular **returns** should be instituted.
3   The system of **management by exceptions** must be applied. This means that only figures and ratios that depart from the standards laid down need to be reported. Like a teacher's register in school, the normal thing is for the child to attend – usually shown by a red line. If a child is absent a black circle shows the exception to the normal – the thing that needs investigation.

4 Wherever possible the control should highlight the weak point in any system which is causing the deviation from normal. If the organisation is such that clear responsibilities are allocated to individuals it should be possible to lay responsibility for an exceptional event at the door of some individual.

5 We must re-examine systems of control on a continuing basis, always suspecting that someone has found a way round the control, and not placing excessive trust in any individual.

10.6 Standard costs

Standard costing is a method of ascertaining costs and checking performance against standards, by comparing actual cost with standard cost and thereby revealing any variation. Such a variation is called a variance and **variance analysis** is the process of analysing a variance to discover the cause. For example, suppose we detect a variance in the cost of direct material used in the production of a particular product. Has the variance been caused by a **direct material price variance** (which is beyond our control because it is an outside influence) or by a **direct material usage variance** (which is within our control because it means poor workmanship, or poor supervision, spoilt work, and so on)? With the price variance the solution is to pass the price increase on to our customers. With the usage variance the solution is to solve the problem by more careful supervision of operations to bring them up to standard.

It is impossible to cover variance analysis fully in this book, but Fig. 10.2 gives some idea of the complexity of variance analysis.

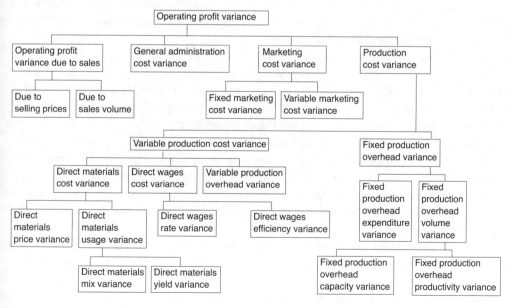

Fig. 10.2   Variance analysis

In order to set standard costs a considerable amount of work has to be done. For example, direct material costs have to be calculated on the basis of price and usage of each type of material, allowing for wastage. The technical expert involved specifies the weight or quantity of each item in the product, and this is then valued at a price which reflects the current or forecast market prices, with allowance for possible trends in prices. It may be necessary to ask for quotations from suppliers to establish these prices. Although the work involved is fairly onerous it does have a useful side effect, that every item or component has to be looked at in detail and this may reveal various savings that are possible, for example, cutting out a multiplicity of thicknesses and weights of materials to reduce stocks to one or two standard sizes may save warehouse space and time.

10.7 Budgeting

Budgeting is the formation of plans for a future period, expressed in quantitative terms, which may be financial or may be expressed in other units, for example, production may be budgeted in units of output. From the accountancy viewpoint, the budget is as many-sided as the business, and individual functions, departments and cost centres must be involved in the budgeting process. It is usual to appoint a **budget committee**, chaired by the chief executive and with a secretary known as the **budget officer**, who supervises the routine work. Most senior executives will be on the budget committee and responsible for preparing the budget for the functional area which they control.

Since budgeting is a control exercise, the allocation of responsibility to various individuals in the preparation process also allocates blame for the period under consideration should the budget prove to be unrealistic or poorly judged. The major functional heads will draw up a functional budget which will be based on departmental or cost centre budgets within the functional area. The amalgamation of these functional budgets into a master budget may reveal the unrealistic nature of some of them, and individuals may be called upon to justify the expenditures envisaged. Cuts may have to be imposed and a review of operations called for to decide what items of activity are to be postponed or what cost savings can be made. It is irresponsible for departmental heads to inflate artificially the activities they propose in order to swell the budget, in anticipation of cuts. The responsible attitude seeks to achieve the optimum budget of benefit to the company from the minimum input of resources. Senior management should take up with the person concerned any under-utilisation of budget in the period, since this is just as bad as going over budget. It either represents a failure to achieve plans which management deemed viable or it is a waste of everyone's time because it leaves the final budget unrealistic as a plan for the period concerned.

Common budgets are the purchasing budget, the production budget, the sales budget, the distribution budget, the plant utilisation budget, the research and development budget, the personnel budget, the administrative expenses budget and the cash budget. The whole procedure is called **budgetary control**. Its advantages are:

1 It compels management to think ahead and set objectives for the company which are desirable and achievable.
2 These objectives then have to be quantified in both numerical and financial terms, which requires costs of materials, components, wages and overheads to be discovered and bargained for at economical prices.
3 It is a morale-raising activity since it requires consultation down to grass-roots levels where cost centres must themselves estimate costs for the period ahead. This generates confidence in the future of the company and interest in keeping it competitive with rivals. It reveals square pegs in round holes, and areas where morale is low, and it generates cost-saving ideas and ideas for expansion which might not otherwise be advanced.
4 It allocates responsibility, and lets each person know what must be achieved if the company's objectives are to be realised.
5 It establishes clear control of cash receipts and disbursements, and provides a system for the proper authorisation of expenditures. It detects variances from budget, probably on a monthly basis. Thus a departmental head who starts to spend money too fast (with the prospect that he/she will be unable to pay the wages of staff in the latter half of the year) is pulled up sharply by the accountant and a stop on all unnecessary orders is imposed until the department gets back inside its budget.
6 Management can be alerted at once to any variations between planned and actual expenditures (or receipts). This is particularly true where the budgeting procedure has been computerised and the computer is programmed to print out warnings of variances as they are detected.

The disadvantage of budgetary control is the amount of work that goes into budget preparation, but again this is much reduced by the computerisation of budgeting procedures.

10.8 The raising of funds

The financial manager has a major role to play in securing funds, and must take into account many considerations when raising finance. The chief methods of finding funds for expansion are:
1 ploughing back profits
2 overdrafts and loans
3 the issue of debentures
4 new issues of shares of various sorts.

We cannot go too deeply into these matters here since they become very technical and specialised, but if we just consider the first two it may help the reader.

Ploughing back profits

Traditionally the founders of companies subscribed the initial capital for the enterprise which in due course, if successful, rewarded them with a dividend at the end of each financial year. This is still one of the best ways of raising capital, but it means that people who know what the objects of the company are and what goods and services it plans to provide must also have the money to contribute to put the plans into effect. If not, they must be persuasive enough to prevail upon friends and acquaintances to put up the capital. Differences in procedure occur around the world, but in the United Kingdom, for example capital is divided into small units, usually £1 in value, called shares, and the owners of shares are called shareholders. They are the owners of the business but, as each share has one vote, effective power lies with the person or persons who control 51 percent of the voting shares. It is therefore possible to have shares in a company but have absolutely no chance of influencing its policies. Minority shareholders are sometimes very poorly treated, because the board will not declare a fair dividend and there is no easy way of compelling more reasonable behaviour. Private limited companies, whose name must end in the word Limited, may not appeal to the public for funds, but financial directors of public limited companies (PLCs) have the power to issue shares to the general public subject to the approval of the Registrar of Companies and the Corporation of the Stock Exchange and, therefore, very large sums can be collected.

Apart from the costs of issuing shares and complying with the requirements of the Stock Exchange Council, the capital obtained in this way is virtually cost-free in that the shareholder is only entitled to a share of the profits made and has no other claim either to a return on the capital invested or to repayment of the sum subscribed. The only way the shareholder can recover the money subscribed is by selling the shares on the Stock Exchange for the market price, which may be above or below the original issue price. This does not, of course, prevent institutions owning shares from bringing pressure to bear on a company that is badly run – and even forcing changes on the board – but they cannot overthrow a board of directors which still retains control by keeping 51 percent of the voting shares. As a general principle a company which wishes to expand its activities should do so by ploughing back profits wherever possible, and it is the usual policy to declare a dividend that is reasonable and unlikely to cause shareholders to complain, but to retain any further profit and use it for expansion purposes. Thus if investors could earn say 8 or 9 percent by investing funds on the money market, they are likely to regard a 15 or 20 percent dividend as a generous reward for taking shares instead. However, if the company is a profitable one, earning (say) 42 percent of profits there is still quite a lot to plough back. This growth is reflected in the value of the ordinary shares, which rise above the original issue price because the 'share' of the shareholder now includes a share of the increased value resulting from the ploughing back of profits.

In ploughing back profits in this way care must then be taken to avoid overtrading. The business needs to grow, and to that end requires extra buildings, plant and equipment, and so on. The profits ploughed in will enable us to buy these assets and produce more. The trouble is that in growing we must expect sales to increase (which means more debtors) and more raw materials to be required (which means larger stocks). These current assets have to be financed, as well as the fixed assets we are buying, as part of the expansion programme. We also need to employ more staff, and pay their wages. In other words, we need not only fixed capital but working capital. Failure to plough back enough profit to provide the working capital required forces the company to borrow from banks, finance companies and so on, at high rates of interest and is one of the commonest causes of business failure.

Overdrafts and loans

Where it is not possible to plough back profits, a company seeking to expand will perhaps turn first to its local bank to provide funds. The bank is the natural lender to turn to for short-term finance to meet cash shortages, and where these have been revealed by a cash flow budget of the sort illustrated in Table 10.1 it will usually be possible to obtain an overdraft without too much difficulty and without providing special security.

Table 10.1 Budgeting for cash

	January		February		March	
Cash flow	Budget (£)	Actual (£)	Budget (£)	Actual (£)	Budget (£)	Actual (£)
1. Cash balance (cash & bank)	5 580		7 527		− 6 643	
RECEIPTS						
2. Sales in cash	22 347		11 800		18 600	
3. Debts collected	450		1 350		220	
4. Other receipts	1 420		1 420		1 420	
5. Loans arranged	—		—		5 000	
6. Total receipts (add 2 to 5)	24 217		14 570		25 240	
7. Total cash available (add 1 to 6)	29 797		22 097		18 597	
PAYMENTS						
8. Payments for business stock	11 340		13 500		13 200	
9. Wages	5 420		5 420		5 450	
10. Other payments	1 260		1 580		1 580	
11. Capital items	—		8 240		—	
12. External payments (add 8 to 11)	18 020		28 740		20 230	
13. Dividends payable	4 250		—		—	
14. Total payments	22 270		28 740		20 230	
15. Final cash balance (7 − 14) (or if in deficit 14 − 7)	7 527		Deficit 6 643		Deficit 1 633	
			Note: see Finance Co. to arrange loan £5000 Also ask bank for £5000 overdraft		This deficit is covered by the overdraft	

For more formal loans, spread over a period of years, the accountant will draw up a more detailed appraisal of the state of the business showing why finance is required, how much, and what relationship this requirement bears to the existing capital in the business. Loans are not intended to be 'risk' capital, and certainly not 'high risk' capital. Loans are made by banks using the depositors' money in the bank, and banks have to be very prudent in making loans from such funds. If the true difficulty a company is in arises from a shortage of equity capital (ordinary shares) then the bank may refer the loan request to its merchant bank department for advice about a new issue of shares, rather than granting a loan.

The loan proposal must include an explanation of how repayment is to be made. The accountant will show how the loan being requested will generate renewed profitability from which the loan repayments can be managed, and will suggest ways in which the bank can monitor events from time to time to judge whether plans are being achieved in practice. In practice, 'sensitivity analysis' by the bank will be anticipated by the accountant. Sensitivity analysis seeks to discover how sensitive the directors are to the possibility that things could go wrong: a downturn in the economy, closure of overseas markets, interruption of imported supplies, and so on. Bankers are good at asking 'What if?' questions, and the accountant will anticipate most of them in his/her analysis of the business's situation.

10.9 The final accounts of a business

It is impossible here to teach the student how to prepare the final accounts of a major business, but we may perhaps assume that most students have studied accounts to some extent already. There are four stages in the preparation of final accounts. They are:

1 *Finding the gross profit on trading* This is done in the Trading Account. Gross profit is the difference between the selling price (the sales figure) and the cost of goods sold.

2 *Finding the net profit* This is done by taking out a Profit and Loss Account. This account starts with the gross profit and then deducts from it all the overhead expenses, rent, rates, and so on. In Table 10.2(a) the Trading Account and Profit and Loss Account are run into one another as a continuous presentation (see opposite).

3 *Appropriating the profit* This is done in an Appropriation Account, or an appropriation section of the Profit and Loss Account. What we do is start with any balance left from last year and add this year's net profit to it. We then appropriate the profit by putting it in various reserve accounts where it can later be used for the purpose for which it has been set aside. Thus the distributed profit will be paid away from the Ordinary Dividend Account in the form of dividend warrants. Profits put into the General Reserve Account may be used for buying assets – the cash represented by these reserves will be available because it has not been paid as dividend to the shareholders but has been retained in the system.

4 *Drawing up a Balance Sheet* A balance sheet is a list of the assets and liabilities, showing the situation at the end of the financial year. In Table 10.2(b) it is presented in vertical style, showing the net assets at the top, and how they were financed lower down. The total assets of £444 254 were financed partly by the ordinary shareholders (with £200 000 of original capital and £104 254 ploughed back). The rest of the funds used were provided by the preference shareholders (£40 000), the debenture holders (£60 000) and tax moneys held in reserve (£40 000).

You should now study Table 10.2(a) and (b) carefully.

Table 10.2(a) The Trading Account, Profit and Loss Account and Appropriation Account of a company

Sunset Products (Cambridge) Ltd
Trading and Profit and Loss A/c for year ending December 31st, 20....

20....			£	20....			£
Dec. 31	Opening stock		72 807	Dec. 31	Sales (Turnover)		504 067
	Purchases		266 376				
			339 183				
	Less closing stock		80 766				
	Cost of stock sold		258 417				
	Gross profit		245 650				
			£504 067				£504 067
20....			£	20....			£
Dec. 31	Rent and Rates		17 200	Dec. 31	Gross profit		245 650
	Telephone expenses		2 000		Commission received		8 000
	Salaries		37 245				
	Repairs		8 600				
	General expenses		29 838				
	Bad debts		1 149				
	Debenture interest		4 200				
	Bank charges due		72				
	Depreciation:						
	Plant	10 680					
	Motor vehicles	5 100					
			15 780				
			116 084				
	Net profit		137 566				
			£253 650				£253 650

Appropriation A/c for year ending December 31st, 20....

20....		£	20....		£
Dec. 31	Reserve for corporation tax	40 000	Jan. 1	Balance	9 888
	General reserve	60 000	Dec. 31	Net profit	137 566
	Pref. dividend	3 200			
	Ord. dividend	30 000			
	Balance	14 254			
		£147 454			£147 454
			20....		£
			Jan. 1	Balance	14 254

Table 10.2(b)   The Balance Sheet of a company

Balance Sheet as at December 31st, 20....
Fixed assets

Tangible assets		At cost	**Less** depreciation	Value
Freehold buildings		150 000	—	150 000
Plant		206 800	39 930	166 870*
Motor vehicles		25 500	17 040	8 460
		382 300	56 970	325 330
Current assets				
Stock		80 766		
Debtors	39 282			
Less provision	1 386			
		37 896		
Cash at bank		60 270		
Cash in hand		1 200		
			180 132	
Less current liabilities				
Preference dividend due		3 200		
Ordinary dividend due		30 000		
Creditors		25 473		
Bank charges due		72		
Debenture interest due		2 100		
Salaries due		363	61 208	
			Net current assets	118 924
			Net assets	£444 254

Financed by:				
Ordinary shareholders' interest in the company			Authorised	Issued
£				£
Ordinary Shares of £1 fully paid			200 000	200 000
Reserves				
Revenue:				
General reserve		30 000		
+ Additions		60 000		
		90 000		
Balance on Appropriation A/c		14 254		
				104 254
			Ordinary shareholders' equity	304 254

(Continues opposite)

		£
		Brought forward 304 254
Preference shareholders' interest in the company	Authorised	
8% Preference shares of £1 fully paid	40 000	40 000
7% Debentures		60 000
Reserve for corporation tax		40 000
		£444 254

Note: In real life of course all these figures come from the closing balances on the Trial Balance at the end of the financial year. As shown in diagrammatic form in Fig. 10.1 (see page 180) the Trial Balance is the starting point for any set of final accounts.

10.10 Internal audit procedures

An audit is a review of an organisation's accounting records by independent persons. Section 384 of the Companies Act 1985–9 requires every company to appoint auditors annually, and the following sections specify many detailed points about their activities. Internal audit procedures are rather different in that they seek to review the accounting records of various parts of a large enterprise to detect any improper dealings, cash handling procedures which are defective, and so on. They are under the general control of the accountant and usually consist of a small team of specialist staff who travel round to various departments and depots making random checks, without warning, on any area responsible for cash, stocks, components or fixed assets. The auditors will report back to the accountant on each investigation and any losses, weaknesses in procedure, and so on, will lead to action by the accountant.

10.11 The annual report: a review of operations

In this book we have looked in detail at many aspects of a company's activities: production, marketing, distribution, information technology, and so on. These various activities add up in the end to a sum total of operations which the accountant, for one, hopes has proved to be profitable. We must be profitable if we are to stay in business, because those who provided the capital on which the whole business relies must be rewarded for their efforts.

In Table 10.2(a) in the Appropriation Account we saw the total profit for the year (£137 566) was added to a residue of profit left over from last year to give a total profit from all operations of £147 454. We then saw that this money was appropriated to certain people who were entitled to take their share. The Inland Revenue was expected to take the government's share, estimated at £40 000 corporation tax. The preference shareholders were entitled to £3200 and the ordinary shareholders to £30 000. The rest was left in the business, some of it in a general reserve account and the rest as a balance on the Appropriation Account.

The figures in this example were small, but the rules are the same for all. At the end of the financial year the directors of a company must hold an annual general meeting (AGM) and the chairman will present a report for the year. He/she will outline the final results of the company's operations, present the accounts for consideration by the members present, propose the dividend to be declared and answer any criticisms made by the members. Usually the accounts will be approved, the dividends payable will be approved, and the affairs of the company for the year just ended will be closed. The new year's activities will already be well under way.

The final accounts of a public limited company are a matter of public record, and a copy will be sent to all interested parties, while supplies permit. After that they may be inspected at the company's offices, or on the company's website.

Part Three

The administrative officer's role

11 Office administration

11.1 The role of the administrative officer

Although we have already mentioned a number of functions within business, such as the production function, the marketing function, and so on, it is usual to appoint an administrative officer who will take responsibility for all the routine aspects of office administration and in many small firms may have a range of functions, including perhaps personnel, wages and accounts. Such a person may have a title of general administration officer.

The role of the administration officer is a wide one and involves supervision of all the routine installations and systems on which the general efficiency of the office depends. Thus the following areas are under his/her control:

1 The office buildings, equipment, furniture, heating, lighting, toilet facilities, caretaking and health and safety at work aspects.
2 The clerical activities including stationery, small office equipment, filing, archiving, office procedures, organisation and methods.
3 The secretarial activities, including any centralised typing facility, correspondence, reprographic department, information technology, filing systems, and so on.
4 The communication system, telephone switchboard and handsets, fax machines, pagers, cordless and mobile telephones.
5 The computer system, or at least certain parts of it, depending on the system installed. There may be a LAN (local area network).
6 A very wide variety of other matters including such things as the use of premises, booking meeting rooms for various activities, refreshment facilities, reception, mail inwards and outwards, chauffeurs, and so on.

We must now study some of these activities in greater detail.

11.2 Facilities management: the 'new look' office administrator

Today the development of information technology has brought the need for new skills in office administration, and the term facilities management has been used to describe the new skills required. Whereas Bob Cratchet could manage Scrooge's counting house with a quill pen and a high stool at a ledge under a window, the new technology has revolutionised the office. People who work at computer terminals and word processors need new kinds of desks and chairs. The screens call for different lighting and the acoustics are different. Some devices are affected by static, so the carpeting has to be different; more plugs and sockets are required for mains and telephone links, and the ionisation of the atmosphere can produce psychological and medical problems.

At a routine level the new techniques give a frightening degree of control to management, counting up every piece of work done and enabling tasks to be set and standards to be achieved irrespective of the variability of work. Some office workers are prepared to 'vote with their feet' when subjected to this kind of tyranny. Tyranny may seem too strong a word for this type of close supervision, but the essence of tyranny is that it is imposed from the very top on the weakest members of society, and this kind of statistical control is essentially control over the lower levels of the office hierarchy. One copy typist told the author that she literally became a nervous wreck by lunchtime if she had not achieved well over half her daily quota, because she knew that the interruptions due to outside calls in the afternoon would nearly always make it impossible to meet the quota, which took no account of the disruptive effect of interruptions on her performance. The daily printout of 'defaulters' who had failed to achieve the standard set, constituted, she felt, an interference with her liberties, since it gave her a bad mark despite heroic efforts to comply with the requirements set by management. In the administrator's new role of facilities manager the premises, the internal facilities and services and the people involved have all to be 'managed'.

The development of information technology may give great advantages to administrators in routine administration but its more important implications lie in the field of management decision-making. Large databases exist which give access to all sorts of stored information. The facilities manager knows what these sources are, what the legal implications are of using such data and the need for data protection. In customer services, in stock records, in financial management, in physical distribution management, in income and expenditure accounting and many other fields the administrator needs to ensure that the necessary support services are available, that the flow of data is efficient and accurate, appropriate to the organisation and in a form where it is readily usable. The administrator needs to develop a thorough knowledge of the technology involved, and should be able to specify what systems are suitable and design systems where required. Such activities call for a highly professional type of administrator able to operate effectively at boardroom level.

11.3   The office and its functions

The location of the office

The administrative officer is usually closely involved in the work of setting up an office initially and in any question of relocation will play a major part in deciding where the office should be located, what form it should take and what layout should be adopted.

Considerations central to the location of an office are as follows:

1 The office should be in as central a position as possible if it is to perform its chief function of controlling the activities of the business. From the sole trader just starting to the captain of industry with a dozen plants to control, a reasonably central location is best.

2 The cost of land may affect office location, and good deal of relocation (for example out of London) reflects the fact that sites elsewhere are cheaper, and a valuable city-centre site can be sold to realise a very considerable capital gain. At one time there was a Location of Offices Bureau which encouraged movement out of London and other big cities into depressed areas, but it was so successful in persuading firms to relocate that some of the city centres themselves became depressed areas.

3 Official aid in relocation is often available and a company which is growing out of its existing accommodation, or wishes to relocate for other reasons, can usually obtain at least some assistance; perhaps rent or rates 'holidays', assistance with housing for key executives, and so on, can be provided by authorities in the new location. Such help has been called a 'golden hello'.

4 Good road, rail and air links are important for some businesses and relocation close to motorways, railways, airports and ports may be advantageous. Some areas are important for other reasons, for example the 'Silicon Valley' sort of location central to an important industry.

5 Staffing is always important. Some firms might relocate in areas of high unemployment where labour will be keen, cheap and cooperative, because in an industry meeting foreign competition labour costs are often crucial. The availability of staff of the right type who can be trained to do all the types of work required is important, and future needs as well as present needs should be borne in mind.

The type of building

Where sites are cheap, buildings can be extensive, two or three storeys at the most. In city centres, taller buildings reduce the site cost per employee, but bring other problems such as the need for lifts, and safety problems in tower blocks. Redecoration is more difficult and car parking almost impossible for anyone but very senior staff.

Internally, offices can be of the open-plan type or they may be the more traditional cubicle offices. They make a surprising difference to the working conditions, which may be summarised as follows:

1 Open-plan offices are cheap to construct (light partitions replace solid walls), and are often single-storey, lit by natural light from overhead. If multi-storey, the walls are nearly all windows.

2 They are democratic, since all grades of staff are on view and accessible. Supervision is simple, managers being part of the general scenery all day long, and not calling in only at intervals (or, even worse, peering in from corridors only at intervals).

3 Layout is simple, natural and easily readjusted to take account of changing patterns of work, with 'project' furniture linked together to ease document flow and rearranged by undoing a few nuts and bolts. The decor is light and colourful, the staff themselves are part of the decor and personal preferences – the odd pot plant, picture or poster – add a touch of individuality.

4 Communication between staff is easy: there are no doors to tap on, no notices saying 'wait' or 'enter', a good telephone system makes person-to-person conversation possible without shouting, acoustic panels reduce noise levels, ionisers reduce indoor static and pollution.

On the other hand, where top-level staff need to discuss confidential matters, especially matters where security is important, or 'insider dealing' and industrial espionage are possibilities, it is better to have cubicle offices. Similarly, where noisy machines, computer printers, copiers and so on are likely to disturb even the open-plan office, a cubicle 'machine room' may be preferable, perhaps at the edge of an open-plan office.

Office layout

Administrative officers are always concerned about the efficient use of resources and the management of office space is no exception. The proper planning of office space includes the following considerations:

1 Each individual needs a personal workstation which is appropriate to the work involved, comfortable and convenient, and adequately supplied with the necessary tools of the trade.

   Illustrated in Fig. 11.1 is a workstation from the flexible King Delta 1 office furniture system. King Delta has a four-legged frame and full cable management facilities. The movable desktop slides towards the user to give access to the generous sized horizontal cable channel; cables are accessed at the back of the desk. Shown here with complementary screen system, King Delta is available in the UK from K & N International. The range includes task lighting, illuminated signs and VDU platforms which all fit on to the desk frame to keep the desktop uncluttered. Such a workstation is comfortable, clean, has plenty of space for a person who needs to turn from one task to another, and yet is at the same time relatively inexpensive.

Fig. 11.1 A clerical/typing workstation (courtesy of K & N International Ltd, London)

2 The office is really a communication machine. If properly planned the parts of the machine (the individual workstations) may be so located that communication between them is direct, with work flowing through from one person to another.

3 The chief types of area to be catered for are reception areas, clerical workstations, secretarial workstations, computerised workstations, technical workstations (in drawing offices and studios), managerial offices and conference facilities. A proper allocation of space for each of these, with linked furniture to give appropriate working surfaces built up from a variety of specially designed modules, gives a pleasant, ergonomic workstation for each which is at the same time flexible should working patterns change.

4 There are always regulations about offices of every sort. In the United Kingdom the rules of the Health and Safety at Work Act 1974 and the earlier Offices, Shops and Railway Premises Act 1963 apply to all offices, and layout must take account of them. Particular problems are the intensive use made of electrical appliances, which in open-plan offices means that there are likely to be cables and wires trailing around if proper design is not incorporated at an early stage. Most of the modular furniture has hidden cable space designed into it, but access to the mains has to come from suitable points which may be at the walls or taken in underfloor gullies to conveniently spaced points in the floor area. Telephone and intercom services needs to be similarly catered for. Plugs must not be overloaded and suitable multiplug adapters should be used if more than one appliance has to be operated from a single plug. With such adapters a single plug leads to a four-way junction box into which four separate plugs can be fitted, so that there is no loose assembly which can be accidentally dislodged. Loose assemblies are a fire hazard, and with computer installations threaten the loss of data if accidentally dislodged.

Gangways and passageways between desks should be kept free of loose packages, furniture, wastepaper baskets, and so on; shielding must be provided for dangerous or noisy machines, and acoustic panelling reduces background noise by absorbing it instead of reflecting it.

Many workstations are not in continuous use, but serve as storage units where a whole host of information is available when required. One firm which specialises in this type of flexible unit, where a variety of types of work can be carried out and all the facilities needed are available, is Flexiform Ltd, 52 Upper Street, Islington, London, N1 0QH. Some idea of the compact nature of their workstation can be gathered from the photograph in Fig. 11.2 and the line drawing in Fig. 11.3. The firm offers a survey and planning service to ensure that systems are custom-designed to meet individual needs.

Fig. 11.2 A Flexiform workstation

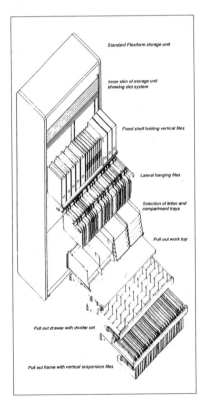

Standard Flexiform storage unit

Inner skin of storage unit
showing slot system

Fixed shelf holding vertical files

Lateral hanging files

Selection of letter and
compartment trays

Pull out work top

Pull out drawer with divider set

Pull out frame with vertical suspension files

Fig. 11.3 A Flexiform storage unit showing the variety of systems housed in the workstation

11.4 The clerical function

Although today the electronic office offers almost miraculous solutions to many clerical activities, the clerical function still persists in countless forms, particularly in new enterprises, in small offices where the volume of work does not justify full computerisation and even, regrettably, as a fail-safe system for dealing with emergencies such as power failures, industrial unrest, and so on, which can render computers useless at times.

The chief areas of clerical activity lie in the following fields:

Routine procedures

There are many situations where a routine procedure must be developed to meet either a temporary or a permanent need. For example, a special offer may bring in countless enquiries for a new product, say a sample lipstick in a cosmetics firm. The procedure starts with an in-tray in the mail inwards department where all such enquiries can be placed when the mail is opened in the morning. This tray will then be routed to Mrs A who records the money received and completes a carbon copy 'counter sales' invoice. The top copy of this invoice may be passed to Mr B who types a label from it and packs up the sample for post, enclosing the top copy of the sales document. Meanwhile the carbon copy has been routed to Miss C who keeps a statistical record of the requests received, showing the advertising medium which produced the response. The mail outwards department will stamp or frank the small packets and dispatch them each day.

This type of activity calls for systematic planning at a low level: the appointment of people to carry out the main tasks, the provision of back-up staff if the response is overwhelming, the design of forms which will expedite the various procedures envisaged, and so on.

Record-keeping

All sorts of records have to be kept and clerical work is to a great extent concerned with the record-keeping procedures. Some of these records are intended for our own purposes, perhaps to build up mailing lists of people interested in future products or to enable us to answer customers' queries and complaints. For example, if a customer complains that a particular product has failed it is helpful to be able to turn up the original order and verify when it was purchased, what quality it was, whether any special circumstances surrounded the sale, and so on.

Other records may be required officially and failure to preserve them may be an offence. VAT records must be kept for six years, and inspectors who ask to see them may bring a charge against the individuals or company directors who have failed to ensure that the records are preserved.

The chief activities in record-keeping are filing and archiving. **Filing is the systematic storing of current records so that they are accessible at any time**. It may mean records on a card index, a visi-index system, where the edge of the cards is raised clear of other cards to give a visible edge where the name of the record can be clearly seen, or a full filing system for correspondence suspended in a cabinet of some sort.

Archiving is the long-term storage of material which is no longer deemed 'current' but which may be required at some future date. Such records may be taken into storage in less accessible areas than the current material. Since legal action on a simple contract cannot be commenced if six years has passed since the date of the contract (Limitation Act 1980), it is common to archive most material for six years (after which it is unlikely that it could be required as evidence in any court case).

More formal agreements such as deeds, indentures, and so on may be the subject of litigation up to 12 years later, and are therefore kept for rather longer, and often indefinitely, since for many organisations which have a sense of history these more formal documents constitute the most interesting materials for historical study, perhaps many years later.

The essential point about filing and archiving is retrieval when required. We must be able to find the information when we need it, though retrieving archived material will be perhaps less easy than retrieving current material. For current material there is much to be said for 'local' filing, that is filing in the department where the records were originally generated, and to which enquiries about them will usually be directed. Centralised filing, by contrast, where records are kept for a whole organisation (for example, a government department) are rarely accessible immediately. Ordinary staff are unable to enter the system to search for a file and would not understand the system anyway. A person who wants a particular file must request it on a special form and in due course it will reach him/her, perhaps several days later. Clearly, with centralised filing, delays are inevitable and those answering an enquiry must get on with other work until the records they need become available.

The administrative officer is naturally very concerned about filing and archiving procedures and with the high costs of the system in terms of the space required, the equipment needed and the labour costs involved.

The rules for filing alphabetically

At this point it is helpful to include a set of rules for filing alphabetically. There are always doubtful points in any filing system, where we are not quite sure what to do about the position of certain names. For example, do we file County of Essex under C or E? Over the years most of these problems have been solved by well-known and established procedures. The best way to bring some order into what is necessarily a fairly complex body of rules is to work through a set of exercises (see *Student Handbook*, p. 70).

Alphabetical filing rules I: Indexing units

The ordinary alphabetical index is used in alphabetical filing to decide in which order the files shall be stored. The sequence is decided by considering the name of the person, or firm, and regarding every element in it as an **indexing unit**. Thus, Margaret Potter has two indexing units, while J.V.H. Knott and Overseas Groupage Forwarders Ltd each have four indexing units.

These indexing units are then inspected to decide which is the first. With personal names the surname is usually chosen as the first indexing unit, and the 'given' names or initials then follow as second, third, and so on, indexing units. With impersonal names, such as the Borough Council of Newtown and the Diocese of Oxford, the first indexing unit is the first word that distinguishes that body from all other bodies. Thus:

Borough (there are many boroughs)

Council (there are many councils)

Newtown (this is, if not unique, at least very distinctive)

We would therefore index the title as: Newtown, Borough Council of.

Two important rules are 'nothing comes before something' and 'short before long'. Thus Potter comes before Potter, H., which comes before Potter, Harry.

Alphabetical filing rules II: Indexing personal names

As already explained, the most important indexing unit, the surname, is placed first. Margaret Potter becomes Potter, Margaret, and J.V.H. Knott becomes Knott, J.V.H. Since K comes before P they would be arranged in sequence as follows:

Knott, J.V.H.

Potter, Margaret

When the surnames have the same first letter, the second letter of the surname is used to decide the sequence or, if necessary, the third letter of the surname. Thus, Tom Driver, Roy Drover and Peter Dimbleby would be indexed in the order shown below:

Dimbleby, Peter

Driver, Tom

Drover, Roy

Where the entire names are identical, the sequence is decided by the address. Thus David Jones, Cardiff, David Jones, Bramhall, David Jones, Stepney, would appear as:

Jones, David, Bramhall

Jones, David, Cardiff

Jones, David, Stepney

Alphabetical filing rules III: titles, degrees and decorations

Titles, degrees and decorations are *not* looked upon as indexing units. They are placed after the name, but are ignored. Thus Mrs Rose Godley, Sir George Godley, Rt Revd Thomas Godley would be listed as:

Godley, Sir George

Godley, Mrs Rose

Godley, Rt Revd Thomas

Alphabetical filing rules IV: names with a prefix

Many names have prefixes, such as O', Mc, Mac, Da, Du, Van and Von. With all such names the whole name is the first indexing unit, so that Peter van Tromp appears as

Van Tromp, Peter

and Leonardo da Vinci as

Da Vinci, Leonardo

Two different methods are used for Mac and Mc. Sometimes a special section in the files is given to these names. If so, Mac and Mc are treated as if they were the same, and all names with these prefixes are filed in the special section under the letters that come after the prefix. Thus Macadam, Macnamara and McCardy would be filed as:

Macadam

McCardy

Macnamara

If there is no special section, then the names are filed as they are written, and the three names listed above would be rearranged as:

Macadam

Macnamara

McCardy

Another group that is often given a separate section is the group of names beginning with Saint or St. If there is a separate section, usually in the 'sa' part of the index, the names are treated as if spelled out in full, that is, Saint, and this is treated as the first indexing unit. Some indexers put all the Saints together, followed by the St's. Others mix them in together, treating them all as Saints and using the second indexing unit to determine the correct order.

Alphabetical filing rules V: hyphenated names

Where a name is hyphenated it is usual to treat the two words which are joined as separate indexing units. There are exceptions to this rule, as shown below, but it holds good for the vast majority of names. Thus Peter Anson-Large, John Wilkes-Browne, John Lampeter-Smythe and Thomas Walker-Upjohn would be filed in order as:

Anson-Large, Peter

Lampeter-Smythe, John

Walker-Upjohn, Thomas

Wilkes-Browne, John

The exceptions to the rule are names which although hyphenated really make a single word, each part being incomplete without the other. Thus Ultra-sonics Ltd or Super-heaters Ltd would be treated as having only two indexing units.

Alphabetical filing rules VI: separate words

Names where separate words occur are treated as if each word was a separate indexing unit, though here again there are exceptions. The rule may be illustrated by:

Make Your Own Board Co. Ltd

Making Merry Wine Co. Ltd

Mending While-U-Wait Co. Ltd

The exceptions are geographical names such as Isle of Man Gas Board. Here Isle of Man is treated as one indexing unit.

Calculations

Another important clerical activity is the field of calculations. True, this may be largely within the accountant's field, since it chiefly takes effect in accounting-related activities such as invoicing, double-entry book-keeping, petty cash, and so on. The widespread use of computers and electronic calculators has made calculating equipment available to almost everyone in every department and has reduced the need for a centralised calculating department where skilled operators check additions, costings, budgets, and so on. However, for major activities where long-term plans are being made, or where the final results of a year's activities are being discovered, there may be a need to check calculations, and this will also be a part of auditing procedures.

11.5 Business correspondence

Business correspondence is to some extent a dying art these days, now that so much correspondence takes the form of e-mail messages. One still receives impeccable correspondence, indeed buckets of it arrive through our letter-boxes every day, but so much of it is junk mail which is immediately filed in the wastepaper basket.

The basic principles of correspondence are still very important and are explained below, but first let us list some of the important aspects of e-mail's intrusion into the correspondence field.

1 E-mail is extremely fast and cheap, arriving in minutes anywhere in the world.
2 It will reach the far corners of the earth in the same time as it takes to reach a downtown address. As most service providers make no charge for e-mail, all it costs you is the cost of your local telephone call. That need not be much, because you do not need to hold on to your service provider while you compose your e-mail letter. Compose your letter, connect to your provider and send the message. The provider will usually check to see if you have any incoming messages, and downloads them. You then disconnect and deal with the e-mail correspondence that has downloaded.
3 Many executives get promoted for their technical, scientific or administrative abilities and not because they are masters of correspondence in English. Such people can feel quite happy with e-mail, which tends to be down-to-earth, brief and informal, and encourages the sender to convey his/her ideas in a more direct and even exciting manner.
4 One often hears people say, 'I wrote to the company and they did not even answer.' However regrettable that may be, executives who are all geared up to answer problems using e-mail may hesitate to respond to ordinary mail, where they may need the help of a secretary. The traditional executive/secretary relationship is much less common than it once was.
5 Many routine letters are avoided these days because a great deal of the information people request is available on a company's web-site and can be downloaded in a few minutes. This is easier than writing in for a brochure and waiting three days for it to arrive.

Despite the above, business correspondence is still important and everyone should be able to write a decent letter which observes the general rules. The administrative officer will often take a supervisory role in the field of correspondence, which is to some extent influenced by the format of business letterheads. It is highly desirable that staff should be trained to write good letters, and a high standard of layout and presentation, which shows uniformity from department to department, is desirable. All new staff may need to be inducted into the use of 'house style', and all staff who are being lined up for promotion may need help in developing this aspect of their work. The best time to insist on such training is in the period leading up to promotion, when attendance at in-house training sessions or secondment for a short course at the local management centre can be seen as a prerequisite to advancement.

Secretaries can have an important role to play in ensuring that the quality of correspondence produced is uniformly high, and for assisting executives who express themselves poorly or spell incorrectly. It should be laid down quite firmly to staff weak in this respect that it is no disgrace to be corrected by a secretary who has been appointed to the post precisely because he/she is competent in the field and able to maintain the standard which is deemed desirable.

Basic principles of correspondence

Business correspondence is the main medium of correspondence between firms. Letters constitute written evidence of the relationship that exists, and it follows that they should be carefully worded so as to be clear and correct. One loosely worded letter to a Greek company with an office in the City of London stated that the price quoted included free delivery. When told to deliver the goods to Singapore, at a cost more than twice the value of the goods themselves, it became apparent that the letter was loosely worded.

Letters should take an appropriate form to suit the subject matter. For example, economy is important in correspondence, and a standard letter which deals with a point that is always cropping up and can be generated by a code from a word processor will reduce correspondence costs considerably. Fig. 11.4 shows such a standard letter.

Other factors affecting the form of a letter are the speed of response required, the degree of secrecy required and the need to include special clauses. For example, where a letter must include a clause saying 'Our terms of payment are cash within 7 days of receipt of invoice', the omission of such a clause has a serious effect on the business relationship established.

Economy is a basic principle of correspondence and efficiency is another. On average it costs about £5 to generate any piece of correspondence, when such costs as executive's wages, typist's wages, stationery, postage, filing, and so on are taken into account. It follows that a 10-second telephone call to answer a query saves money and is more efficient from all points of view. Today correspondence should be reserved for the more weighty aspects of business communication, particularly those where we seek a pattern of business activity which established a contractual relationship with suppliers or customers.

Letters should begin with an appropriate salutation of a formal kind, unless a very personal relationship with a business associate has already been established. In this case the

MEGAPOLIS MAIL ORDER CO LTD

27 The Quay, Megapolis, Hampshire, England.   Tel: 75402

Your Reference: Letter dated 17 October 19--
Our Reference: MOB/ab

21 October 19--

Dear Sir/Madam

The answer to your letter is given on the line marked X below.

Please note
the line marked
X below

1. Your order has already been sent. It left
   our Cayton Street depot on ....

2. Your order was sent today. We regret the
   delay which was caused by ....

3. Your order has been delayed due to difficulties of supply overseas. We hope to be
   able to fulfil it by ....

4. Your order has been held up on the instructions of our credit controller. She tells
   me that you were written to about this
   matter on .... Would you please
   check your files on this matter. In case
   of difficulty please phone Mrs Taylor on
   Extension 291.   ....

5. We can find no trace at all of your order.
   Please send us further details and if
   necessary consult your local post office
   if a loss of money in the post may have
   occurred.   ....

Yours faithfully

M O'Brien
Sales Department

Fig. 11.4 A standard letter which permits a variety of responses

salutation is left out by the typist and the executive writes a free-hand salutation of the 'Dear Bill' or 'Dear Amanda' type.

A subject heading is a great start to most letters, for it ensures that the mail inwards department can route it to the correct person at once. Thus a letter with a sub-heading 'Safety helmets: new design' is going to reach the safety officer more quickly than one with no such sub-heading.

The introductory paragraph should be relatively short, but should set the tone of the letter. It should be followed by a number of paragraphs which deal with the true subject matter of the letter in logical order, lucidly expressed and developing the proposal or argument clearly and concisely. The final paragraph should, if possible, state clearly and concisely what response the writer hopes for from the letter.

The letter should end with a 'complimentary close'. This takes the form usually of two words only, 'Yours faithfully' or 'Yours truly' for an impersonal letter, and 'Yours sincerely' for a slightly more personal, but still formal, close. For example, a letter which begins 'Dear Sir' or 'Dear Madam' would end with 'Yours faithfully' or 'Yours truly', while a letter beginning 'Dear Mr Jones' or 'Dear Mrs Smith' would end 'Yours sincerely'. For warm, personal relationships the closure would not be typed, but the typist would leave a space for a hand-written closure, of a slightly more personal nature. The final part of the letter shows any enclosures, and the distribution of the letter if copies are to be sent to other people than the addressee.

11.6 Mail inwards

The administrative officer will usually supervise the arrangements for receiving mail inwards, which should always be dealt with early in the day if the company receives a considerable volume. In such situations it is usual to collect it from the sorting office in a lockable bag which is opened in the presence of a small team of middle management staff. An array of trays for the various departments should be available, and a letter-opening machine or paper knives, date stamps, paper clips and desk lamps should be available. The mail is then opened and the contents date-stamped to show the date of receipt. The end of the letter should be looked at since it indicates any enclosures, and these should be checked. Special care should be taken of any money, cheques or other financial documents, and any shortage should be witnessed by others present to confirm that the contents are incomplete. The contents should be clipped together if necessary and placed in the appropriate departmental tray. The envelope may be attached to the contents or, if this is not the usual practice, it should be held up to a desk light to confirm that it is empty, before being put in the wastepaper basket. Some offices delay the disposal of such envelopes for one day in case a query arises from any department.

Important documents such as registered letters, recorded delivery letters and so on should be recorded in a mail inwards register and, if it is the agreed practice, cheques and money should be recorded in a remittances inwards register. This will be signed by the cashier when he/she takes delivery of the tray containing the remittances.

11.7 Mail outwards

The post department is an important part of any organisation and a sound system for collecting mail throughout the day and processing it before dispatch is essential. The administrative officer will usually exercise general control over the staff in the post department, who may need support if departmental heads do not lay down strict rules about procedures.

The basic rules are:

1 Mail that is posted early in the day reaches its destination sooner, and escapes the overloading that can occur around evening time when the 'rush hour' for mail causes delays. Early posting is therefore essential.
2 An adequate system of mail trays in all parts of the building ensures that letters and packets are collected regularly throughout the day and can be dealt with systematically.
3 A last collection made at about 4.30 p.m. will mean that other non-urgent mail waits until next day, but 'emergency' correspondence can still be handled by arrangements with the chief clerk in the post department. Those people who habitually abuse the 'emergency' arrangements must be cautioned about it and if necessary reported to the administrative officer who will take the matter up officially.
4 Departmental staff must be trained to indicate which type of postal service is required: first class, second class, recorded delivery, registered post, and so on. They should also be trained to check the contents of letters before sealing them, for example, are all the enclosures actually enclosed, and so on.
5 Private correspondence should not be posted at the expense of the company.
6 Procedures for preserving receipts of registered letters, recorded delivery and express items should be established.
7 Executives who delay signing letters until late in the day seriously hamper the work of the post department. Secretaries should be instructed to build into their executives' diaries short sessions between other appointments when letters can be signed, while if mail is not of major importance it should be signed pp (*per pro*) the executive using a subscription of the type 'Dictated by… and signed in his/her absence'.
8 Franking machines (postage meters) should be used wherever possible to reduce the use of postage stamps. It is now possible to reset them electronically over the telephone.

11.8 Systems for producing business correspondence

Most offices are now so heavily computerised that the traditional secretarial posts where typing, audio typing, dictation systems and the personal secretary/executive relationship existed are much less common. There are a number of packages available which enable the computer to be used for ordinary correspondence, report writing etc, and more sophisticated presentations are possible with a spreadsheet facility. These have made it possible for almost anyone to produce good quality correspondence and documents. Everyone can become his/her own secretary. The following situations arise:

E-mail

As mentioned already many executives have an e-mail address and type their own e-mails on their computer terminals. Top level executives may save time by using secretarial help with e-mails, but everyone should be encouraged to handle e-mails themselves, and staff in line for promotion should be sent on in-house training courses or short courses at local colleges or training centres to develope computer literacy in this respect.

Word processing

Word processing is now available to almost all staff through a computer terminal. Once available as a dedicated word-processing machine, the move to generalized word-processing software has made the many advantages of word-processing available to all PC users. Administrative officers are key personnel in ensuring that most members of staff have been inducted into the use of word-processing software. The great advantage is that text can be changed as often as you want before printing off the final document or correspondence. The rought draft of a letter, or a report, can be saved on the computer while we circulate it to interested parties calling for comments and criticisms. When they arrive the text can be amended to give a finished product. The style and layout can be varied, headings and sub-headings can be inserted and changed, you can edit the text on the screen and WYSIWYG (what you see is what you get) applies. This means that if you use special printing effects, bold print, or italic, justified right hand margin (a straight right hand margin) etc you will actually see it on the screen. What you see on the screen is what you will get when you print out the final letter or document. The term WYSIWYG is pronounced 'wizzy-wig'. Many universities and schools make word-processing facilities available to all students in a first term compulsory computer literacy course. Familiarisation with computer hardware and software is a basic need for all staff today and the resulting improvement in the legibility of student coursework makes this initial introduction well-worth while. Further refinements are the attachment of spell-checkers and grammar checkers, while a thesaurus (treasury of words) enables students to consult lists of synonyms or antonyms to find the best word for their essays. With a dictionary you know the word you want, and wish to check its spelling or meaning. With a thesaurus you know what you want to say, but you can't think of the best word to say it. The thesaurus will lead you to it. Once the course is completed students are free to use the word-processing terminals provided around the campus for their own needs, and many will of course set up their own computers in their own rooms on campus.

Back-up secretarial support

Secretarial assistance may still be required by staff in many firms but the traditional presonal secretary/executive relationship is likely to be reserved for very senior staff, with the secretary being designated personal assistant (PA) and fulfilling a very broad range of activities. At lower levels, with so much work being done by staff themselves, what secretarial help is provided may well be of a group nature, one secretary doing work as required for a number of executives. In many situations this is an advantage. For example a laboratory may call for secretarial help which has a particular scientific vocabulary, and the secretary doing work for the staff will become familiar with the terms used and develop his/her own shortforms which speed up dictation on such matters. The danger is that a lazy executive will throw a bigger burden on the secretary than is really fair, and an admin officer may find it necessary to restore the balance with a quiet word. A genuine need for extra secretarial help can be met by an audio-typing system.

Audio-typing

This technique can be centrally organised, with a large number of executives linked to central banks of dictation machines. The service is impersonal, with the executive separated from the typist. The work is allocated by a supervisor to a suitable typist, whose work is checked before returning it to the executive. Naturally a time lag occurs, correspondence being part of a routine activity which proceeds at its own pace unless special arrangements are made for emergency treatment. The executive needs to be trained in the use of the equipment, for example, letters are best dictated in small batches, the executive breaking off contact with the machine after a few letters and reconnecting again. This enables the supervisor to remove one cassette and pass the work to a typist who is free, while the executive's next batch of letters has been connected to another machine.

Audio-typists must be able to type at a good basic speed, and to spell and punctuate correctly. Typing from the headphones directly on to the word-processor requires accuracy in spelling, judgement of where a new paragraph is to begin and a good grasp of display.

Personal secretaries and personal assistants

At these levels the secretary is a highly competent person.with first-class secretarial skills, able to control staff and to represent the executive he/she serves in many ways. The executive/secretarial relationship becomes one of partnership, with the secretary knowing everyone in the organisation on the executive's behalf, and behaving in a professional manner at all times. This ensures the executive is highly regarded and fully informed about all matters likely to be of interest to him/her. The secretary can make an extremely effective (and cost-effective) contribution to the work of the company by ensuring that the executive's time is used in the best possible way, routine matters being attended to without any need for consultation and the more important work being fully anticipated, fully prepared and followed up in the greatest detail to make the best possible contribution to the total efforts of the company.

11.9 Meetings

Meetings assist communication within the firm or company and help with decision-making in a particular area of activity. They often promote democracy within the organisation, by turning what would otherwise be board decisions imposed from above into consensus decisions reached by a group delegated to attend as representatives from various departments. There are many different types of meetings, ranging from statutory meetings required by law (such as the annual general meetings of companies), board meetings, standing committee meetings, *ad hoc* meetings and departmental meetings. Standing committees are those which meet regularly to consider special sectors of work, for example health and safety at work committees or welfare committees. *Ad hoc* committees meet to consider a particular problem, and once it is solved the committee is dissolved. Thus an industrial accident, or the dismissal of an employee, or a redundancy situation might call for an *ad hoc* committee to be appointed.

Generally speaking, all meetings should show some degree of formality, for example, there should be a chairperson in charge, to whom all speeches are addressed. Two people cannot speak at once 'through the chair' and private conversations between groups are not allowed, if only because they cannot possibly be minuted by the minuting secretary. Most meetings will follow a set agenda agreed in advance between the chairperson and the secretary of the committee, and minutes will be kept. Minutes are a written record of the procedures, but need not include detailed summaries of everything said. They should list the resolutions proposed, and the results of the votes on these proposals. All meetings start with the minutes of the last meeting, but if these have been circulated to members beforehand it may be proposed 'that the minutes be taken as read' and the rather tedious business of reading them be avoided. Where a meeting is called to allow people to air a grievance and speak their minds freely without fear of victimisation, the taking of minutes may be dispensed with.

The administrative officer will often take the chair at meetings and it is important for him/her to know the proper procedures and to keep the members of the committee in order and the discussion relevant to the matters in hand. Important points in the organisation of meetings are:

1 *Preparation of the agenda* The agenda is prepared by the secretary, who sets up a system for enabling all members to propose items for it, with a deadline for submission. The items will be discussed with the chairperson and arranged in the best order. The agenda will then be circulated, together with the minutes of the last meeting and any special documents or reports which are to be considered at the meeting. If a report is not ready it will be shown as 'to be tabled', which means members will find a copy on the table at the meeting.

A special agenda called a 'chairman's agenda' is prepared for the chairperson. It contains more details about the agenda items than would be required by an ordinary committee member, for example, a brief summary of the position with regard to an agenda item, the names of any persons who are to attend to give a report, and room for the chairperson to make notes about the decisions taken or any matters to be attended to as a result of today's meeting.

2 *Items at the start of a meeting* These include 'apologies for absence' and 'minutes of the previous meeting' (unless it is proposed that they be taken as read). The chairperson will sign the minutes if the meeting agrees that they are a true record of the previous meeting. The next item is 'matters arising'. Thus it may have been agreed that Mr A should undertake to interview a particular person, and he needs to report back. Any member may ask for clarification of any matter, but if it is the subject of an agenda item further down the list, the chairperson will ask that it be left until that point in the meeting.

3 *The main agenda items* Each agenda item is now dealt with in turn. Sometimes non-members are called in to give information or opinions upon matters under discussion and the chairperson will introduce them, and thank them at the end of the discussion before they leave. The chair's job is to keep the discussion moving ahead as briskly as possible, and to draw out what is the consensus view of the problem. This will result in a resolution being proposed, seconded, discussed, perhaps amended, and finally passed in a form which will lead to positive action before the next meeting.

4 *The final items on the agenda* These are AOB (any other business) and 'date of next meeting'. The former gives any member who is aggrieved because an item he/she proposed was not accepted for the agenda the opportunity to speak about the matter. It is also a suitable point to give items of news to committee members on matters unrelated to the work of the committee. The 'date of next meeting' enables members to have advance warning for their diaries. Some people are very busy, and if a date can be agreed for which most members are available it ensures a successful next meeting.

The minutes

The minutes of the meeting should be taken by the secretary but sometimes a special 'minuting' secretary is appointed to leave the secretary free to make reports, join in the discussion, and so on. The minutes should be couched in temperate language which will not colour them. For example, the statement 'a violent argument then began' would not be appropriate language (even if it was true), and the discussion would be better described as 'a lively debate'.

After the meeting the minuting secretary should write or type the minutes as soon as possible, while the significant features of the discussions that have taken place are fresh in his/her mind. They should embody all the resolutions that were proposed, with the result of the voting, and particular activities to be carried out by individuals or subcommittees should be mentioned for follow-up at the next meeting. The chairperson should be shown a draft of the minutes, in case he/she feels they are in any way defective as a true record of the meeting. The corrected version will then be reproduced in sufficient copies and held ready for circulation just before the date of the next meeting.

Follow-up activities

A number of activities follow from any meeting and the chairperson and secretary will usually confer about these. For example, if particular members have been asked to make certain arrangements or collect certain information before the next meeting, it is helpful to put this in writing to them as soon as the meeting is over. It confirms that a responsibility has been placed upon them, reminds them what they have to do and instructs them to liaise with the chairperson (usually well before the next meeting, so that the item can become an agenda item).

The smooth working of committees is assisted if a high standard of courteous conduct is observed, and the secretary and chairperson will usually cooperate to ensure that letters of appreciation are sent to members, people who give special reports, catering staff, and so on. Although these may seem trivial items they build the confidence of junior members of staff and are appreciated by other members who perhaps have volunteered to do a job which others in their departments preferred to avoid.

Terminology at meetings

Every activity has its special terminology and it is essential to know the vocabulary of meetings. A **quorum** is the minimum number of members that must be present at a meeting under the rules, if any resolutions passed, or decisions made, are to be valid. A meeting cannot be allowed to start without a quorum, and a poorly attended meeting where some members leave may be forced to adjourn if the attendance falls below a quorum. Some members are appointed *ex officio* (because of the office they hold). For example, the personnel officer will usually be an *ex officio* member of a welfare committee, whereas the works representatives will be members because they have been elected to attend by colleagues in the departments where they work. A **motion** is a proposal to be considered by the meeting. The **proposer** speaks to the motion and advances the arguments which led him/her to propose it. The **seconder** follows to support the proposal. The debate then opens up, and members may speak when the chairperson gives them permission. If an **amendment** to the proposal is suggested, this will be voted on first and, if carried, the proposal is reworded to take account of it. Finally the proposer may reply to the debate before a vote on the proposal, or the amended proposal, is taken. The proposal then becomes a **resolution**, which has been proposed, seconded and carried, that is, passed by a majority vote. The vote may be unanimous or *nem con* (no-one contradicting it), or by a majority, for example 16–5. An exactly equal number of votes may be resolved by the chairperson's **casting vote**, a second vote allowed to the chairperson to resolve the difficulty.

If a matter is allowed to **lie on the table** it means that it cannot be pursued any further on this occasion and will be left open for the present, pending developments before the next meeting. A motion 'move next business' appeals to the chairperson to leave the matter under discussion since agreement seems impossible, and to move the meeting on to the next agenda item.

Every committee over the years builds up a collection of rules for the conduct of its affairs which become known as **standing orders**. They originate in the constitution of the club, or organisation, but new rules are added by general agreement as experience dictates. If a member feels that the rules are not being observed, he/she may interrupt the proceedings 'on a point of order' and object to the way in which standing orders are being ignored. If the **point of order** is established, the chairperson will ensure that the meeting follows the usual procedure from that point onwards.

To **adjourn** is to suspend the proceedings until another time. If time runs out, or if it seems unlikely that the agenda can be completed for any reason, the chairperson may propose an adjournment, and if the meeting agrees the proceedings come to an end until they are resumed at a further meeting, of which proper notice has been given.

11.10 Conferences and functions

The general administrative officer will usually have a large part to play in any conference or function that takes place, and will almost certainly supervise the general arrangements, even though the details may be delegated to others. Generally speaking, the work involved in such activities is enormous, and it is common to find that there are too many chiefs and too few subordinates on the day of the event. For this reason a very senior member of staff is required who can order heads of departments to delegate an adequate staff for the activity, and ensure their attendance and effort to make the whole thing a success. A small subcommittee may be formed especially for the occasion, and well before the date. Its first job is to think the whole thing through, stage by stage, so that the entire procedure is known and preparations are made well in advance. Everything – from booking the venue, finding the speakers, sending out invitations, down to a bouquet for the lady mayor who declares the function open – has to be considered and planned.

Preparations for the event

A file should be opened which will contain details of all the conference activities and divided into sections which will enable each aspect to be considered separately, and also as part of the whole. Some of the activities will be delegated to particular members of staff – for example, responses to invitations, the collection of fees, invoicing, and so on – but at the end a short report on the final outcome and the success (or weaknesses) of the system should be incorporated in the file for future reference. Some of the more important preparatory activities are given below, but they will vary with the type of function.

1 Preparation of a programme of activities with the executive who is acting as the conference organiser. This programme may need to be approved by the board or senior members of staff.

2 Finding and ensuring the cooperation of leading figures who will speak, or perform, or be members of panels, and so on.

3 Booking accommodation and ensuring that all the facilities required are available should any defect in the arrangements manifest itself on the day. Arrangements may require conference rooms, seminar rooms, telephone, fax, photocopying, computers,

overhead projection facilities, canteen or restaurant arrangements, car parking, toilet facilities, and so on. These should all be inspected.

4 Preparation of invitations, programmes, folders of conference materials, car stickers, tickets, personal badges, and so on, preferably all bearing a distinctive logo. This is helpful for identification purposes and general security, assists staff who are attending to car parks and reception areas and generally assists conference delegates in finding their way around.

5 Transport often presents problems at such exhibitions, both for VIPs and ordinary delegates who may need to be taken on trips to inspect installations, works and so on. Penny-pinching on transport is likely to cause trouble, and an adequate budget is essential so that reliable firms can be booked who have the range of vehicles necessary.

6 The costing of such events is important; the budget must be adequate and must be approved well in advance. The expenses incurred must be fully documented (external receipts and petty cash vouchers for all disbursements wherever possible, and internal petty cash vouchers countersigned by a senior member of staff if an external receipt is not possible). The final report should include a detailed statement of income and expenditure, and an evaluation of the whole exercise from the financial point of view.

Activities during the event

The chief administrative officer has many tasks to perform each day of a conference or other function, and peace of mind is essential as far as the routine organisation is concerned. Everyone should know what his/her job is and should be on hand punctually to do it. Careful selection of reliable staff well in advance ensures that all posts are manned on the day. This should leave the administrative officer free to act as host/hostess, and as a reference point for all problems. Each part of the programme has its difficulties to be overcome, and several snags may occur at once, so the presence of an adequate back-up team is essential, to whom some of the problems can be delegated.

The worst aspect of all such events is the final clearing-up session when the work-shy will slope off on some pretence or other and a few noble souls are usually to be found facing a backbreaking series of activities. It is essential to reduce the strain as much as possible by clear instructions about the dismantling of the activity; timely reminders to those who have particular areas of responsibility; a word of praise for all those playing their proper parts and a bit of help to those who are most hard-pressed. Since the administrative officer gets much of the credit for a successful event it is helpful if those lower down the hierarchy know that the praise is well-deserved because they have seen the efforts for themselves. In general it is advisable to stay to the very end, and thus ensure that no-one has been more imposed upon than oneself.

Follow-up activities

A wide variety of follow-up activities is necessary after any major function and the administrative officer will be responsible for many of them. They include such matters as letters of thanks to the celebrities and personalities who played a major part in the event, and the payment of any fees or expenses agreed; letters of thanks to members of staff who bore the brunt of the extra effort required; and a report in any in-house journal or in the trade press may need to be written or approved. All hired or loaned equipment should be returned in good order, and any breakages or defects should be reported and if necessary an accommodation made for losses or repairs. The file on the activity should be completed, including reference notes for future functions about things that went wrong or went particularly well. Useful notices, posters, signs for car parks and so on should be safely stored and their whereabouts recorded. Sales documentation or other material likely to be of use should be passed through to those needing to take action upon them, and the very broadest view should be taken. For example, delegates to a conference in the course of questions and discussion may reveal that there is an export opportunity or a personnel problem in their own countries which the firm or company could readily solve. The person most likely to be able to take advantage of such an opportunity should be officially alerted to it, and if the bottom of the letter reveals that copies have been sent to the managing director and the chairman, it is more likely that the person concerned will take an interest.

One final activity is to record in the filing system somewhere the names, addresses and telephone numbers of any organisations that proved useful or helpful during the event. Thus if there is a departmental system for filing such records – for everything from the names of future speakers, possible chairpersons for future seminars, subjects which seem to interest delegates, and so on, down to the names of plumbers and electricians who were helpful in some crisis moment – all these should be recorded in the system.

11.11   Delegation

The chief administrative officer has to oversee many activities and must delegate some of the work to subordinates. *Delegation may be defined as the transfer to lower level staff of the responsibility for performing a given task or set of duties, and for making management decisions consistent with the duties to be undertaken.* Once responsibility has been delegated, the subordinate should be allowed to act without officious monitoring of the area of responsibility, while at the same time the senior member of staff is available for consultation should any problem arise.

Delegation is essential to the operation of large-scale businesses, and enables senior staff to free themselves of routine activities to concentrate on the more significant management tasks. Delegation puts a subordinate in charge of an area of work which is believed to be within his/her capacity. It helps staff to develop, to take responsibility, to gain experience in a new field and it promotes self-esteem and peer-group recognition. It reduces bottlenecks, defined as situations where one person is retaining control of too many areas of work, so that some areas are starved of attention and consequently cannot make progress. It distributes the work-load more fairly and enables decisions to be made at lower levels. It gives people the chance to make mistakes and to be held accountable for them, which is part of the business of gaining experience and developing prudence and caution in business affairs.

At the same time, delegation does not mean that the senior member of staff has shed all responsibility for the delegated activity, which is still within his/her span of control. The senior member of staff must still bear the responsibility for errors made (and still takes the credit for any successes achieved, though with due recognition of the subordinate's efforts). The senior must support the junior member of staff where problems arise, and help to resolve them. A periodic review of the area of work delegated gives the executive control without day-to-day supervision.

Delegation is most effective where it is properly announced or promulgated so that everyone is aware of the measure of responsibility conferred upon the subordinate. The authority to act comes from the public designation of the subordinate as a fit and proper person for control of the area concerned.

12 Other responsibilities of the administrative officer

12.1 The organisation and methods department *procedures, process, systems*

From time to time all aspects of business administration should be re-examined to see whether they are effective, or are due for revision and for computerisation. There is practically no area of activity that cannot be computerised to some extent, so that any reappraisal calls for consideration of this aspect in particular. In large organisations it is usual to set up an organisation and methods department charged with the responsibility of keeping methods of work under review and devising new systems as required. Usually the department will be a separate 'staff' department, perhaps responsible directly to the board, or the managing director or general administration officer as representing the board and making its recommendations to him/her. It will tackle problems:

1 When referred to it by the board because some concern has been expressed at board level for a variety of reasons (for example, bottlenecks in production or distribution, complaints by the public, suspected overstaffing, and so on).
2 When requested to do so by department heads concerned with
   a a new procedure or
   b an expensive procedure which they feel can be improved or
   c low morale because of tedious procedures or
   d difficulties in recruitment, and labour turnover to more attractive posts elsewhere.
3 When complete reappraisals *analisis* are ordered so that an amalgamation or a reorganisation *merge* can take place.
4 When an area of work comes under scrutiny *minuoso* simply because its turn has come as part of a process of review which systematically examines all areas of activity.

Conducting a review of organisation and methods

The basic principles of such a review are: ~~Laying~~ *writing* down what to do.
1 *The terms of reference* The appropriate authority (the board, the managing director or the general administrative officer) will notify the department to be investigated and send a set of terms of reference to the head of the O&M department and to the head of department concerned. The terms of reference must be clear, detailing the area to be investigated, giving any reasons for the review, calling upon the two departments to

cooperate in a proper manner and specifying the degree of authority granted to the O&M department during the review period. It should call for a clear time limit on the investigation and for a report and recommendations.

2 *The existing situation* The first stage is to discover and record the present situation. A preliminary meeting discusses in general terms what is done at present in the area under investigation and broad headings will be drawn up which will become the subject of detailed examination later. We seek to discover what is done, and why, who carries out the grass-roots work, how he/she does it, what use is made of it, where it takes place and so on. Detailed examination will follow procedures through the company, discover at what point the work of one department triggers another department into activity, and so on. In the process the various machines used, inputs to the system (such as forms bought in from outside), filing systems and archiving procedures will all be noted. These will then become the subject of detailed appraisal and reports. Care is needed to ensure staff cooperation in these investigations, and reassurances of staff positions may be necessary.

3 *The analysis of the present situation* Once the O&M department knows what is done and the investigated department concedes that it is a true and fair view, the whole procedure will be analysed strictly in the light of the terms of reference. Is a particular procedure necessary at all? If so, is it soundly conceived? Are the staff employed on it working in the best way, or could the system be improved? How many problems arise with the procedure, and what is the cost of correcting the errors? How serious is the backlog of work (if any)? Is there any idle time, either of staff or machines?

4 *Proposals for changes* When the analysis has led to conclusions about the changes that are needed and will best meet future needs, a clear specification has to be drawn up of the proposed new system and the documentation, personnel, equipment and so on which will be required. The effect on output, costs, machine utilisation and efficiency should be evaluated and a detailed report should be drawn up. This should include detailed statements of the procedures to be followed which should then be open to discussion and comment from those actually involved. They should be asked to submit written comments where this seems necessary. Finally, the whole plan should be presented to the authority that commissioned the investigation, and after discussion, if adopted, plans to implement the new procedures should be made.

5 *Implementing the new procedures* So far as possible, the new procedure should be phased in 'in parallel' with the existing system, records being kept by both methods for a few weeks so that any defect in the new system can be discovered and sorted out without any loss of data or information. It may be necessary to bring in the new system in stages, to develop staff familiarity with it and the manual of procedures associated with it. Prompt feedback of any difficulties to the O&M design team so that they can sort out any teething problem is essential. Ultimately a full evaluation of the new system is made, and conclusions are drawn about it.

12.2 Security aspects of business

All enterprises are subject to security risks. The commonest risks are the security of cash, stocks and other valuables, but the security of information, ideas, inventions, new products, and so on, is just as vital. Confidentiality in personal and business affairs is essential and terrorism is always a possibility. The general administration officer is the most likely person to assume responsibility for security matters, though he/she may liaise with other senior staff in areas where the risks are high. Generally speaking, we cannot be too vigilant and a security aspect enters into almost every type of business activity.

Theft

Theft is the dishonest appropriation of the property of another, with the intention of permanently depriving the other of it (Theft Act 1968, s.1). Theft can be prevented by a security-conscious attitude towards any areas where money, stocks or capital assets are handled, stored or used. Much theft is opportunist theft – the thief sees an opportunity and takes it, despite the risk of being caught in the act. Doors should not be left open, goods waiting to be loaded or in the process of unloading should not be left unsupervised, careful checking of loading bays, exit gates and so on should be the rule and a documentary system which gives control should be introduced. For example, invoices can have an extra 'gate copy' showing what has been purchased by a customer. This is presented by the customer to the gatekeeper who does a visual check of what is being taken out.

Where money is concerned, safe systems for handling petty cash, such as the imprest system, provide a framework of control. The imprest system gives the petty cashier a known sum of money (usually enough to cover an average week's expenditure) called the imprest. Sums spent are recorded, and a petty cash voucher obtained for each outlay (for example, a post office will give a receipt for postage stamps purchased). At the end of the period the petty cashier strikes a balance on the book, which must agree with the balance of cash in hand, presents both the book and the money to the chief cashier, who checks them and restores the imprest (that is, makes up the cash available to the agreed imprest figure) for a further period.

In supermarkets and in garage forecourt shops, where considerable sums of money are taken from customers, it is usual to remove large notes at intervals (say, every hour) from all tills. The arrangement leaves the cashiers less vulnerable to raids, and speeds up the banking process since large amounts of the takings can be cashed up and the book-keeping entries made during the ordinary working day, rather than after closing time. It also means less temptation for cashiers, since most of the money available is in small-value coins and the valuable, portable notes have been removed.

Burglary

Burglary is entry to premises to commit theft or cause grievous bodily harm. Premises should preferably be protected by a caretaking or security guard system. If this is not possible, attention must be paid to the locking up of premises, the safe custody of keys, burglar alarms of various sorts may be installed and a local keyholder whose name and address is known to the police should be available. The general administration officer should liaise with the local crime prevention officer and take advice about vulnerable aspects of the premises, security locks on windows and so on.

Industrial espionage

Industrial espionage is theft of expertise by people who are knowledgeable in a particular field for sale to rival manufacturers and traders. It is a well-known fact that Paris fashions can be on sale in London, New York and elsewhere within days of the latest styles being revealed. Similar copying in the technological field is a source of loss to many inventors, research organisations and so on. Electronic bugging, concealed cameras and natural ingenuity (in that many people have photographic memories and only need to see something for a few seconds to remember every detail) are responsible for many of these losses. The detection of such espionage is not easy and requires systematic records of visitors and callers, staffing of reception areas at all times, security doors which only admit visitors who have proved their identity, and so on.

Without being paranoid about such matters, we should suspect everyone: customers, competitors, applicants for jobs (who subsequently perhaps do not take up the position offered them but simply applied to get into the building and have a look around), past employees, and so on. A record of visitors should be taken and preserved because later (when the industrial espionage becomes apparent) it may be possible to pinpoint certain suspects who could have been responsible.

Letter bombs

Today the terrorist is to be found in all walks of life – every conceivable kind of bee is to be found buzzing in every type of bonnet, and there are people in positions of power around the world who are only too quick to show the bees how to sting. The ordinary mail is a particularly easy way to introduce bombs into unsuspecting premises, and often the person who addresses the letter or parcel bomb has made some simple error which means the wrong target altogether has been selected. All incoming mail should be scrutinised, and the best guidance is that given by the Metropolitan Police of London. Their hang-up card, which is available for display in mail-rooms, is self-explanatory and embodies years of experience of dealing with hundreds of bombs of every sort.

Bombs in the post – be alert
Look for the unusual:

- Shape
- Size
- Thickness
- Sealing

- Wrapping
- Grease marks
- Signs of wires or batteries
- Postmark

- Writing
- Spelling
- Wrong name, title or address
- Unsolicited mail

If you are suspicious:

Don't

1 Don't try to open it
2 Don't press, squeeze or prod it
3 Don't put it in sand or water
4 Don't put it in a container
5 Don't let anyone else do any of these

Do

1 Keep calm
2 Look for the sender's name on the back
3 Check with the sender
4 Check with the addressee

Still think you've got one?

- Leave it where found
- Evacuate the room
- Lock the door and keep the key
- Send for the security officer
- Phone the police – dial 999

12.3 Risk management

Risks are inseparable from business activity. The taking of calculated risks is a day-to-day part of every decision-maker's life. Probably the new enterprise is the most vulnerable one, and the number that do not survive the first year is indicative of the serious risks that have to be run. Insurance is one way of reducing risk. All insurance policies reduce risks considerably, or at least reduce the consequences of misfortune considerably, but we cannot usually afford to obtain cover against every eventuality, and some risks in any case are non-insurable risks. A non-insurable risk is one that is insusceptible to statistical calculation. Insurance depends upon the calculation of future risks by statisticians called actuaries, and if there is no evidence on which the calculations can be based the actuaries cannot predict the probability that a loss will occur. Thus the risk that I shall prove to be a fool in business or the risk that the product that I deem to be desirable will prove unpopular with the public cannot be calculated, and I must bear the risk myself. That is why ordinary capital in a limited company is called risk capital. If the uses to which it is being put prove to be badly conceived, losses will be made and the persons who contributed the capital will lose their money. Profit, say economists, is the reward for taking risks, and losses, by contrast, are the penalties for poor risk management. All business risks may be said to be 'economic' risks.

The chief types of risk are as follows:

Physical risks

These are the risks of physical destruction of assets, such as premises, motor vehicles, plant and machinery, furniture and fittings, work in progress, finished goods and stocks of every kind. The physical destruction may be caused by fire, flood or inherent vice (machines rust, fruit decays, cattle get ill, paper gets damp, vital employees have accidents and their services cease to be available, and so on). Risks like burglary, theft and theft by employees are akin to physical risks in that the use of the property is lost to the owner even though it is not physically destroyed.

Physical risks can be reduced by proper systems of work, security, training of staff, and so on. For example, theft by employees can be reduced by proper accounting and recording procedures, as explained in the security section. Proper training of staff to develop merchandising skills and husbandry skills will reduce inherent vice problems. Stock losses can be reduced by careful buying and refusal to take speculative positions with stocks. A speculative position is one where, because it appears that a profitable opportunity will develop, more stock is purchased of a particular type than would normally be disposed of in a trading period. If the speculation does not in fact prove correct, deterioration of stock will take place before the sale can be made.

Adequate precautions must be taken against fire, and if they are the risks will be reduced and the losses also. A small fire may be quickly extinguished and the loss suffered will be reduced. Consequential losses (loss of profits during the period of reconstruction) will also be reduced.

Insurance cannot in itself reduce risks, except that an insurance company will usually inspect premises and advise on the adequacy of the facilities available to fight fires, prevent burglaries, and so on. Insurance spreads the losses suffered over a great many potential companies and firms, by pooling the risks. Those at risk pay a contribution, called a **premium**, into a pool of money. The premium varies with the cover required and the probability that a loss will occur. The unfortunate ones who suffer the loss are compensated from the pool. In this way the heavy losses of the few are compensated out of the minor losses of many (the premiums contributed).

Some physical risks can be reduced by dispersal – a number of small depots is better than one central warehouse – for it is unlikely that all will catch fire or be burgled at the same time. The individual losses will therefore be smaller, while the ability to bring stocks in from other depots reduces the disruption that occurs.

Technical risks

Technical risks are those which must be faced in any sort of technical or technological work. The ideas of 'mad' inventors do not always work; even when they do they may be superseded by a better idea before they are off the drawing-board. Years of technical expertise with mechanical calculators were wiped out almost overnight by the electronic calculator. To reduce such risks it is necessary to keep up-to-date in the whole technical field in which we operate. It is essential to keep training and education going so that an adequate core of staff is available, and to encourage innovative ideas and the application of knowledge to solving the practical affairs of the company. Outside consultants should be brought in if there is a real need to solve some technical problem quickly.

Marketing risks

There is always a risk that the products we manufacture will fail to achieve the sales we hoped to achieve. Market research beforehand may prevent the development of a product which is unlikely to appeal, and marketing activities during the initial period, if skilfully done, may ensure the success of a product which otherwise might stumble.

Personal risks

Fate knocks on someone's door every day. We are all at risk personally: 'Never ask yourself for whom the bell tolls, it tolls for thee.' For this reason it is usual to take certain precautions to protect a business from the loss of key personnel, and all businesses have an insurable interest in the lives and well-being of staff, managers and directors. Taking partnerships as an example, there are two situations which develop from the death of a partner: firstly, there is a loss of his/her skill and judgement which will need to be replaced by taking on a new partner or an employee; secondly, the partnership is dissolved by death and the deceased partner's share will almost certainly be withdrawn in cash. There must be cash available sufficient to meet this need, and this requires life assurance on each partner for the benefit of the other partners (not the widow or dependants). The death of the partner produces a lump sum which is used to pay off the deceased's heirs. Similarly a company may take out a 'death in service' policy on a key director to ensure that, should the director die, a lump sum will become available which could be used to employ a consultant, or act as an inducement to a person of similar skills to join the company.

External risks

External risks are those which are inherent in the nature of business generally, for example, wars and civil wars may interrupt supplies from a traditional supplier or make it impossible to sell goods to a particular overseas market. A general trade depression may reduce the market for goods or may delay payment or prevent it altogether. Such events as the rise in oil prices demanded by OPEC countries in 1973/74 not only made petrol more expensive but drastically reduced the demand for cars, and entire tanker fleets were laid up with a consequent depression in shipping and other transport industries. Such risks are very difficult to predict, are largely uninsurable and the chief safeguard is to be as widely diversified as possible. Thus it is never wise for the purchasing officer to be totally committed to a single supplier, or for one sales area to be developed to the total neglect of others.

In almost all sections of the commodity markets it is possible to make 'hedging' contracts. A hedging contract is one that shelters a trader from the bitter winds that blow in all markets at certain times. It is usually arranged with a speculator who is prepared to speculate by offering forward prices which will be honoured even if the price moves adversely. Thus A, a flour miller, may buy forward wheat at a price which will enable him to mill it into flour at a profit. If the price rises, the wheat on the market when the due date arrives will be more expensive. In theory the speculator would have to buy the wheat at the market price and supply it at the contract price. In fact the speculator would leave it to A to buy the wheat on the free market, but would pay him the difference in price, the speculator having lost money. If the price fell before the due date, A would still have to pay the agreed contractual price, and the speculator would have made a profit on the speculation. Either way, A gets the wheat at a price at which he can make a profit by milling it. A wants his normal business to operate in the normal way at a normal profit, and not be affected by market swings.

Financial risks

There are many types of financial risk. The risk of bad debts is one, and the solution to it is a sound system of credit control (see p. 118) and unhesitating resort to court action where payment is slow. Where dividends are kept low to provide funds for the replacement of depreciating assets or for the expansion of the business it means that the funds which otherwise would have been paid to shareholders are available in cash form within the business. They may easily be used unwisely, or even embezzled, if left 'sloshing around' in the financial system. It is best to invest them in a sinking fund, a balanced portfolio of shares and other securities which will themselves earn dividends or interest pending management decisions about the purchase of new fixed assets.

In export trade the risk of non-payment by foreign debtors, or of default by foreign state buyers, or of official action to prevent the release of foreign exchange, is fairly large. It is possible to take out cover against these and other eventualities with an official body, the Export Credits Guarantee Department (ECGD). Your local BusinessLink will advise on such cover. Such a policy is relatively economical, and clear terms of compensation will mean that payment of the vast majority of the invoice value will be made if the risks covered should occur.

Another type of financial risk is the risk of losses by staff mis-use of the telephone and computer links made available. Now that we can dial anywhere in the world it is very easy for staff to make personal long-distance calls to friends and relations abroad. Through the voicemail system it is even possible to do this from home, dialling in to the voicemail system and then out again at company expense. It is even possible for telephone hackers to do the same thing by accessing the voicemail system and then dialling out.

Night security guards have been known to while away the time by listening in on chat lines at premium rates. Such activities must be controlled by the administrative officer. A system of call logging is available which detects what extension made particular calls, and enables the matter to be taken up with the member of staff concerned. Misuse of the telephone has been declared judicially to be theft. All new staff should be warned on induction that mis-use of the telephone for private purposes will be treated seriously, and an occasional reminder in house journals is advisable.

Similarly, where access to the Internet is available, staff may browse the net for all sorts of private reasons, and download matter which may, or may not, incur a fee. Perhaps the most serious 'cost' in this is the time they spend browsing the net when they should be getting on with their work.

To conclude, we may say that risk management is inseparable from business activity, and requires constant vigilance, with the full implications of each aspect of business being thought through and action taken to reduce risks and minimise losses.

12.4 The environment of organisations

All organisations operate within an environment which assists them in their business or other activities and also acts as a restraint upon them by curtailing activities which are antisocial or adversely affect the environment. We may divide these environmental influences into four parts or fields, the economic environment, the legal environment, the social environment and the political environment.

The **economic environment** is the pattern of demand for goods and services, and the resulting supply situation. How shall wealth be created? When it has been created, how shall it be shared out? This part of the environment has a profound effect on business activity, influencing what is done, how it is done, and so on.

The **legal environment** reflects the society in which we live, a series of nation-states. Each lays down laws for the guidance of human conduct which must be obeyed by its citizens. Where several states combine, as in the USA or the European Union, states' rights naturally must be subordinated to some extent either to federal law or community law.

The **social environment** influences what organisations do. The unfettered behaviour of firms in the *laissez-faire* era of the industrial revolution described by Adam Smith in his famous book *The Wealth of Nations* proved to be socially unacceptable. *Laissez-faire* means 'leave things to work themselves out', and implies that organisations should not be interfered with, for fear of discouraging production and reducing the output of useful goods and services. This idea has long been abandoned and the social environment in which firms work now places grave responsibilities and heavy costs upon them. Have these costs become so heavy that the goose has given up laying its golden eggs? It is certainly a matter for debate.

Eventually, the **political framework** of society is the most powerful environmental influence at work. Its control of financial resources and its ability to legislate and compel adherence to its laws makes the political system all-powerful. Within the framework of the constitution established in the past, and limited by the checks and balances imposed upon it by the electoral and judicial systems, the political forces determine what type of economy we shall have, decide what 'mix' we shall have in our mixed economy, and ultimately decide how the aims and aspirations of the nation in the economic and social fields shall be achieved.

Looking more closely into the environment in which firms work, we find that all sorts of organisations, institutions and individual people claim in some way on the business. Business administrators find that they are constantly subjected to claims for help of one sort or another in areas which are only connected in the most tenuous way with their true business affairs. The **concept of the claimant** is quite an important concept in considering the environment in which firms work. It holds that a firm or company is constantly beset by claims from parties in and outside the business which it must take into account in any plans it makes.

Whatever the claims of various claimants, decisions have to be made about each claim at an appropriate level. This decision-making process involves three elements. First an **informational system** detects the environmental influences at work, or monitors those that have already been located. Such an informational system may have a formal framework such as Technical Committee on Competitors' Developments. Alternatively, it may just be the designation of one administrator as a press officer who reads the local press for any developments in the community and handles any correspondence, complaints and so on, on behalf of the organisation. Secondly, the information has to be processed. **Information processing** takes many forms. It may mean case work in personnel, or consideration by an appropriate committee and reporting upwards and downwards. Finally, there has to be a **decision output**. Decision outputs do not need to come from top level; they can be made at every level. Discretion within a policy is an almost universal practice, which speeds up decisions at any given level, and throws the more difficult ones up to a higher level and, finally, to board level. Routine decisions are made within the agreed policy laid down by the board as it conceived the organisation's objectives at the time. The cases which need decisions which do not fit the existing policy come up to the board for top-level decisions which are then promulgated as new policy developments.

12.5 What is a claimant?

The survival of organisations in many cases depends upon their proper appreciation of the many claims that are made upon them. They exist to fulfil the purpose for which they were founded, but they can only do so if managers appreciate that those ends have to be met in an environment that presents countless obstacles to be overcome. The least understood element of any organisation is this total environmental framework, and the claims which it makes. Countless examples could be quoted of organisations which failed because they were too intent upon their own activities to appreciate the impact they would make upon their environment. We cannot regard responsibility for employees as ending at the factory gate, if we wish to avoid rapid staff turnover and costly training programmes. The cost of recruiting staff is very expensive. We cannot proceed with plans if there is a likelihood that governmental opposition or local opposition will be aroused. Capital costs are high, and an abortive project can ruin a prosperous company.

A claimant is an individual, firm or institution which is making, or may make in the future, a justifiable demand upon the organisation, which it would be illegal, morally wrong or merely unwise for the organisation to overlook.

An environmental model can be built up for each organisation, which lists the claimants upon the organisation, the nature of the claim, the proposed method of meeting the claim and the method of conflict resolution to be adopted should it be impossible to reach an agreed settlement. Such an **organisational claimant model** is presented in Table 12.1, but the reader should note that it cannot be more than a general model. The crucial thing for the management of any organisation is to draw up such a model in the correct order of priority of claim, specific to the organisation. The mere preparation of such a model is a salutary exercise which will throw up areas of difficulty which have been under-appreciated hitherto. The reader should now consider Table 12.1.

Table 12.1 An organisational claimant model

List of claimants	Nature of the claim
(This list is a general list and not arranged in any special order. Managers should draw up their own lists in proper order of priority for their own organisations.)	
(Further columns should be added to any chart drawn to suit the claims upon a particular organisation, showing (a) method of satisfaction envisaged and (b) method for resolving conflicts, if any.)	
1 Ordinary shareholders	a Claim to share in the profits
	b Claim to vote at the AGM
	c Claim to a share of the assets on liquidation
	d Claim to take up additional stock offerings
	e Claim to ask for investigation of the company
	f Claim to receive copy of directors' report and accounts
	g Any other rights accorded in the prospectus or other contractual arrangement with the company, or in legislation such as the Companies Act 1985–9
2 Preference shareholders	a Claim to receive the agreed rate of dividends if profts are available
	b Claim to vote at meetings if dividend is in arrears or variation of rights is proposed
	c Claim to prior return of capital if authorised by the issue originally
3 Minority shareholders	a Claim to fair treatment in dividend policy
	b Claim not to be defrauded under the exceptions to Foss *v.* Harbottle rule
	c Claim for investigation under Section 431 of the Companies Act 1985–9
4 Debenture holders	a Claim to interest on debenture
	b Claim to secured assets in event of default
	c Claim to receive copy of directors' report and accounts
5 Secured creditors	a Claim to receive payment in the agreed manner
	b Claim to petition for bankruptcy and deal with security according to law, in the event of non-payment
6 Unsecured creditors	a Claim to receive payment
	b Claim to petition for bankruptcy and a receiving order in the event of non-payment

7 Suppliers	a Claim to be considered as accredited supplier, especially if he/she has adjusted his/her business to suit the organisation
	b Claim to be paid in the agreed manner (see 5 above)
	c Claim by suppliers of professional services to be treated in a professional manner and possibly with ***uberrima fides*** (utmost good faith)
8 Customers	a Claim to be supplied in the agreed manner, at the agreed time, at the agreed price, etc. as per contract
	b Claim to receive service as required for the product
	c Claim to be able to obtain spares during product lifetime
	d Claim to take advantage of customer credit as advertised
	e Claim to technical information on use of product
9 Employees	a Claim to realise self-respect, the respect of others and the full development of individual personality in the working situation
	b Claim to a satisfactory reward for the factor labour, in money form, on an appropriate scale and with prospects of economic advancement
	c Claim to be free of arbitrary or capricious behaviour on the part of supervisors and managers
	d Claim to be represented by an appropriate union, and to exercise rights to act freely in accordance with the law in the pursuit of legitimate aims
	e Claim to know the terms of any contract of service and have them in writing
	f Claim to participate in the planning and organisation of his/her own job
	g Claim to participate in management at an appropriate level and be aware generally of the trends within the organisation and its position in the mixed economy
	h Claim to enjoy a safe system of work
	i Claim to enjoy staff welfare facilities and other fringe benefits
10 Unions	a Claim to represent groups of organised workers
	b Claim to engage in collective bargaining
	c Claim to participate in drawing up job descriptions
	d Claim to participate in drawing up codes of practice for (i) health and safety, (ii) disciplinary procedures and (iii) industrial relations
	e Claim to participate in management and to know full facts on profit calculation and allocation
	f Claim to be informed of all developments likely to affect security of employment, redundancy, expansion, take-overs etc.
11 Trade associations	a Claim to represent the industry at all levels
	b Claim to impose levy on organisation for funds
	c Claim to discipline organisation for breach of agreed code of practice

12 Local community

    a Claims for improper environmental behaviour by organisation

    b Claims for nuisance from parking, traffic access, noise, interference with television signal, etc.

    c Claims for provision of local amenities of a social, religious, educational or recreational kind

    d Claims for raising aesthetic overtones of the organisation's buildings, grounds, workshops, etc.

    e Claims for participation of organisation's officials in local affairs, local institutions, rag weeks, festivals, charities

    f Claim to supply a reasonable proportion of local produce

13 Local government

    a Claim to know what company proposes in so far as law requires or mutual interest makes this desirable

    b Claim to business rate contribution as levied, promptly paid

    c Claim to participation of organisation in projects of mutual or public importance

    d Claim to release of employees who become elected representatives without loss of payment

    e Claim to service of organisation's senior staff on local panels, committees, boards of governors of institutions, etc.

    f Claim to compliance with both the law and the spirit of 'fair trading' legislation, advertising standards, consumer protection and weights and measures controls

14 Competitors

    a Claim to pursue a line of production or service previously conceded to lie within the organisation's brief

    b Claim to diversify into an area which is a manifest duplication and waste of capital

    c Claim to compensation for alleged deliberate poaching of ideas, staff, etc.

15 Business community

    a Claim to support in financial or practical terms for mutually advantageous schemes

    b Claim to membership and service by organisation's officials on local committees and panels

16 Central government

    a Claim to have the legislative requirements on health, safety at work, trading standards, quality controls, documentation and statistics, codes of conduct in industrial relations, worker participation, disciplinary procedure, taxation, VAT, exporting, etc., met by the organisation

    b Claim to interfere in matters of monopoly trading, price control and other administrative aspects

17 The general public

    a As customers (see 8 above)

    b In general the claims are environmental and ecological, and require the organisation not to impose social costs on the community which should be privately borne (such as clearing oil from beaches)

    c Claim that organisation should fulfil its social purpose (especially if it is a public sector body)

12.6 Assessing the impact of claimants

Having identified claimants in-house and in the environment, the management team have to turn the mental model into quantified details about the impact of each claim upon the organisation. The organisation's planning and decision-making will be influenced by its estimates of the time and money it must spend to meet the present and the developing claims of each class of claimant. It will equally be influenced by the returns it anticipates from the environmental improvements achieved in the process. Thus a strike-free plant should more than offset the cost of achieving good industrial relations; staff fringe benefits may cut labour turnover and the cost of training; customer satisfaction should increase market share; good community relations should increase goodwill and bring reciprocal benefits in such local matters as community college bias in favour of the industry, improvements in transport infrastructure, and so on.

It may be that claims are unreasonable, or deserve to be side-stepped because they seek to take advantage of the organisation's availability. Appetite grows with feeding, and a concession to support a particular aspect of local life may snowball into demands to support a wider and wider range of activities. It may even be necessary to fend off adverse trends by publicity, or appeals to local and central government to reach a more reasonable consensus on measures to be adopted. Organisations cannot fall in with every proposal just because it has been made. The organisation's original objectives are still the *raison d'être* of its existence. Pressure groups exist to preserve a vested interest and protect it from assailants who may not fully appreciate its value to the community at large, or the extent of the capital sunk in it at great expense to the community as well as to the owners. For example, every port in the UK is vitally interested in any new proposal to install new facilities anywhere else. There is only a certain quantity of trade to go through our ports, and a new facility may only take trade away from existing facilities. If the capacity of our ports is already adequate, further capital investment is nationally wasteful, even if it would be locally profitable, for any profit it earns will be at the expense of facilities elsewhere. This is not to deny that new types of facility may create trade by competing with foreign ports.

Index